For the Love of God's Kids

In Brazil: A Jesus-like Role Model to the World

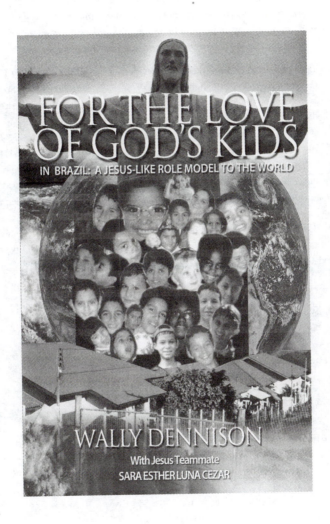

FOR THE LOVE
OF GOD'S KIDS

IN BRAZIL: A JESUS-LIKE ROLE MODEL TO THE WORLD

WALLY DENNISON

With Jesus Teammate
SARA ESTHER LUNA CEZAR

Belleville, Ontario, Canada

Library and Archives Canada Cataloguing in Publication

Dennison, Wally, 1933-

    For the love of God's kids / Wally Dennison.

ISBN 978-1-55452-109-8
ISBN 978-1-55452-110-4 (LSI ed.)

    1. Street children--Services for--Brazil--Campo Bom. 2. Baptists--Missions--Brazil--Campo Bom. 3. Missions--Brazil--Campo Bom. I. Title.

BV2616.D45 2007   266'.68165   C2007-900001-0

For more information or to order additional copies, please contact:

Wally Dennison
Sheriton Apartments, 208 - 543 Rowcliffe Ave.
Kelowna, BC V1Y 5Y8

Guardian Books is an imprint of *Essence Publishing,* a Christian Book Publisher dedicated to furthering the work of Christ through the written word. For more information, contact:

20 Hanna Court, Belleville, Ontario, Canada K8P 5J2
Phone: 1-800-238-6376 • Fax: 613-962-4711
E-mail: info@essence-publishing.com
Web site: www.essence-publishing.com

Dedicated to all those adults and children throughout the world who give so selflessly of themselves for the love of God's kids.

(All proceeds from the sale of *For the Love of God's Kids* will be donated by the author and his teammate to the CHAIN of Love ministry in Campo Bom, Brazil.)

TABLE OF CONTENTS

From any perspective, the CHAIN of Love is a lively testimonial to God's love and ministry to His kids.

Rev. Ken and Jerilyn Bayer, co-founders of the CHAIN of Love, celebrate Jesus every day in their ministry of love to God's kids in Brazil.

1

KIDS THRIVE IN A BEEHIVE ALIVE WITH GOD'S SWEET LOVE

On a grassy slope in Campo Bom, Brazil, is a thriving and expanding domestic community as buzzing with love for God's kids as possibly anywhere in the universe outside the heart of Jesus Himself.

The spark that ignited this consistently widening fire of love was the murder in 1993 of a homeless fourteen-year-old street kid known only by the nickname of Rusty. He was Amilton Renato Ternus. Subsequent chapters will unfold the story of how the shooting of this kid, whose name remained unknown for almost six years thereafter, triggered everything now transpiring over this 107,600 square-foot site in Brazil's southernmost state of Rio Grande do Sul. Here are *Lar Colméia,* or "beehive homes" in Portuguese. Within the walls and sheltered under the red-tiled roofs of these seven white-marble homes are about seventy-five children rescued from the most abominably loveless plights imaginable, now tasting motherly, fatherly, brotherly, and sisterly love as sweet as honey itself. In other neighborhoods, another fifteen children salvaged from similar situations are accommodated in two private homes under the same Christian ministry.

While the numbers of children and homes on and off the *Lar Colméia* campus are in constant flux, the ministry, in 2005, was retaining a quota of roughly ninety children, at least temporarily. All ninety were being nurtured in the loving heart of the *Lar Colméia* complex, which includes large playgrounds, a bocce-ball court, a gymnasium, fruit and vegetable gardens, a plant nursery, and a technical-vocational center where the children are taught skills and trades equipping them for productive lives.

Lar Colméia is *not* an orphanage, however. It is, in fact, as the Portuguese title denotes, "a beehive of activity" where young souls from six to eighteen years of age share work, play, family, and community responsibilities in a growth process guided by houseparents, volunteers, and professionals dedicated to shaping their lives in the image of Jesus.

The English-counterpart title for this unique operation is CHAIN of Love, and it functions as a ministry of North American Baptist Conference International Missions. And what a wonderfully precise acronym it is: Christian Homes for Abandoned Infants in Need of Love. Links in forging that ever-lengthening CHAIN of Love are the North American Baptist churches and individuals whose donations of money, skills, labor, and child-sponsorship have continued powering it to greater momentum since its official birth in July 1994, when aldermen of the City of Campo Bom donated the land.

This inspiring ministry conceived of and led by Canadian missionaries Ken and Jerilyn Bayer has operated from day one without a formal budget, banking its investment wholly on God. CHAIN of Love arose from God's soil without a red cent in the bank to start. The dedicated Bayers simply decided the need for action was urgent. The time had arrived to prayerfully take that bold initial step. They felt compelled to build a life preserver of Christian hope with which to pull in homeless and abandoned children from the dangerous urban streets of neighboring Novo Hamburgo (population 250,000) and other Brazilian cities.

In May 2004, after twenty-five days of interviewing children, houseparents, the Bayers, and virtually every key player involved in this marvelous CHAIN, the author and his teammate translator, Sara Esther Luna Cezar, were absolutely convinced that Jesus Himself is piloting the project. We visualize Him displaying this CHAIN of Love ministry in His hands as the global prototype, indeed the world's role model, for churches and assemblies of worship wherever they are and whatever their denomination. By using this pattern as a basis for their own mission plans for ministering to deprived children, they can extend that loving chain into every corner of the world.

Thus, to Sara and me, it's hardly news that the Bayers' lead and model is already being followed and taken to a higher level. Their global outreach has started thirty-one miles to the south in Porto Alegre, a city of 1.5 million, where the Christian and Missionary Alliance is several years off the ground constructing homes for boys and girls. As this is written in 2005, there are two structures, each about six times the size of a single house in the Campo Bom complex. "They can accommodate more of the children who would have come here," Rev. Ken Bayer notes, pointing out that the greater metropolitan area of which Campo Bom, Novo Hamburgo, and Porto Alegre are municipal components has a population total of 3.5 million. Pastor Ken's administrative assistant, Clovis Scheffel, offers Alliance leaders advice and information as the CHAIN's liaison.

After roughly thirty interviews and being awestruck daily by the joyous love exuding from the children themselves and everyone wired into their lives, Sara and I wholeheartedly endorse a judge's declaration to Pastor Ken: "If every church would do what you are doing in Campo Bom in all of Brazil, the problem of homeless children would be solved." Indeed, Sara is as convinced of that as the Bayers are themselves. This thirty-three-year-old Mexican-born daughter of missionaries to Mexico served as Ken's administrative assistant for a few years and is married to the son of one of *Lar Colméia's* housemothers. My teammate's answers to interview questions in a subsequent chapter will spotlight the impact being made locally by the CHAIN of Love.

So, if one Brazilian judge confidently asserts that the problem of homeless children can be erased in his country with each church determinedly stepping up to the plate, then why not the plight of street children throughout the world? That's not impossible. You answer the question. What could happen if, in fact, each worship assembly on earth actually marched out as faithfully and fearlessly as did the Bayers? After all, hasn't the Christian and Missionary Alliance successfully taken the cue? Impossible and too daunting? Think about it. Not to the Bayers, whose Good News Baptist Church in Novo Hamburgo was originally, and continues to be, the propelling force for CHAIN of Love. Not if the countless hundreds of thousands of churches and worship enterprises across Earth each ventured out as the power of one plus one...plus one...plus one...in an unending chain for the love of God's kids.

If worship assemblies united in a cooperative assault on one of this planet's most disgraceful problems, the possibilities would be infinite. Even a blight as globally mountainous as street-kid homelessness could be conquered. Sara and I feel reinforced in that conviction by the encouraging insights outlined in a recent "Focus-on-Faith" newspaper column in the *Kelowna Courier* by Dr. P. Tim Schroeder, senior pastor of Trinity Baptist Church in Kelowna, British Columbia, Canada. Paraphrasing Pastor Tim's words, churches compete seriously—not against each other, however, but as an army of competitors battling on the same side against all the godless afflictions besetting humanity. And, as he emphasizes, they also "joyfully coexist to see the love and grace of God advanced."[1] Sara and I contend that with God and prayer guiding the ingenuity of faithful humans, the possibilities are infinite. So, what's to prevent the world's worship assemblies from saturating the map with loving homes of hope for street children? Such an international campaign could materialize into the most spectacular, yet thoroughly individualized, effort ever launched under the banner of global ecumenism! The CHAIN of Love would serve only as the global prototype and role model for guidelines. Ken and Jerilyn Bayer would be more than pleased to assist. Each congregation, using the collective imagination of its members, could target its resources to pattern whatever type of domestic community it envisions for God's kids and establish it wherever it wishes. In fact, a church in one country could even decide to pair with a "brother" or "sister" congregation in another nation in establishing a children's complex in each of their homelands—an Australian congregation building one in the United States, for example, and the U.S. church doing likewise down under, or a Canadian church constructing one in Brazil while the Brazilian worshippers build in Canada. Yes, the ideas and possibilities are endless.

The very fact that CHAIN of Love thrives as an infinitesimal blip encircled in a colossal global ocean of self-absorbed myopia and violent inhumanity magnifies its excellence as a prototypical role model of Jesus-like love to all mankind. For a few months in 2004, for example, CHAIN of Love had cause to sadly inform child sponsors how "heartbreaking" it was having to turn away at least thirty children for lack of available accommodations—such is the demand in just one small section of Brazil. Multiply that number ad infinitum across the world's seven continents, and maybe, just maybe, one can visualize the millions of children's hands reaching out desperately for helping hands such as yours, dear reader. No doubt about it—the daily diet of mass media is alarmingly and increasingly bloated with crises and conflict. What's our planet like as these words are written? Humanity stands horrendously shamed and besieged by the following atrocities: more than one million children and families displaced and on the verge of mass starvation in Sudan in the world's worst humanitarian crisis (prior to the Southeast Asian tsunamis December 26, 2004), AIDS decimating hundreds of thousands in the Third World nations of Africa and elsewhere, and war and terrorism raging on in Iraq and the Middle East.

But the cumulative formula of one plus one, plus one, plus one in a lengthening chain of love is overpowering emotionally and financially in the lives of children yanked out of a hopeless abyss. The brightly colored heart-shaped cameo images of children's faces on CHAIN of Love leaflets are genuine representations of the children day in and day out. The author knows. He felt the joyous warmth of those smiling faces daily for several weeks at *Lar Colméia*—and he especially knows how the sunshine of Jesus-generated human love is contributing to the healthy growth of his own sponsored boy, fifteen-year-old Alexandre da Silva Fonseca. You will meet this impressive live wire as we talk with him in a later chapter.

All the children come to CHAIN of Love legally as placements from Brazil's court system or social-services system. Operating under strict but sensitive guidelines, the Bayers' ministry accepts children from birth to age twelve and retains legal guardianship of them until they become mature enough to function independently, normally at age eighteen.

Pastor Ken explains that the CHAIN runs entirely on donations. The amount continually varies because of fluctuating exchange rates and other operational variables. The money comes from individuals sponsoring one or more specific children and from churches, organizations, and individuals whose generosity enables continuing construction and upkeep of infrastructure and buildings and furnishings, plus promotion, marketing, and development of programs tailored to fortifying children for self-reliant futures. For example, CHAIN of Love offers computer education as just one of its technical and educational skills programs and recently developed a second Web site.

Each sponsor contributes $300 US ($360 Canadian) annually to underwrite the food, shelter, medical, educational, and other needs of his or her assigned child. All of the children have multiple sponsors, and they benefit and grow as human beings through the special attention that flows naturally from a one-to-one relationship of loving concern with their benefactors, receiving birthday and Christmas presents, letters, and even, occasionally, visits. From this money pool, each housemother is allocated a monthly sum covering the needs of her flock. Housefathers both add to the family income and, more importantly, solidify and reinforce the sense of family through their paid jobs outside the home and as a working partner with housemothers in nurturing the children. Professionals, such as a social worker, a psychologist, a private tutor, a speech therapist, doctors, and dentists, are on fee-for-service contracts but also give freely of their skills whenever possible.

More than twelve years since its inception, this incredible example of love for God's kids has been graced by the skilled hands and minds of people from North American churches and groups who gave freely of their time and labor. First they assisted Brazilian workers in clearing the site, then in constructing the buildings, making the furniture and all other physical amenities at *Lar Colméia,* and instructing the children in manual skills and trades programs. Year after year, these servants of Jesus keep coming in teams of selfless servanthood for the love of God's kids. Some will talk with us in subsequent pages. Note that the frequent absence of full names in our narrative is purposeful and not unusual. Brazilians, as Pastor Ken explains, consider their usage unimportant and superfluous, since about half the nation's population is either a Silva or a Santos. In our view, this shouldn't mar what amounts to a truly spectacular tale of love that keeps expanding in breadth and depth with no discernible ending.

For now, we can only extol the many current heroes and heroines at CHAIN of Love, who come in various ages, shapes, and sizes. They range from Pastor Ken—whose tigerish physique befits the ferocity with which he charges each day, laboring for his Work Superintendent, Jesus—to sweet-faced thirteen-year-old Paulo Ricardo do Amaral de Assis, whose courage even as a five-year-old on the streets and amid the garbage dumps, looking after his younger sister and baby brother, shone with the light of Jesus. They include Jerilyn, Pastor Ken's wife and the CHAIN's unfailing tower of patience, sensitivity, and compassion; and housemothers Romilda and Deny, whose love-infused work and play with their flocks encapsulate motherhood at its finest.

From so much misery, and now to so much hope and so much love, children thrive gloriously, thanks to the CHAIN born out of tragedy and a missionary couple's determination to take action on behalf of Jesus.

2

HOMELESS RUSTY IGNITES A FIRESTORM OF LOVE

Credit Amilton Renato Ternus as the conscience-jolting, earth-moving force that drove CHAIN of Love into existence and thereby opened the doors through which hundreds of miserably deprived and outcast Brazilian children have passed into joyously transformed lives for more than a decade. He was just a filthy, hungry, homeless waif of fourteen, begging and scrounging for food and scrambling for a spot to sleep nightly on the mean streets of Novo Hamburgo—until fatally shot through the heart at three in the morning by a downtown bar owner allegedly fearing robbery. But by his death and through the example of his short, pitiful life, Rusty—as he was called by everyone around Good News Baptist Church in Novo Hamburgo—provided the spark that ignited the church congregation led by Ken and Jerilyn Bayer into pioneering a CHAIN of Love mission aimed at saving homeless Brazilian street children from dead-end futures.

In life, church members nicknamed him Rusty—or, in their native tongue of Portuguese, *Foguinho* ("little fire")— because of his fiery red hair. Rusty was a tolerated nuisance, a habitué around the church whose glue-sniffing would kill the hunger pangs until he was fed, most often by a compassionate woman caretaker who lived at the back of the church. Thanks to her, Rusty also was allowed to shower and bathe himself temporarily clean and then sit and talk with her in church.

To this kindly lady, he was really an angel with a dirty face to be shined. You can call him a guiding angel now; had it not been for the circumstances surrounding his tragic death, this ministry of love for street kids probably would never have been considered. His demise, when read about in the local newspaper of April 24, 1993, rattled everyone who had been at the church the previous evening for a fifteen-year-old girl's birthday party. Rusty had turned up, was fed some leftovers, and then wore out his welcome by lingering past church-closing time. Their last view of him was as a silhouette in the dusk loitering forlornly outside the front door of the locked, darkened church.

That last scene and Rusty's tragic aftermath were the triggers of all that followed. Prodded by the Bayers, the Board of Missions of the North American Baptist Conference approved the CHAIN of Love project at its annual session only days later. Committee members from Good News Baptist Church envisioned one group home to start and just a month later organized a board of directors to lead the charge. In that same month, the CHAIN was recognized, registered, and officially incorporated as a philanthropic society by the cities of Novo Hamburgo and Campo Bom. The seeds had been planted quickly, and in July 1994 they were nurtured by Campo Bom's grant of 107,600 square feet of land for the society's institutional development. Construction began in October 1994, and the first children began arriving into care the following month.

Today, Rusty's aura radiates through both the physical facilities and those most intimately involved in the day-to-day operations of the CHAIN of Love. In its entirety and its continuing growth, the CHAIN is a pulsating monument to Rusty's legacy and what can be accomplished when adults energized by Jesus go to bat for deprived children because of the eternal lesson they learned from one. It's a global prototype, indeed a divinely inspired role model, for any worship assembly of any faith anywhere bent on hurling life preservers to hopeless street children like Rusty.

Novo Hamburgo's Good News Baptist Church and its creation, CHAIN of Love, as noted previously, have taken the lead and laid out an already long-proven and enormously effective route to follow. Admirable as their progress has been, however, it is only a tiny footstep up the towering mountain of challenge worldwide. Who knows what could happen if all worship assemblies across the globe launched similar team efforts for the love of God's kids.

God only knows what could result, but undoubtedly, there's so very much to do. Data gleaned from the Internet and other sources illuminate that challenge. One study from 1997 reported that forty million children roam the world's urban streets, Brazil accounting for fully eight million, or 20 percent of that total, just in the city of Sao Paulo alone.[2] Two to six children are assassinated daily on the streets of Rio de Janeiro by "death squads," because citizen groups and businesses want the streets "cleaned up" to ensure "public safety." According to juvenile court statistics, most of the more than 3,000 eleven-to-seventeen year olds who died violently in Rio between 1993 and 1996 were murdered by death squads, the police, or various gangs. In São Paulo in January 1999, minors were victims of 20 percent of the homicides committed by police. Across the nation, 4,611 street children were executed, some mutilated almost beyond recognition, between 1988 and 1990. Head counts on one particular night showed 900 children asleep in the center of Rio and another 600 in São Paulo, with at least fifty of the latter number under twelve years old and alone.[3]

Estimates of the number of Brazilian street children range wildly from 200,000 to the eight million cited above, but a report as far back as 1989 presented to a conference in the nation's capital of Brasilia said about twelve million lived in the nation's streets. That same report noted that 624 abandoned children under seventeen were murdered in the nineteen months between January 1988 and July 1989.[4] Grimly ironic is the fact that the conference, focusing on the plight of street children and reported by Reuters news agency, was sponsored by the United Nations International Fund for Children (UNICEF)—you know, that compassionate charity that those adorably cute and costumed North American trick-or-treaters collect for each Halloween. For street children, though, it has been all horrific, deadly tricks and absolutely no treats worldwide, according to the National Movement of Street Boys and Girls, which presented the report. It is grimly ironic, too, that the 765 attending the conference were those who know all too cruelly the mean street realities—750 street children representing Brazil's twenty-seven states and another fifteen from seven Latin American countries.

The report emphasized that 24 percent of the 624 Brazilian street children murdered in the nineteen-month period of 1988-1989 were victims of death squads, composed of *justicieros* (justice seekers), who are often off-duty police officers hired by businessmen to kill their enemies. Most of those "eliminated" were between eleven and seventeen years old. A total of 430 under seventeen years old, most of them boys, had been shot, and seventy-three had been stabbed.[5] Even the beloved nineteenth-century English urchins of Charles Dickens' novels fared better in day-to-day survival and life expectancy than the ragamuffins roving Brazilian streets do. Such is modern Brazil and mankind's so-called progress.

Granted, street-kid misery is a worldwide tragedy. But the Brazilian millions stand out because most expect to be killed before age eighteen. This is hardly surprising, considering their options: finding food in rubbish or garbage dumps; being exploited by street sellers; eking out a few cents by shining shoes, cleaning the windshields of vehicles stalled in traffic, or entertaining sidewalk traffic with stunts; begging; stealing; becoming drug runners and drug takers. They're often beaten by citizens or police, and their prospects include prison, malnutrition, and every conceivable disease, including, of course, AIDS. A teenager in Rio is twice as likely to be murdered as one in Bogota, Colombia, reputed to be Latin America's most violent city.[6]

This was the uncaring, unloving milieu in which Rusty moved. To him, it must have seemed his existence was as insignificant and of as little value as that of any stray dog or cat. Stray, unwashed, unwanted children do think that way.

Weren't other children being gunned down like animals? Still, from his eternal reward, Rusty had the final say about his worth—six years after his death his murderer was sentenced, thanks to a jury convinced by the prosecutor's Scripture-quoting declaration that every person has value.

Not until 1999 did the members of Good News Baptist Church learn the real name of the boy they knew only as Rusty, whose violent death was the seed from which *Lar Colméia* and the CHAIN of Love germinated. By then CHAIN of Love was a vibrant and expanding entity staffed by people stretching themselves for the love of God's kids. So, maybe, just maybe, a grateful, gleaming smile shone across the spiritual face of Amilton Renato Ternus from his perch in eternity at the instant his full identity became known to Jerilyn Bayer. A scruffy street kid's life had been of everlasting value.

Perhaps it was divinely devised that his legal identity came to Jerilyn in a discarded newspaper amid the garbage, so much like the days of Rusty's life had been. That newspaper, dated October 6, 1999, was taken along with others from a neighbor's recycling bin to line the cage of a pet rabbit acquired recently by the Bayers' daughter, Julissa. While folding the paper into the cage, Jerilyn's eye chanced upon an item headlining the sentence of man convicted for killing a minor. Her curiosity piqued, she unfolded the paper and read further, suddenly realizing that the recounting of grim facts described the killing of Rusty. "I was amazed how God had put this into my hands, because it reinforced our decision of years earlier regarding our change of course." That altered direction in ministry by the Bayers will be detailed in chapter four, along with the deep soul-searching and the overwhelming support of Good

News Baptist Church that brought it into motion and then accompanied it. That same chapter will chart the sequence and significance of the moves the team generated for the love of God's kids.

But, for now, let's just imagine the "nobody" Rusty of planet Earth as a "somebody" in Christ's kingdom looking down proudly at what his death has inspired—former street kids like himself romping happily and being nurtured in a loving atmosphere he never knew, children like Paulo Ricardo do Amaral de Assis, mentioned in chapter one. When Jerilyn Bayer's eye tripped upon that newspaper article giving Rusty's name, fourteen-year old Paulo had already been with *Lar Colméia* for more than two years. Like Rusty, Paulo had suffered all too long the street-kid indignities of having to claw through urban garbage dumps like some stray animal, desperate to wolf down any available scrap. His heroic voice and story follow.

3

DRILLMASTER JESUS SHAPES UP HIS TROOPS

Early in their mission of starting Baptist churches in Brazil back in 1983, Drillmaster Sergeant Jesus must have already been shaping up Ken and Jerilyn Bayer with the basic training that would fortify them for the eventual launch of CHAIN of Love as the haven in which suffering homeless street kids would reap new, healthy lives.

Street-kid homelessness is so pervasive and indelibly stained into Brazil's social fabric that it's visible to varying degrees everywhere—even in the small coastal beach city of Torres where the Bayers devoted three years to beginning a new church. But the real eye-openers that moved their hands to start reaching out earnestly and fervently to these deprived wanderers began afterward, in Novo Hamburgo. It was in that city of 250,000 where haunting scenes of homelessness bombarded them. They had returned there in 1988 to start another church after a year-long furlough in

Canada. In chapter four, we'll detail those five years from 1988 to 1993 in Novo Hamburgo that worked up to the CHAIN's birth and how the Jesus-emulating dynamism of the Bayer personalities brought it to life. You will get a close-up of how Ken and Jerilyn, assisted by thousands of helping hands, persevered diligently over its rocky roads of infancy and have continued steering it to its present and expanding status. But, for now, for purposes of contrast, let's get acquainted with four lives on both sides of the ministry turning point triggered by Rusty's murder. Note the healing, nurturing power of love as we meet Ivan and Paulo from pre-CHAIN days, and note especially its vastly strengthened potency later as we engage with a younger, different Paulo and Leonardo, two boys growing joyfully in the *Lar Colméia* family.

Actually, the success tasted by the Good News Baptist Church family with Ivan was a notable forerunner to the later defeat church members agonized over upon Rusty's violent demise. This feeling of victory rescuing one young soul at the congregational level may have been a blueprint later for ever-enlarging expectations. Fourteen-year-old Ivan, Jerilyn recalls, was found living in the streets by his aunt, a church member, who had gone searching for him after learning that his mother had been imprisoned for drug-trafficking. This was a teenager who had never gone to school, whose teeth had never been brushed, and whose body had never slept upon a bed. Black rags were all that clothed him—excellent camouflage for hiding at night from police eager to nab a food-and-money thief. Ivan's road to a new life began when his aunt was awarded legal guardianship and took him into her home. She immediately trashed his clothes and shaved his head to destroy lice. Thereafter,

Ivan wore brightly colored clothes fashioned and sewn by his aunt. He learned to read and write, thanks to a man from the church, and then was enrolled in school. "The remarkable change in Ivan really touched us," Jerilyn says. "He was so open to the gospel."

From so much misery to so much hope, so much love, for Ivan, all because of the power of love from one—an aunt who reached out and started the ball of one plus one, plus one rolling. Ivan was surrounded by love for the remaining years of his life. Sadly, he died after he and his aunt moved back to Brazil's interior.

Love's embrace of Paulo through Pastor Ken and Jerilyn Bayer is also one of astounding measures—basic training, surely, from Sergeant Jesus for a couple who subsequently became and remain the fulcrum of a remarkable chain of love. In those early days, because they possessed the only car and telephone in the congregation, the Bayers were the emergency-response team for anyone ill or injured requiring an emergency run to hospital. Thus, several times they were saviors for twenty-year-old Paulo, a street wanderer since being orphaned as a child. Thanks to their compassionate care, he eventually became a Christian. As Jerilyn recalls, "Because he felt like we were family, he came to us whenever he was hungry, needed clothes washed, or simply wanted our company—and that was often." Jerilyn taught him such basics of daily living as how to comb his hair and eat at a table. "In a sense, he began living with us."

In Paulo's eyes, Jerilyn became his mother—although both were about the same age. "He even brought me a rose on Mother's Day." Although he was always welcome, the responsibilities of tending to Paulo sometimes stressed Jerilyn. She was mother also to her two little daughters in a small, cramped apartment and was undergoing a difficult pregnancy with her third. It was tough going, considering that Paulo was on the verge of death several times, once from gunshot and knife wounds. "Ken rushed him to the emergency center in Porto Alegre, and, would you believe, they didn't want to accept him because he didn't have a dime to his name. So, we paid.

"And another time when death threatened, doctors thought Paulo had leukemia, since his bone marrow wasn't producing Vitamin B-12. The final diagnosis, however, was that the deficiency stemmed from extreme malnutrition. Ken paid for the medications and vitamin injections that cured him." Happily, Paulo landed a job when he returned from hospital to Novo Hamburgo, but he always turned up at the Bayers' apartment when a crisis arose. They were family. Today, he is a missionary whose kindness is a Jesus-inspired outgrowth of the love showered upon him by the Bayers in times of desperation.

Flash ahead to roughly nine years later on September 8, 1997, when another Paulo—Paulo Ricardo do Amaral de Assis—arrived just a month and a half shy of his fifth birthday at *Lar Colméia,* which had been up, buzzing, and continuously expanding for almost three years as a loving refuge for God's kids. Then flash ahead to July 23, 2002, when six-year-old Leonardo Geraldo da Silva arrived to a still larger "beehive" complex of love. In both time-frame snapshots are two children unchained from horrible sce-narios and welcomed into the loving arms of a house family and a community family that have literally saved their lives from futures of hopeless despair, if not death, on the streets. As a hospital poster in this author's city of Kelowna, Canada, so perceptively declares, "It takes a community to raise a child." How true! How especially true with Paulo and Leonardo, as their stories will reveal in the following paragraphs. So, dear reader, as you reflect upon their tales of survival, rescue, and currently ongoing nourishment in both family and community environments, please remember that we in North America, as the poster implies, bear that responsibility for the love of God's kids lost on this continent's streets.

Paulo Ricardo do Amaral de Assis, a courageous little hero, with his younger sister, Vanessa Amaral da Silva.

Paulo and his younger sister and baby brother were repeatedly abandoned for periods of up to several days by their mother, a prostitute. Our stocky little hero, at the age of four, had responsibly taken charge and looked after the welfare of his two younger siblings and himself until social workers were alerted, discovered their misery, and arranged for them to come under the legal guardianship of CHAIN of Love.

Paulo, sister Vanessa, and brother Sidinei had been at *Lar Colméia* almost seven years when we interviewed him in May 2004. The three children, Paulo recalled, lived with their mother in their grandfather's shack near a municipal garbage dump. While she roamed the streets soliciting at all hours, Paulo, Vanessa, and Sidinei were almost totally neglected by an alcoholic grandpa habitually bombed out by moonshine-guzzling bouts. Then one day the children found him dead in bed. He had drunk himself to death. Paulo said that the very day all had returned from his burial, their mother abandoned the children in the middle of a Novo Hamburgo street and walked off in search of male customers. Fortunately they knew how to get back to the family hovel. Paulo admitted that he doesn't even know his mom's name, nor does he care to know it. "I never think of her, and I don't care to see her. I love living here." Sadly, she long ago abandoned her three older children for the same unsavory purposes.

Amazingly, Paulo and his siblings survived their mom's gross negligence during that year in which the family would move from one abandoned hovel to another around the garbage-dump area. During their mother's frequent absences, Paulo, as best he could, fulfilled a three-way role as father, mother, and older brother to Vanessa and Sidinei. For their food, Paulo scoured the garbage dump, gathering scraps. As he told a judge, he routinely relieved his own hunger by eating grass. Another reliable food source was an avocado tree known by Paulo because it was on land where his grandparents had lived. Drink came from any accessible liquid source. Paulo did not disclose how that basic need was met.

Whenever the three were caught unexpectedly in a downpour far from the shack, or even under its leaky roof,

Paulo would fetch discarded newspapers and shield them under the porous umbrella of newsprint. For warmth, Paulo huddled the three into a large jacket he had urged away from a compassionate gentleman while panhandling.

Thankfully, their appalling plight was finally discovered because of a concerned neighbor. Several days of constant crying told her that something was amiss. Checking out their shack shocked her to tears—Vanessa and Sidinei were bawling, seated on a floor of filth. Her call to Social Services brought a social worker so disgusted by the stench drifting out of the hovel that she had to cover her nose and mouth with a cloth before entering. By then, Vanessa's and Sidinei's crying had risen to screams. Paulo was gone—as usual, out scrounging for food to fill their stomachs and wash away their tears. As the social worker reported, the mess was indescribably sickening, with the little ones literally up to their necks in excrement. How could Paulo, then just four months short of his fifth birthday, know how to change diapers? The children were rushed to hospital, so severe was their dehydration. A hospital report the next day stated that Sidinei, despite all of Paulo's loving efforts, would have died of dehydration just a day later had their plight not been reported, officially discovered, and immediately acted upon.

Little did the three children know it then, but in just two months God in His merciful love would be gifting them with a set of two parents for the first time in their lives, with Pastor Ken and the CHAIN of Love arranging everything. Meanwhile, during those two months, they were cared for in a state-run halfway home. Typically, in his ever-so-practical manner, Ken Bayer had devised an solution. He accomplished this by offering to have a construction crew from the CHAIN build a few more rooms on the Novo

Hamburgo home of a couple from Good News Baptist Church, should they accept becoming Mom and Pop to the abandoned Paulo, Vanessa, and Sidinei. José and Iraci, whose family included their own three children of about the same ages, agreed. *Lar Colméia,* as Pastor Ken had explained, was already filled, and until the new homes being built there were opened, it could not accommodate any more children. Less than eighteen months later, in early 1999, veteran houseparents José and Iraci and family would move into a newly constructed fourth home on the growing *Lar Colméia* campus. By then Paulo, Vanessa, and Sidinei had been lovingly woven into a family's heart.

Flashing back, though, few moments in Pastor Ken's ministry could have been as heart tugging as on that first day of September 8, 1997, when the three ex-street waifs arrived at the newly renovated home of José and Iraci. He was there, smiling, with everyone. And Paulo? So excited was this beaming, dark-eyed, stocky little barrel of a four-year old that he dashed into the arms of both Ken and José, calling each "Dad." Of course, even the halos of angelic street children bear some dirt to be scrubbed away from their do-or-die days of survival. Right off, there was that street-kid pattern again when Paulo grabbed all the other children's toys later and hid them for himself. But with the warmth of an affectionate family, he has long since learned the value of sharing among brothers, sisters, and parents infused with the love of Jesus and each other.

One huge step along that path came just a month and a half after their arrival, on October 21, 1997, Paulo's fifth birthday. Iraci asked him if he had ever had a birthday party. Arranging a birthday party, naturally, is just one of the zillions of things good mothers do for each kid in her brood. Birthday party? Paulo's face went blank—a wordless non-expression saying, "What on earth is a birthday party?" He didn't know. His face lit up, smiling, as Iraci explained that his family would be honoring him for the day he entered the world. "And, oh," she added, "we eat a whole lot of special things."

Iraci had been planning to cook and bake a smorgasbord of dainties and sweets, but Paulo's concept of special food was altogether different. "Are you going to make me some cabbage?" No kid had ever made such a birthday request to a housemother. But, then, that was special to a street urchin who had never eaten dessert or anything supposedly yummy. Today, as each new birthday arrives, Paulo laughs when virtually every gift bearer cracks the standard yearly joke that the party dessert of cabbage should be a super treat.

Roughly a year after Paulo, Vanessa, and Sidinei came under the CHAIN's guardianship, José and Iraci bought a farm and passed the mantle on to new houseparents, Cida and Renato. By then José and Iraci had been with the CHAIN for several years, and they adopted one of the children, Luis Paulo de Oliveria, whom they had received as a seven-month-old along with two older sisters.

Life goes on, and Paulo and his two younger siblings had long been blossoming, thanks to the nurturing showered upon them by José and Iraci. Then, with Cida and Renato, that unfailing stream of caring guidance and love continued for the dozen children on the lower level of House Four at *Lar Colméia*.

Paulo captivated us when we interviewed and observed him in May 2004. His jolly smile never seemed to shut off and neither did his bouncy step. On the playground swings and in games with other children, he was consistently the joker, igniting others into laughter. Everything was going gloriously uphill for this fireball of unquenchable curiosity, six years and eight months after being linked into CHAIN of Love. Grade five at Santos Dumont Elementary School in Novo Hamburgo was providing academic adventures, but physical education was really special—Paulo loves playing cricket, the Brazilian version of baseball.

He was also quick to help with household and community chores—volunteering, for example, to clean up for instructors of the shoemaking course at *Lar Colméia's* technical-vocational center. Meanwhile, even if his fingers were yet too small for guitar playing, Paulo remained determined to eventually play both guitar and keyboard. Piano lessons would be ideal, but they were too expensive at that point for a lad whose sights were set on becoming a professional musician.

The week's highlights to Paulo's young eyes were Sunday church services and Sunday school at Good News Baptist Church. Now, that's family; that's community! It was thrilling just observing Paulo's heartfelt musical passion flaring joyfully in hymns to his Savior.

Hearing Paulo's burst of worship in Portuguese hymns got me reflecting: what a amazing kid!—a dynamically packaged barrel of seventy-seven pounds, just short of five feet tall. Imagine his dead seriousness and scrawniness of almost seven years earlier, scavenging garbage dumps for the survival of Vanessa, Sidinei, and himself. Imagine the fantastic stamina, endurance, and self-sacrifice of that pint-sized Paulo, whose heart and lungs are now belting out "Jesus Loves Us," his face aglow. And I'm so inspired, so proud, knowing that Paulo, not even five, had, by the time of his rescue, already gone the distance, completing a biblical assignment of which millions of us adults could never boast. He's the mini-embodiment of its message—a hero by any definition. It's from Paul's second letter to Timothy (2 Timothy 4: 7): "I have fought the good fight, I have finished the race, I have kept the faith."

Love does that, and thank the Lord that Paulo's own concept and expression of it earlier is now being sustained and rewarded in the outpouring of love he receives from his houseparents, Cida and Renato, his house brothers and sisters, and everyone in CHAIN of Love.

It is miraculous how a thunderous flood of love from all directions can drown all chances of children like Paulo and Leonardo Geraldo da Silva becoming jaded into lifelong bitterness because of their horrid experiences before rescue. Like Paulo, Leonardo knows the terrifying face of adult alcoholism, but unlike Paulo, he had at least experienced a decent, loving mother until the day an unbelievably gruesome fit of rage stole her from him and his four siblings.

Picture the childlike innocence and bewilderment of Leonardo, now ten, as a six-year-old arriving home from school and wondering why his mother wouldn't respond as he tried to shake her awake. Picture that same facial innocence as Leonardo, youngest of the five da Silva children, tells Pastor Ken later that she wouldn't even talk to him after some people had removed her from bed and placed her into a black box.

Fortunately, those innocent eyes and those of older sister Jenifer and older brothers Dionatan, Davi, and Leandro hadn't witnessed the bloody horror a few hours earlier when their drunken father burst into their home and swung an ax into their mom's head, her body crashing to the floor amid a gush of blood. This insanely jealous and delusional maniac then telephoned a neighbor, admitting the slaying and justifying it by alleging his wife had been "seeing another man." Then the madman forewarned the neighbor that he also intended to kill his children, then in school. Mercifully, that alarmed neighbor immediately phoned relatives, who rushed to the family home and, swallowing their shock, had the presence of mind to cleanse the victim and mop up the gore as best they could, place her into bed, then pick up the children from school. Meanwhile, an aunt made funeral arrangements.

The awful preface to this grisly tragedy is that, after years of being violently abused by this lout, the victim had kicked him out of their home, saying the family could no longer tolerate his violence. In contrast to their father, here was a woman the five children loved dearly—a dedicated, conscientious, and industrious mother whose days were spent sifting through garbage dumps for items that she could sell as a street vendor. Those trivial sales earnings and whatever aid she could squeeze from the government were all that brought food onto the family table for seven mouths, including the drunken coward who escaped. One wonders about the quality of Brazilian justice, considering that, although apprehended a few days later, he inexplicably eluded imprisonment. According to Pastor Ken, that father also sought to reclaim the children, who refused to see him for even a minute. His current whereabouts are unknown.

Meanwhile, for the five children he so wickedly deprived of a devoted, loving mother, there are scars that will remain throughout their lives. Still, Christ's compassion never fails, even in the most profound grief, so those scars have been healing since July 23, 2002, under generous daily applications of nurturing love from Marli and

Cezar Mello, servants of Jesus and their new "mother" and "father." That date is when the da Silva brood were brought into the guardianship of CHAIN of Love and welcomed into the arms of houseparents Marli and Cezar at their rented home off the *Lar Colméia* campus. The four da Silva brothers and sister Jenifer quickly took to Cezar, at last experiencing the loving warmth and concerned decency of a genuine father. Marli, though, had some tough sledding initially, trying to fill the devastating hole left in each of the children's hearts by the horrid demise of a mother so overwhelmingly loved. But eventually they felt Marli's love enveloping them and were heartened by its radiance upon everyone else in the family of twelve children. That feeling of genuine family does work wonders! And wonders never do cease in a thriving, close-knit, Jesus-loving family of mother, father, brothers, and sisters. Growth such as that now being experienced by the da Silva children is precisely what Pastor Ken and Jerilyn Bayer had envisioned and prayed for when they embarked on their unique enterprise for the love of God's kids.

Now, for chapter four, we'll return for more of that gripping story of the life and death of Rusty, that nameless street kid whose death inspired the birth of CHAIN of Love. He was the first link in a chain now so interconnected with success that it shines as a prototype for what can be accomplished in rescuing homeless children. Naturally, as its organizers, the Bayers are the next two links. From an overview perspective, we are convinced that Rusty, the Bayers, the housemothers, the housefathers, the children, and everyone involved now or in the past have been chess pieces moved uncannily and with flawless timing by that Supreme Chess Master, Jesus, in a team effort on behalf of God's kids. So, back to Rusty, some deep talk with Ken and Jerilyn Bayer, and how the Bayers' powerful personalities are carrying out God's loving work for children so magnificently.

4

Born Out of Tragedy:
A Divine Ministry of Love

Unquestionably, the jolting news of Rusty's murder on April 24, 1993, was the flashpoint that swept Ken and Jerilyn Bayer into a cause as passionately aflame as the orange-red color of Rusty's hair.

The Bayers had been in Brazil for a decade. Their prime responsibility had been starting and nurturing new churches, but so shaken were they by Rusty's early morning death from a bar-owner's bullet that they determinedly adjusted the focus of their missionary sights toward rescuing homeless Brazilian street children from lives of lifelong despair and the likelihood of deaths such as Rusty's.

As Jesus surely would say, the harvest is bountiful for a worldwide outreach of love for God's kids. Perhaps worshippers everywhere should ponder that challenge as we recount both that fateful night of Rusty's arrival at Good News Baptist Church and all that followed. He had walked in just as the festive birthday party for a fifteen-year-old girl was ending. It was an inconvenient arrival, since everyone was stacking chairs back into place for the next day's service. Yet there he was, filthy, hungry, glassy-eyed as always. Could anyone refuse such a hangdog, imploring look? A kindly lady motioned Rusty to sit down. She filled a plate of leftovers and placed it in front of him. Eating ever so slowly, he watched everyone hustling to finish and leave quickly for tomorrow's workday.

Finally, with everyone else gone, just as Rusty had digested his last bite, Pastor Ken gently urged, "Rusty, we need to close the church now, and you'll have to leave." Shuffling out of the building, Rusty sluggishly dragged on to stop at the gate, a figure of utter dejection. Again, Ken spoke softly. "You'll have to get out of the gate so we can lock up."

So there Rusty remained, outside the gate, forlornly stepping back and forth in the shadows. Church members walking home could see his loitering and merely shrugged. As the Bayers were stepping into their van, their eldest daughter, Jenise, wondered, "Where will Rusty sleep tonight?"

"I don't know," Pastor Ken replied, "but he'll find a place to stay." Ken knew that street-smart children like Rusty always manage...unless and until...

The next day a front-page article in the local newspaper delivered a blow as crushing to a Christian conscience as that of a sledgehammer to the head—Rusty had been shot to death. And the whole congregation was blown away. Everyone who had been at the party suddenly felt like "Bad News" Baptist Church because of that night's grim outcome. They felt searing, torturous, wrenching, gnawing, collective guilt.

So anesthetized had Pastor Ken and his flock become to an almost-daily news diet of urchins being shot that victims were casually dismissed as another statistic in the normal morbidity of Brazilian street-scene homelessness. Not this time. This statistic was once-breathing flesh and blood—Rusty—and his fate battered at their hearts and heads. "We punished ourselves," Ken recalls, "asking such questions as 'What kind of Christians are we?' We knew he would spend the night downtown." Similarly, church members were berating themselves. In effect, their words were, Ken notes, "We all live in our comfortable homes, and we left Rusty in front of the church. We could have saved him by taking him home with us. We are all just too comfortable as Christians."

For the Bayers, Rusty's death was a life-changing turning point. God had dropped a huge problem into their laps. They could either shy away from doing anything for the love of God's homeless kids or swing into action on their behalf, rallying their church flock behind them. As faithful Christians, they really had no choice but to aggressively take on the Lord's challenge—and the turning point of Rusty's death would develop into the ministry milestone of CHAIN of Love. God and His people do have a knack for fashioning loving masterpieces, even out of extreme human pain and tragedy!

Reviewing the earlier lives of Ken and Jerilyn Bayer, one senses that God, as the Master Chess Player, could have been preparing them for precisely this momentous undertaking triggered by Rusty's death. He shaped them through the faith-blessed backgrounds of their parents and how each is uniquely wired as a human being, how uncannily certain lives intersected with their own life journeys as a couple, and how their own initial meeting during college days ultimately blossomed into a marriage bound securely to Christian missionary partnership.

For starters, there is that take-charge, go-go, pioneering drive of Ken's, which delights so many day after day at *Lar Colméia* and for which he is routinely, but admiringly, kidded. He was no less spirited as a boy in Winnipeg, Manitoba. For example, one summer while his parents were away on holiday, he dismantled a red wagon and, with drill and screwdriver, rebuilt it into an even flashier four-wheeler. Meanwhile, Ken's boyish ears would perk at the stories told by missionaries who were regularly accommodated in the Bayers' home. "Living under primitive conditions, they would tell how they improvised or invented things needed for everyday living." As he points out, they never complained but told of making things out of virtually nothing. "That kind of mentality inspired me."

That industrious, make-it-happen spirit was very much ingrained, as well, in Ken's father, Leonard, and mother, Irma. They had emigrated separately from then Russia's Ukraine to Canada, married in Morris, Manitoba, and then moved to Winnipeg when Ken was three. There, his entrepreneurial father organized Bayer Electrical Co., a commercial and industrial firm now headed by Ken's two younger brothers, both electricians like their dad.

"Dad," forty-nine-year-old Ken says, "never had to teach me how to do things. I'd watch him do all sorts of things—electrical, mechanical, carpentry work—you name it, he could do anything. So I grew up with that mindset as well."

After graduation from Winnipeg's Mennonite Brethren Collegiate Institute, Ken entered the two-year Bible Studies program at North American Baptist College in Edmonton,

Alberta, uncertain as to whether he would return for the second year or join his father's company instead. Not only did he return, but he also switched into the four-year bachelor of arts program, the prelude to the master of divinity degree he acquired in 1983. All in all, it seems God held the logistical timetable for Ken and Jerilyn Bayer.

Jerilyn Bayer is a perfect complement to an unstoppably dynamic, full-speed-ahead husband. She's an understanding tower of patience, sensitivity, and compassion whenever expectations of people and events temporarily veer off course—the rock of stability who counsels and comforts everyone toward weathering setbacks and navigating back on track. This couple blends into an incredibly awesome force, the power of which is demonstrated daily in the CHAIN of Love.

Not only has Jerilyn been a maternal angel partnered in the raising of three daughters, but all along she has led and sung with worship teams wherever the couple has started churches. Moreover, she has shared counseling in crises, formed children's ministries, and headed leadership-training ministries and women's prayer groups. The appeals from those prayer groups, incidentally, are scheduled so that God is hearing them around the clock, seven days a week. Indeed, the strongest armies march on their knees both in defense of God's kids and in championing the welfare of all people being prayed for.

And that missionary spirit has passed on to the three Bayer daughters. Jerilyn and Ken proudly note that Jenise, Jessica, and Julissa are deeply involved in activities both at the church and CHAIN of Love. Jenise and Jessica are moving toward potential careers motivated by the fruitful work they have observed being accomplished by their parents and so many hundreds of others united in a loving commitment to God's kids. The two attend Ulbra University in Canoas, where Jenise, in 2005, was a fourth-year psychology major and Jessica was in her second year of prenatal nursing. As her mom was being interviewed for this book, Jenise was out collecting data from two Chain of Love children on behalf of a university instructor whose nine-kid study sample would provide answers to a doctoral-thesis question on whether physical abuse affects intellectual development. Some of Jenise's other field work was with several children at *Lar Colméia*, children assigned to her by the CHAIN's psychologist.

Sara and I marveled at hearing how the torch of Jesus was being passed from generation to generation. Take Jerilyn's education and training for the CHAIN of Love challenge and the Brazilian cultural and environmental milieu in which it continues growing. Everything must have been divinely ordained and mapped. "Brazil is mostly home to me," she points out. "My brother Allan and I spent our formative years in Brazil. I was only six and he was just eight when Dad and Mom came here as missionaries to plant churches, so Allan and I attended Brazilian schools and learned to speak Portuguese." And Dad and Mom thoroughly involved them in starting churches and participating in daily church life.

"The biggest influence on what Allan and I are today came from Dad and Mom," Jerilyn continues, referring to Dr. Herman and Ardath Effa, now of Edmonton, Alberta. (Many years later, while Ken and Jerilyn were starting churches in Brazil like Jerilyn's parents had done before them, her dad became director of international missions for the North American Baptist Conference and served several years before retiring.) "To this day, they are sold totally on kingdom work. They taught us everything, from telling biblical stories to discipleship." As a result, few brothers and sisters could be more like-minded and closely connected in spirit than Allan and Jerilyn. Allan served for many years as a missionary in Nigeria and now teaches on missions and cross-cultural studies at Taylor University College and Seminary, which operates under the North American Baptist Conference in Edmonton, Alberta.

It is typical that, little more than a decade after Ken's graduation and ordination, both his parents and those of Jerilyn would be in Campo Bom to help build the first home at *Lar Colméia*. And should it really be surprising that the senior Bayers and Effas labored every year since 1994 in construction of the first seven homes? Moreover, the Effas were again gearing to colead a volunteer team from their church for two weeks of repairs, renovation, and building in July 2006. This author gratefully gives thanks to Allan and his father for their answers as a team to e-mail questions on Brazil's spiritistic movement, and to Dr. Effa and Ardath for information and comments they provided on CHAIN of Love in telephone interviews and letters.

When one reflects upon the sequence of events, one can see how God, as the Master Chess Player, linked specific people of compatible chemistry in specific places at specific times to produce the first link of that ever-lengthening chain and, ultimately, the inspiration for the words now being written. Links include like-minded Christian parents, similar attitudes and outlooks, and that first meeting between Ken and Jerilyn in a cafeteria lineup during a youth conference at the University of Manitoba in 1977. "I was behind Ken when he turned around and offered to help place food items onto my tray," Jerilyn recalls, smiling.

"He was very gallant. Then he carried my tray from the counter to the table where I had been seated with some friends and placed it in front of me. We introduced ourselves, and he recognized my name, since, as coincidence would have it, his roommate then at North American Baptist College in Edmonton [now Taylor University College and Seminary] was my brother Allan. So I said, 'Well, I'll see you there, because I'm going to begin there in the fall.' His last words as he walked away were 'See you there.'"

They started double-dating as the school year began since, again coincidentally, a classmate friend of Ken's, Allen Mertes, was dating Jerilyn's roommate, Shirley. Those double dates led to two marriages. The Mertes family, until June 2006, lived in Kelowna, British Columbia, where Pastor Mertes was senior high youth pastor for twenty-one years at Trinity Baptist Church, of which this writer is a member. The Mertes family is now in Three Hills, Alberta, where Pastor Mertes teaches at the Prairie Bible Institute.

As Ken and Jerilyn studied toward their respective degrees (Jerilyn has a BA in Christian education), they planned both for marriage and later striking out as a missionary couple. Ken suggested Japan or Brazil; Jerilyn recommended Brazil because of her wealth of experience there, her ease with the people, and her facility in the Portuguese language. Each was praying for direction as to their destination.

In the meantime, Ken had been appointed youth pastor of Edmonton's McKernan Baptist Church in 1979. Following graduation in May 1980, he prepared to start into the college seminary's three-year master of divinity program that fall. First, though, there were wedding bells with

Jerilyn on August 2, 1980. Then, as the two continued cracking the books, they supported their partnership with income from Ken's youth ministry at McKernan Baptist and Jerilyn's earnings as a department-store clerk.

By May 1983, the Bayers knew where they were headed. They had been commissioned for missions and assigned to Brazil. "I guess I had prayed harder than Ken," Jerilyn chuckles, adding that she would also have been happy to go to Japan. In just one week in that month, Ken took his final exams, graduated, was ordained, and, with Jerilyn, was commissioned for missionary assignments.

Graduation, ordination, and farewell celebration were packed into one day, perfectly in the tempo and style of Ken Bayer. Jerilyn quotes, with a smile, the church moderator who ordained Ken at McKernan Baptist: "Ken always gives the impression he has a whole lot to do in a short time."

More than twenty years later, Pastor Ken's intensity would be captured in a pithy comment from Clovis Scheffel, his administrative assistant at CHAIN of Love: "Whatever he decides to do prospers."

To which Jerilyn, after twenty-six years of marital observation, proudly adds, "He's totally driven, very ambitious to get things done for the Lord. And absolutely every day is that way."

But possibly no other period in the good pastor's life has been as supercharged as that from May to November 1983, part of which saw the Effas' Edmonton home as the couple's domicile. In those six months he shuttled between Edmonton and Winnipeg, where he packed and crated goods for shipment to Brazil. As well, he completed all the Bayers' documentation from the Brazilian consulate in Toronto, underwent cultural adaptation training in

Farmington, Michigan, and, with Jerilyn, raised financial support for their Brazilian mission in Edmonton, Winnipeg, and the province of Saskatchewan.

On November 15, 1983, the Bayers arrived in Brazil, on the holiday celebrating the declaration of the Brazilian republic. Jerilyn was four months' pregnant with Jenise. The couple ministered in the small beach town of Torres for three years, and, typically, the go-go pastor was quick off the mark, becoming fluent in speaking, reading, and writing Portuguese. Attending a course in a nearby city was sandwiched between ministerial and family responsibilities. He also led church volunteers in building a parsonage.

Then, after a year's furlough in Canada raising financial support, the Bayers were back in Brazil in 1988 to renew their assigned duty of planting churches. Now it was in Novo Hamburgo, where ministering over the next five years would indeed prove to be both extremely challenging and eye-opening. Originally a German settlement, Novo Hamburgo is home to 250,000, and the Bayers' church was a shack of just 26 1/4 by 19 1/2 feet in one of the city's poorest areas. Again, Pastor Ken's mechanical giftedness shifted into high gear as he quarterbacked a church-volunteer team in reconstructing the wooden house and adding two rooms and a parsonage over the next four years. Worship leader Clovis Scheffel recalls that the earlier version of Good News Baptist Church had literally been on its deathbed with just a few members. Clovis had volunteered along with a few others to keep that tiny, last-gasp shack of a church going, having transferred from Good News Baptist's mother church of Central Baptist six months before the Bayers arrived to complete the job of resuscitation and lead it to today's vibrancy. By the beginning of

1989, the congregation had grown to 270 members. It now attracts up to 400 people for Sunday evening services in a newly constructed building capable of seating 700, which was formally dedicated at its new location on May 2, 2004.

Soon after the Bayers arrived, God's short-term plans came rather dramatically into focus. Jesus may have been laughing along with Pastor Ken and others witnessing lively stepping song leader Clovis, then much heftier than today's slenderized fireball, stomping through the rickety floor-boards of that old shack and winding up viewing everyone sheepishly from a waist-high stance of red-faced embarrass-ment. It's funny how a divine sense of humor has a way of expediting construction action. First stage of the church expansion included ceramic-finished flooring. You will hear much more of bouncy Clovis' inspiring walk with Jesus in chapter thirteen.

Those early months in Novo Hamburgo brought the Bayers face to face with wretchedly degraded humans mired in the hopelessness of unbelievable poverty. Ken and Jerilyn reached out into the neighborhood with home visi-tations, each accompanied by a newly professed Christian. Jerilyn went out on Tuesday mornings and Ken on Friday nights, the roughest night of the week. And were they over-whelmed by the needs! Talk and prayer often ended with some drunken, cursing, and knife-wielding family member barging in and shouting at them to get out. "That's when we started forming a vision for reaching the poor," Jerilyn says. As she notes, large families suffered miserably because of unemployed breadwinners. Outright abuse and lack of food and clothing were the daily social norms, expected to prevail over entire lifetimes. "It was obvious why the older children made their homes on the streets.

Those streets were preferable. That's how many young people got into drugs."

Many people from the so-called more privileged classes and even some missionaries might have shrugged uninterestedly and turned blindly away from the glaring panorama of daily despair. Not Ken and Jerilyn Bayer. That would be alien to their makeup. "We had to do something," Jerilyn says. Even government workers, who are actually paid to serve their people, dismiss these poverty-scarred neighborhoods and focus their sights wholly on "development" and "modernization." Eliminating the problem of street children would please them enormously, and that's why officials routinely overlook the murders of these irritable urchins. Gathering from this author's own research of published articles, their killings are viewed merely as a process of necessary extermination, comparable to that of a business owner's use of pesticides against insect infestation. For example, since so many of these waifs shoplift to survive, their crowding around storefronts turns potential customers fearfully away. Thus, shopkeepers hire thugs to "remove" these "trade barriers" with gunfire.

Digest another example: on July 23, 1993, almost three months to the day after Rusty's murder in Novo Hamburgo, three Brazilian military policemen shocked the world when they machine-gunned forty-five homeless children sleeping in front of a church and art museum in a fashionable section of Rio de Janeiro. Seven died instantly, and so thunderous was public outrage that the suspects were arrested three days later. That, as one journal editorialized, was the "real news" in a nation where many police officers who have killed street children admit they feel it to be no different than gunning down a stray dog. Reportedly, bullets have also ended the lives of people who tried to help street children by campaigning to bring trigger-happy police to justice.[7]

In business jargon, the harsh bottom line is that Rusty's heartless demise in 1993 was equal to that of a stray dog in a year that saw more than four million Brazilian children not attending school, 10 percent of adolescents unable to read, 700,000 children living without their mothers, and 460,000 of that total not living with either parent.[8]

Jerilyn, because of her training, education, and lifelong experience working with children, indeed had sweepingly fertile ground in which to contribute and cultivate her abilities for the love of God's kids. She immediately organized a children's ministry at Good News Baptist. Vacation Bible School was emphasized, attracting a mixture of middle-class and desperately destitute children. Jerilyn was aghast at the many street kids arriving with lice-infested heads of hair. "We're going to have to either send these kids home or do something about their lice," she told her ministry workers. Jerilyn feared the children from better homes would be withdrawn by their mothers should one or more come home with lice. But, as a ministry assistant swiftly pointed out, "Well, they need Jesus just as much as our neighborhood children do."

The slum children were quickly separated from the others and escorted to bathtubs at the back of the church. Soon, Ken was back from a pharmacy with a shopping bag full of lice shampoo packages. As the ministry women scrubbed the children's heads with the tub water, they assured the children that they themselves were not ugly because of the bugs defiling their hair. On the contrary, they explained, it would be ugly not to eliminate the condition. Eliminating it would prevent other children's heads from being infested.

Jerilyn confesses, "I wondered if I was going to have to wash their hair and asked myself if I was willing to do so." But the ladies offered to do it, and she sighed with relief. Nonetheless, Jerilyn knows, as all of us should, that it's sometimes incumbent to dirty your hands doing the Lord's work.

Following the head-washings, the women carefully—and tenderly—combed out the lice and nits. What a sight classes were that day, shampooed heads bobbing and faces wreathed with smiling faces! As Jerilyn says, "I was really challenged by these women who wanted to do something so those children could stay and hear about Jesus. And they reminded those children to wash their hair before coming the next day." They came to class the next day clean and proud and continued on through the entire semester of Vacation Bible School. And no children got infested. The women and children had given the bugs the boot! To Jerilyn, the shampooing process is now old hat. She laughs, recalling how often she has shampooed her own daughters because they had picked up lice from hanging around with Brazilian friends.

Thanks to the Bible school programs, ties between the Bayers and the children deepened. During trips downtown, for example, Ken and Jerilyn would often hear children excitedly exclaiming, "Oh, there's the pastor and the *pastora*." "They would dash to our car wanting to talk," Jerilyn says, "and I would always remind them, 'Now, don't forget to come to church—you need to learn about Jesus.' And so they came—enthusiastically and joyfully."

For the Bayers, it seemed every day in those early 1990s brought a new observation or insight into the havoc wreaked by poverty and street-kid homelessness. One incident in particular was a jolting preface to the soul-searching precipitated by Rusty's death. It occurred while Jerilyn was undergoing a difficult pregnancy with their third daughter, Julissa. Miscarriage was possible, so the doctor warned against the slightest exertion, even walking. Yet Jerilyn had no choice but to walk Jenise and Jessica to school every morning. Ken had to drive the car, the only available vehicle, to oversee construction at the church.

Above all, the doctor warned Jerilyn not to let anything upset her. "That was fine, as I don't easily get upset." She had to go with the flow, even when a volunteer construction team from Canada was quartered with the Bayers, with bedding and belongings strewn in the living-dining room. Then, one evening, there was a body-rattling boom as Ken's mother was serving supper. "Something fell on our balcony," Jerilyn yelled. A lady attempting a suicidal leap from the fourth floor had landed on the Bayers' balcony. "And I was not supposed to become stressed out! I called for help, and we quickly brought the bleeding woman in. We had already phoned emergency when the lady's husband and daughters came screaming into our apartment."

At that point, the Bayers were scheduled for furlough to Canada and had been preparing to turn the church reins over to a Brazilian pastor. Yet they sensed that the entire succession of events involving children, adults, and poverty added up to a question being posed to them by the Spirit of God. So they prayed together and discussed their concerns with church members, praying with them as well. Then, with Rusty's death, it seemed that everything previously experienced coalesced into one cataclysmic tragedy hammering at their consciences. For the love of God's kids, the Lord was insisting they must strike out in a new ministerial direction.

5

Seizing the Day and Mapping the Way for the Love of God's Kids

So emotionally disturbing was Rusty's death to Ken and Jerilyn Bayer that it drove them to transform the scars on their hearts into stars of love for other children like Rusty. In the words of Dr. Robert H. Schuller, pastor of "America's television church," "The Hour of Power," they turned their scars into stars. The power of God has turned what many others might have avoided as an impossible dream into the bricks and mortar of loving reality—the CHAIN of Love ministry. Today, the ever-growing *Lar Colméia* community of homes centered at Campo Bom, Brazil, shines as a global role model of what can accomplished to salvage the lives of homeless and abandoned street children.

Initially both Ken and Jerilyn struggled fiercely with doubt and hesitation. They seriously questioned whether their respective abilities, minds, and temperaments would be strong enough and blend harmoniously enough to actually create havens of love for homeless and abandoned children. They would have to abandon the prime focus of their ministry, planting churches, for twenty-four-hour on-call crisis work. Rusty's murder had created only a vague notion of venturing in that direction.

Uncharacteristically, even tough-minded Ken was apprehensive: "Oh, I don't really work well with children." Meanwhile, Rusty's image preyed upon their minds. In turn, their praying was that of beseeching God for divine guidance. God's answer to Ken's earnest questioning came soon enough. "I sensed Him saying, 'I will enable you to do what you need to do.'"

Jerilyn, though, was leery and held back. As she recalls,

"We were already going non-stop starting churches, with everybody on call. I thought, if we started this, it would absorb us completely. After all, we were the only couple with a car and a home phone. Just think if someone had died in those years of starting churches and we hadn't gotten there. We did everything then from making funeral arrangements to helping dress the body and carrying the coffin. And we had small children, too. It was hard enough handling emergencies. So, now, it would really be scary, trying to continue ministering to the church and handling crises with children full-time. I kept questioning God, 'Are You sure I am ready for this?'"

This was a relevant and perfectly understandable question from her perspective. Jerilyn is the family's emotional rock, and she knew that she, not Ken, would be wrestling far more strenuously and in much more detail with all the volatile problems affecting children.

"When you are church planting, you are doing church work, helping people spiritually and counseling them. But then you go home. Not, however, with what we envisioned. Everything, and I mean everything, would 'go home' with us, and particularly with me. Around the clock, and it seemed I was already going around the clock."

Ken, meanwhile, stubbornly held fast. "I was the rebellious one," Jerilyn admits. "Well, Ken—he just continued making his plans."

Her words told this author that husband Ken was a person whose vocabulary and outlook on life exclude the word *impossible.* And his own words verify that. "I envisioned the construction long before we broke ground. Those who say 'impossible' often have no desire or ambition." In Pastor Ken's mind, no doubt, was the solid assurance that Jesus would be the Foreman and Friend at his side, along with his sweet-hearted partner, Jerilyn.

As for Jerilyn's hesitation, Ken sensed that she could not help but embrace the challenge before long. Fourteen years of marriage had shown him how sensitive and people-focused Jerilyn had been in meeting crises, both in their family and with children and adults involved in their church-planting missionary work. Jerilyn chuckles about that now, adding, "And the minute I see Ken with a measuring tape, I think, 'Uh oh, here we go again—another building plan.'"

Summarizing all that has happened to date, Jerilyn observes,

"It is such a neat experience to be in the center of God's work. You just go through open doors, work hard, obey and trust, because all the resources are in God's hands. All our changes have been from good to better. We have seen the children graduate into forgiveness and new lives after rebelling in protest over all they had suffered and endured before coming to us. We have seen children change completely. Following forgiveness, they blossom in all areas—social, spiritual, educational, you name it. So, whenever I look back wondering whether it has been worth all this work, all I have to do is observe the differences in their lives. Always, I say, 'Yes! Yes! Yes!'"

And, Jerilyn emphasizes, it's not just decent clothes and wholesome food that dress these children of God with such joyful demeanors but the spirituality with which they're nourished by houseparents, Good News Baptist Church, Sunday school, Bible studies, and Bible camp.

Still, consider that none of these blessings would now be showering on these Brazilian children of God had it not been for the boldly faithful action that Ken and Jerilyn Bayer finally agreed on. In the next chapter, you will read how consistently Jerilyn, in particular, shone in overcoming the many kid-centered crises that have confronted the CHAIN of Love ministry to date. In doing so, Jerilyn corroborated Pastor Ken's unwavering confidence in her.

No doubt the Bayers, in evaluating and projecting their ministerial course following Rusty's murder, were asking themselves that oft-quoted Christian question, "What would Jesus do?" Now, in 2006, it appears that in their little corner of the world, the Bayers are emulating Jesus for the love of God's kids. As the author of "One Solitary Life,"

Dr. James Allan Francis wrote that Jesus' humble life lacked any of the things normally associated with so-called success: political office, home ownership, going to college, writing books, traveling widely.[9] To which this author adds: by the self-centered yardsticks of this short-sighted, materialistic speck of a planet in God's cosmos, perfectly selfless Jesus was dirt poor in what sociologists label the three P's—power, property, prestige—while those who possessed those zealously prized three P's in the greatest quantities were precisely the ones who spat upon, cursed, mocked, humiliated, and, ultimately, crucified Him. "Yet," as Dr. Francis declares, "all the armies that ever marched, and all the governments that ever sat, and all the kings that ever reigned have not affected life upon this earth as powerfully as that One Solitary Life."[10]

Well, from their one little spot on the globe at Campo Bom, Brazil, Ken and Jerilyn Bayer are demonstrating to worship assemblies throughout the world what can be achieved for the love of God's kids by seizing every second of every day. For more than twelve years at *Lar Colméia* and CHAIN of Love, the Bayers have seized day after day...after day...after day...without let-up.

Back when Jerilyn was still nervous about changing course and Ken was charging ahead anyway, Jerilyn realized she could no longer forestall a decision. She knew Ken was already sounding out politicians and governmental bureaucrats on land availability and other child-related matters. She felt a negative decision would be rejecting God's wishes. "I knew I could not do that, and I heard God telling me, 'Go ahead; I will be with you through the people at the church.'" So the Bayers poured out their concerns to the family of Good News Baptist Church, explaining that they felt God was calling them to undertake "social work" with children. They received the church's wholehearted support. Without exception, church members vowed they would do whatever it took to go the distance with the Bayers. They organized a decision-making board of directors and agreed to supply whatever was necessary to kick-start *Lar Colméia* into reality. The Bayers' vision was their vision. To Ken's eyes, it was a win-win deal, since sharing in the ministry was certain to make his church flock grow in their walk with Jesus.

And, as always, Ken became the spark plug igniting people into action. "Less talk and more doing" is a phrase Ken lives by, says administrative assistant Clovis Scheffel, one that he quickly learned under Ken's direction. The swiftness with which Ken moved is revealed in his recruitment, even before a shovel of dirt was turned or a workforce organized, of several church couples to take homeless children into their homes and become housemothers and housefathers. This is another example of why this energetic, trim expediter, who in earlier years lifted weights and routinely ran ten miles daily, would be the perfect poster guy for the Young Men's Christian Association and its advocacy of striving for optimal mental, physical, emotional and, most importantly, spiritual fitness.

Ken and Jerilyn immediately began researching the various institutions caring for children sent in from the streets. They explored the Assembly of God institution and three other facilities in Porto Alegre, thirty-one miles south, before going to Ijuí in the interior of their state of Rio Grande do Sul. There they stayed a weekend, hosted by Baptists from Germany whose ministry involved raising children in a family-style environment. A major lesson learned was how extremely important two-parent home settings are for the children's healthiest growth into adulthood.

They interviewed housemothers and housefathers, some of whom had served more than twenty years and raised an entire generation of lost children into successful Christian adults. These dwellings are called home by the many former residents who return regularly with families of their own for visits. Interviews with these one-time street children inspired the Bayers, providing them with a wealth of insights that supported statistics they had gathered. Their informal, in-depth talks with directors reinforced and increased their enthusiasm. As they watched the children, particularly the boys, playing soccer and engaging with their "dads" in various other ways, Ken and Jerilyn became convinced that housefathers would be crucial to the operation they envisioned. A father figure is even today the critical missing piece in institutional settings in Brazil and many other nations. In Campo Bom, most of the children the Bayers would take in had never lived with a father. Ken and Jerilyn knew the children would grow up properly only if they were blessed by the presence of good housefathers as models and partners with housemothers. Growing up in a foster-family residential setting would enable these children to march out into the world with a healthy concept of family life.

While the Bayers left Ijuí more encouraged, they had a few different wrinkles in mind for *Lar Colméia* and CHAIN of Love. They rejected having a large central laundry like that at Ijuí where hired workers washed and mended all clothes and returned them neatly folded and packaged to the housemothers. Having seen the children play at Ijuí, Jerilyn concluded the mothers there didn't fret over how dirty, stained, or ripped clothes became, since the laundry would remedy everything. Jerilyn knew that housemothers at Lar Colméia would become more responsible in their maternal roles if they washed and repaired all the laundry. Besides, this duty in just one small routine of daily family living would promote rapport between mother and child and bind them more securely in love. The children, for example, would recognize how deeply their moms felt. In turn, that would make them feel better about themselves. They would take pride in their clothes and even walk more confidently in spotless attire—at least until the next playground dirt fight. It was far more economical, too, they calculated, to equip each home with a washing machine rather than to purchase massive commercial washing machines and be burdened with a regular payroll for the hired help.

The Bayers also planned to manage food resources with far more cost-effectiveness than at Ijuí, where a main industrial-size kitchen with hired staff prepared the noon meal for children Monday to Friday. The lighter meals of breakfast and supper were eaten in the homes, and all meals were consumed there on weekends when the main kitchen was closed. To the Bayers this was wasteful—high overhead for a large kitchen, needless wages, and the volume purchase of food in quantities exceeding that actually consumed. Ken and Jerilyn had a sound business sense for the bottom line. As the homes operate now at *Lar Colméia* and CHAIN of Love, housemothers are paid a fixed monthly allowance based on the number of children being cared for—an allowance designed to cover their purchases of food for the entire family. Housefathers supplement that allowance with income from jobs or their own business enterprises in nearby communities.

Unlike Ijuí, the *Lar Colméia*–CHAIN of Love homes do not include a separate home for adolescent boys and another separate residence for adolescent girls. At Ijuí, which had 120 children in twelve homes when the Bayers visited, boys and girls would be transferred at age fifteen from a family of brothers and sisters to the one housing solely their gender. The Bayers felt this could prove detrimental to both the children and houseparents of the single-gender homes. Leaving their original home could be traumatic for the children, and any parent, however well-intentioned, could be strained by caring solely for a pack of children individually coping with the innate struggles of their age. For housemothers particularly, mixing children of all ages would be much healthier and more conducive to family bonding by all.

For several years, however, *Lar Colméia* had Erolnilda, a grandmother, caring exclusively for her own granddaughter and four adolescent girls—but what distinguished that arrangement as an exception to the Bayers' plan was the fact that the four had come into care from sexually abusive situations. Beloved Grandma (Vó) Nida, now sixty-six, was compelled to leave *Lar Colméia* because of a heart condition, and now a couple resides in the house as houseparents to nine children of both sexes, including girls originally cared for by Nida. As Pastor Ken explains,

> "The girls came here fearing any male, as likely would any girl who had suffered what they did. But, with maturity and love, that has changed. Lacking a male figure would inhibit their development. In fact, the girls longed for a father figure, and, in time, they started calling me 'Dad.'"

Without males in their lives, as Ken points out, such girls could enter womanhood unable to relate to any men and particularly a potential husband.

"It's not by chance that God created man and woman. It's human nature, regardless of culture, for man and woman to unite for the formation of families. And what we have here in Brazil are so many broken homes because of broken families. The thrust of our CHAIN of Love ministry is to break that pattern so that the children under our care do not repeat it. And living in a family is the key."

Thus, back even while they weighed the pros and cons of the Ijuí operation in 1993, the family plan turned up as the most desirable option for the Bayers' overall strategy for rescuing abandoned and abused children. Couples approved as houseparents would have their own rooms and bathroom, while their own children would share rooms with children legally brought into care as placements from Brazil's court system or social services system. Less than a month after Rusty's death, Ken and Jerilyn and two other church couples sharing their vision had spearheaded the formation of the first CHAIN of Love board. The entire concept was on track when the Bayers left on a year's obligatory furlough to North America in May 1993. There, after some vigorous persuasion, they convinced an initially reluctant home missions board to permit the launch of this new ministry. Its first reaction to the idea was that continuing to plant churches was more important than the uncertainty of charging into a "social gospel." Now, more than a decade later, leaflets published by the International Missions office of the North American Baptist Conference at Oakbrook Terrace, Illinois, hail the accomplishments of the CHAIN of Love ministry and urgently invite people to link into that chain and keep it growing through child sponsorship or other financial pledges, emphasizing the great need. Featuring the heart-framed colored images of smiling children in the CHAIN's family of families, those heart-tugging leaflets prod us with biblical passages such as Lamentations 2:11: "My eyes fail from weeping, I am tormented within…because children and infants faint in the streets of the city."

Having convinced the board, the Bayers then journeyed from church to church and city to city to gather support. That, indeed, was challenging as well, since the congregations would have to recognize their envisioned ministry as legitimate and worthy of their backing. The congregations also had to believe that Ken and Jerilyn would be capable administrators. After a year, they returned to Brazil with eighteen sponsors pledged for children—without a single child yet placed into care. The sponsors had been assured that they would be immediately informed once the project was operational and children were coming into care. Everywhere the Bayers spoke, people agreed that their proposed CHAIN of Love sounded wonderful, but some felt it prudent to await evidence of a successful startup before committing church support. Still, the Bayers plunged ahead faithfully, knowing God's voice was driving them toward rescuing children from the streets. "What He wanted led us into situations that surprised even us," Ken says. As they would discover, many trials and much needed prayer would fuel the days and years ahead.

6

Driven by the Nails of Faith, a Loving Foundation Is Laid

Faith—what a wondrous way of life! As the biblical letter to the Hebrews puts it, "Faith is the substance of things hoped for, the evidence of things not seen" (Hebrews 11:1, KJV). Moreover, "Faith is the force of life," as Russian literary great Leo Tolstoy declares. That firm trust in God governs the lives of Ken and Jerilyn Bayer almost as much as love does, and certainly rare is the couple anywhere who packages it as dynamically day in and day out as the Jesus-driven Bayers. Faith motivates them twenty-four hours a day, and they consider it as vital as their very breathing. Without it, they would not have been able to pioneer the CHAIN of Love ministry. And, of the two Bayers, that faith in action is most visible in Pastor Ken. He's always raring to go to work, a carpenter and a builder of just one little kingdom for the love of God's kids in Brazil, his head under a construction helmet and his hands gripping a hammer and saw. "We didn't really know what we would need or how to get started," Ken recalls. "What I didn't know, I learned," he says, pointing out that, by necessity, he appointed himself to oversee all administrative responsibilities as chief developer. He secured blueprints, gathered the construction materials, and plotted the construction schedule.

The land on which Ken and hundreds of volunteers would contribute their talents and labor into the twenty-first century consisted of 107,600 square feet donated in 1994 by aldermen from the City of Campo Bom, with permission to begin construction in October of that year. Most influential in obtaining that municipal land in the first place was Volnei Ferrari, an architect and urban-development specialist thoroughly versed in the city's master plan, who attended Good News Baptist Church and knew of the Bayers' new ministry vision. Talk about God putting the right people in the right places at the right time to team with other people also deliberately positioned to fulfill His plan for His children! Under Campo Bom's master plan, 10 percent of municipal land was to be reserved for institutional use. Knowing that, deal-maker Ferrari first persuaded his three co-owners to sell what is now the *Lar Colméia* site to the city. Then he, with the newly organized and passionately devoted CHAIN of Love board, sold Campo Bom aldermen on the idea of donating that land to mesh with the institutional-use component of the city's master plan. As important, if not more so, their presentation underscored the social-services benefit to the city, state, and nation of having a privately run Christian enterprise bringing in homeless children. As the Bayers emphasize, governmental administrations undoubtedly have saved untold thousands of dollars by having the CHAIN of Love as a refuge for homeless children rather than having their bureaucracies oversee that responsibility. Incidentally, Ferrari was eventually baptized by Pastor Ken. It is amazing how God scripts His work, both personally and globally!

Perhaps because of the CHAIN's obvious success, Novo Hamburgo has also offered land for homes. However, Ken says the board would rather not have the larger city's tracts at this point. The land at Campo Bom is more ideally suited to the CHAIN's purposes currently, he notes. "In retrospect, the plan of God was for us to be here."

Even as the deal with Campo Bom was nearing completion, the Bayers rented a home in the city's downtown and placed their first board-approved houseparents there, ready to receive children. A Caterpillar started clearing land on the *Lar Colméia* site during the first week of November 1994. The Cat slashed through brush growth and leveled enough space for the construction of a work hut and the first two houses. The second and third weeks were devoted to drilling a well. That job took twice as long as had been expected, since the water source wasn't tapped until 295 feet down. Doesn't help, either, when the work crew is dead drunk most of the time. Subcontracting is always a gamble, but then, as Ken points out, you don't always have a choice.

Such was the Bayers' initiation into the trials of construction, merely a foretaste of the countless tests that would press upon their faith, endurance, patience, perseverance, and determination to hammer out their vision for the love of God's kids. Ken, always time-conscious, partially neutralized those downtimes from crew drunkenness. He led those not nursing hangovers in building the work hut and a shelter for the cement mixer, then marked off the foundation.

Next, they poured and shaped the seventy-two-inch pilasters of the foundation. As Ken notes, a house consisting of steel, concrete, and brick is a mighty heavy creature and must be sturdily supported. Some piles were poured closely together and a pad poured over all of them, with a column rising out of the middle. Some of the pads would sustain thirty-three tons each. It was not exactly a cool picnic, as November and December are summer months in Brazil. Temperatures reached 42 degrees Celsius, 122 for the crew working so closely to the baked earth. After the foundations were sunk, a crew of five full-time Brazilians from Ken's church labored for more than a month into the new year of 1995 laying the grid in preparation for the first pouring.

In January, a church volunteer group of fourteen people from the Canadian provinces of Alberta and British Columbia and one fellow from the province of Manitoba devoted a month to the construction and electrical installation. It was mighty handy to have an electrical company owner and jack-of-all-trades like Ken's dad working, along with his mom, Irma. Women in the group conducted Daily Vacation Bible School for children of Good News Baptist Church and sewed clothes for the three children already being cared for by CHAIN of Love in the rented home near the site. Besides the electrical circuitry, that month saw Ken's crew get the walls up, the framing stripped from under the house, the basement poured on one side, and the frame built overhead for pouring of the ceiling. But again a test of patience intervened: the group would have poured the ceiling had the cement truck and company arrived as scheduled, but they didn't, and most of the volunteers had to fly home. The truck and crew turned up a week later with no explanation except that carnival time had just ended. Such is life wherever a *mañana* attitude prevails.

With most of the North Americans gone, the pace slowed somewhat. Those who stayed on, however, still made good progress. Water installation began; the local Brazilian crew began building the roof; parts of the sewer system were started under the house; and the brick basement fill-in walls were raised, enabling the construction of a workroom. With that, another trial smeared things. Landscaping had not yet begun, and the dirt embankment was higher than the door that opened into the basement, so mud poured in whenever it rained.

By the first week of April 1995, about 5,000 roof tiles weighing four to five pounds each had been placed, and the ten bunk beds built would be enough to furnish the first two homes when completed. One bed went into use a few days later by three additional children brought into the CHAIN's care.

Early April also brought several unpleasant intruders to the job site: snakes. A coral interloper was killed one day and three days later another unidentified critter four feet in length. Ken nearly stepped on it going to the work hut for a glass of water.

Progress during that first construction year indeed fulfilled the Bayers' hopes as expressed in their newsletter to contributors in April. By Christmas 1995, the first home had been completed and a second was being constructed. That first home, which would now house the houseparents and the children being cared for by them in the rented home near the work site, is an everlasting memorial to all those American and Canadian church members whose contributions financed it. House one was constructed entirely from the $70,000 U.S. collected from blessing boxes in churches. And, speaking of divine blueprints, guess who designed that first *Lar Colméia* home and the five others of the same design that neighbor it today—none other than Volnei Ferrari, the deal maker baptized by Pastor Ken. As the Bayers' newsletter to contributors back in April 1995 glowingly reported:

> "Our internal space is large, seeing that there will be twelve or more people living in each residence. With our basement, the space for occupancy exceeds 3,220 square feet (large for Brazil). The bathrooms are also very large, as well as the verandah that wraps around the kitchen. Can you just imagine what would happen on a rainy day if the house lacked an area like this in which the children could play?"

Meanwhile, the CHAIN of Love board was devotedly considering who to approach as prospective houseparents. While no dramatic crises arose during those early days of selection—and few, in fact, did over the next decade—judicious guidelines and much praying blessed the board in recruiting a truly God-given assortment of housemothers and housefathers. The major criterion was personal knowledge of the candidate couples by one or more board member. And the very fact that the board itself was comprised of six couples, most of them from Good News Baptist, empowered it with basic insights into which people would probably work out and which might not. The search was never advertised, and the board seldom took recommendations. When praying as a group, potential names would come up for discussion.

Faith again was the yardstick that guided decisions on who could prove suitable.

The board would then approach the couple considered capable, and, in Jerilyn's words, render its offer: "We thought of you as possible candidates for the ministry of houseparents. What do you think? But, before you say yes, pray about it, and then we will sit down and talk further about it." Some refused, while others who readily accepted were ultimately rejected. Those turned down included an alcoholic husband who had recently gone "dry" and another husband not of the Christian faith. The board felt it crucial to select only couples united in faith and solid marriages, since the loving welfare of God's kids was in the balance. Potential houseparents, then and now, are told that they are being called by God into a long-term commitment, just as the Lord recruited the Bayers for the long haul. And that's not for just a few dedicated years but at least until children who arrived as little ones have matured to legal adulthood and can venture out into the world confidently and independently. True to the board's faithful selection and almost without exception, going the distance for the love of God's kids has been the record of houseparents to date.

For example, because they have had stability, security, consistency, and, above all, the nurturing and loving care of two sets of houseparents since late January 1996, Ana Paula de Oliveira and her sister Taís, now nineteen and seventeen respectively, have progressed remarkably, considering the conditions from which they were freed after Jerilyn answered the alarm, sacrificing her own thirty-seventh-birthday cele-bration with her family that January 26. Jerilyn's response was every bit as noble and dutiful as that of a gallant fire-fighter, rushing to rescue God's kids from harm.

Perhaps, too, as much as any of the children's histories at CHAIN of Love, the story of sisters Ana Paula and Taís epitomizes the stick-to-it-ness of a ministry commitment that has never flagged. In chapter eight, you will meet Ana Paula, speaking exuberantly of her life now and her goal of becoming a gospel singer. Her comments from our interview represent only a fraction of the heartwarming expressions that erupt daily from these adorable CHAIN of Love children. There's a joyful treasury of human interest in Ana Paula's interview answers and the initially sad and then touchingly hopeful stories of other children to which that same chapter is exclusively devoted.

For now, picture their fearful and desperate circumstances as we flash back to that missed birthday celebration. Jerilyn was alerted by a telephone call from a social worker, telling Jerilyn of her dilemma. She was without a vehicle and needed a ride immediately to the garbage dump where two young girls had been discovered wandering aimlessly without their mentally ill mother. Ana Paula, age eight, and Taís, age six, were being threatened by some men who lived there. Earlier that month, the social worker had been assured by the Bayers that the CHAIN would accept the two sisters whenever everything was legally finalized. A couple from Good News Baptist had already agreed to take in the pair. This would be crunch day.

Jerilyn's quick call to Ken ascertained that it was impossible for him to drive the social worker because of crucial obligations at the *Lar Colméia* construction site. Thankfully Ken's mother, Irma, was there from Canada and could pinch-hit looking after the girls while Jerilyn was out with the social worker. "Sure didn't realize what I was getting into," Jerilyn recalls. She drove the social worker over little trails to what seemed the middle of nowhere on Campo Bom's outskirts. There the city dump, popularly—and flatteringly—nicknamed "Shopping," wilted under the intense heat of Brazil's January summer. The air boiled with the gagging stench of rotting garbage. Here at this recycling site, desperately poor souls live in shacks pieced from anything they could sift out of the trash. For adults, teens, and even the smallest children, sustaining life hinges on digging through the piles for anything they might eat, sell, or use. And the dump's soil is the bathroom for all. Pigeon flocks attack the garbage and excrement, and fires are ignited frequently by the combustible gases. Here at this dump, too, is where lustful men prowl as beasts, raping women such as the violent and unbalanced mother of Ana Paula and Taís. Besides collecting the children, Jerilyn and the social worker were to pick up their mother and drive her to an institution for treatment.

They found the two girls playing on a garbage mound. Then, back at the shack, the social worker grabbed the mother's hand and said, "Today, we're going." The girls' outraged grandfather, known to have beaten them frequently, was placated only by a lie—the mother and girls would be registered in a special school.

As they rode to the police station, the car became permeated with the awful stench arising from the rags worn by the mother, Ana Paula, and Taís—rags dug out of the dump. At the station, the mother showed officers the many body marks proving that she had been beaten and raped repeatedly. Then she signed papers releasing Ana Paula and Taís into the legal custody of CHAIN of Love. Rambling on, the mother told the police and social worker how her live-in man not only routinely beat her but chained the children and whipped them as well. Meanwhile, waiting in the car outside, Jerilyn's attempts to befriend and entertain Ana Paula and Taís were feebly received until Ana Paula, pointing to Taís, finally blurted out, "She doesn't speak." Jerilyn thought the child could not be more pitiful—in addition to rotted teeth and matted clumps of lice-infested hair, adding up to a revolting physical appearance, she was wordless.

With the police report seemingly going on into eternity, the heat and stench encasing the car became oppressive almost beyond endurance. So Jerilyn asked the girls if they wanted a Pepsi. The eyes of both sisters sparkled joyfully as their faces broadened into smiles. "Oh yeah!" Ana Paula exclaimed. After a quick drive to the nearest store, Jerilyn purchased the drinks, then knelt and handed a Pepsi to each sister, who were seated at a patio table.

"Both jumped out of their chairs smiling and smothered me with hugs and kisses. Neither had had their own soft drink before. They were used to sharing sips from the same soft drink—that's customary there, and a very rare treat even then. Each was just so delighted to drink her own Pepsi, and I could see their lips shining with happiness."

Driving back to the station, though, Jerilyn mused, "Not exactly how we planned to spend my birthday."

Back at the station, true to form, the official paperwork was still in progress, and as Jerilyn waited, news of yet another crisis came via a telephone call from Ken. Leandro, a boy in the CHAIN's care, had run away, Ken reported, requesting Jerilyn to drop by his grandmother's house for a look. That was likely where Leandro would have gone. So Jerilyn was off again with Ana Paula and

Taís, while the social worker and police continued with their legal documentation.

At the grandma's, she did not exactly receive the warmest birthday welcome. A twenty-year-old uncle of Leandro's burst out of the home and wielded a horsewhip as Jerilyn approached. As she fled, he was yelling, "Get lost! You are not taking this boy again!"

"He was cracking that whip on all sides of me, and just barely missing, while the girls froze, terrified as they watched from the car's back seat."

Angered, Jerilyn jerked around and, facing him, shouted, "If you don't stop that right now, I'm going right back to the police station and report you! I just came from there, you know!" Speechless, the uncle brought the whip to his side while Jerilyn set him straight: "Our homes are for children who don't have a place to live. If your mother will care for Leandro, we will not take him. We are not a jail, and we are not keeping him against his will. If you wish to be responsible for Leandro, go to the Social Services offices and complete the paperwork. But right now we're responsible, and we are only making sure he's all right and looked after." With that, the uncle promised he would go to Social Services and sign for Leandro.

Finally, with the police paperwork completed, they drove to the psychiatric institution to admit the mother, then to the rented home near the CHAIN construction site. There, the surprised housemother, Iraci, was aghast at the sight of the two sisters in filthy tattered rags that reeked with foul odors. Her jaw dropped as Jerilyn announced, "I brought your girls."

Staggered, Iraci asked, "Today?"

Close to tears, Jerilyn managed, "Yes, now. You don't know what I've already been through today, so please take them. I need to go home for a while, but I'll be back later."

At home, a heartsick Jerilyn poured out the day's distressing experiences to her mother-in-law while Ken was at Iraci's home checking on Ana Paula and Taís. He returned with a horrifying report: the girls' legs were scarred with burns, their feet encrusted with chiggers, and their heads full of lice. "Get over there fast with lice medication and your other medicine. Those chiggers have to be dug out of their infected toes." (Chiggers are the larva of various mites, several of which are parasitic. The egg under the skin produces a white maggot within a bubble sac.)

Observing the girls as they were being showered by Iraci, Jerilyn stood horrified by the sight of multiple cigarette-burn scars on both and one knife-inflicted scar on Taís. Later, Ana Paula said Taís had been repeatedly raped by men who knew their victim couldn't expose them. She was an innocent child, defenseless because her mouth couldn't utter a word.

Jerilyn recalls,

> "I choked back tears while I treated the burns on their legs, and it took so long rooting the chiggers and worms out of their feet. Their legs were a mass of open wounds. Just think, all of this from living in garbage day after day! And those awful burns were from the hot plastic melting in the garbage mounds. The sad and terrible truth is that they were now being treated to the first shower of their lives. Iraci and I teamed bathing and cleaning them from lice. Then I backtracked home about 10 A.M. to collect some clothes for the girls. Since we still didn't have any donated handmade clothes in supply, I grabbed some of my daughters' clothes and drove back to

Iraci's home. Can you imagine, an eight-year-old still sucking on a pacifier and actually wearing her mother's underwear! This dear child had never even worn underwear of her own."

When she was back home at last for the night, Ken and their daughters were gearing up for a birthday celebration. But, groaning, Jerilyn said, "Oh please, no supper. Let's just go for ice cream. My stomach might handle that."

Six days later, the sisters' seven-month-old baby brother, Luis Paulo, came into the CHAIN's care, joining Ana Paula and Taís at the home of José and Iraci. Until that day, Ken and Jerilyn had been unaware of his existence. The social worker told the Bayers that Luis Paulo had just been released from hospital and, in his mother's absence, was being cared for by a woman living at the dump. So Jerilyn gathered a stack of diapers and baby playthings, drove to the woman's home, and brought Luis Paulo back to the Bayers' place, where he was picked up by Iraci. "He had no reflexes at all," Jerilyn says. "He just lay limp, not able to hold his head up." Within days, though, this beautiful child began to improve, thanks to the strong, vitamin-packed formula being given to him by Iraci. Meanwhile, Ken continued checking his progress daily with a simple test—holding out his fingers to him. Then one day the baby grabbed those loving fingers, and an elated Ken brought the exciting news home.

Still, other worrisome problems were apparent in both Luis Paulo and Taís. They babbled incoherently, and they lagged in learning and speech development. Doctors blamed their condition on toxoplasmosis, a disease caused by eating food contaminated by rat, cat, or bird waste. The *Oxford Dictionary* points out that it is dangerous in unborn children, noteworthy because the Brazilian doctors told the Bayers both children had been infected prenatally when their mother ate tainted food. Had toxoplasmosis been detected earlier, treatment would have helped, but it was now too late.

Compounding that neglect for Taís was her speechlessness and slowness in learning. A government-appointed doctor's physical examination confirmed that brutal sexual abuse was to blame. Later, the Bayers would learn that her chest scars were from sharpened barbecue skewers held by an uncle to keep her pinned flat while neighborhood cronies violated her. The enormity of those emotional wounds was dramatically impressed upon Jerilyn in an incident at the hospital while Taís was undergoing cranial X-rays. She made no fuss when the male nurse technician first X-rayed her lying on her side, but when he started to gently turn her around for a back X-ray, Taís erupted into terrified screaming, shaking, and sobbing. Jerilyn managed to ask the nurse to leave, then embraced Taís and broke down sobbing with her. "It was awful driving home with this poor girl beside me and my insides wrenched with pain. How could anybody treat a human being so horribly simply because she was unable to tell anyone about them?"

Now, more than ten years later, Taís has blocked that savagery from her mind, Jerilyn says. "She doesn't remember anything beyond the CHAIN of Love. For her, life began here, and she has made amazing progress." For that incredible growth, Jerilyn thanks and credits Mariene Tammerik, the CHAIN's psychologist, who drives in twice weekly from Porto Alegre to counsel children in her office at the *Lar Colméia* complex. In chapter fifteen, readers will meet and hear from Mariene and other professionals helping the children. Taís, as even this author heard, now speaks more clearly and understandably. As Jerilyn observes, when asked to draw something, Taís will studiously and colorfully sketch her most prized object, saying, "This is my house." Taís can also now write her name and read some letters. Still, she requires consistent reassurance of her place as a family member who is actually loved. Her housekeeping is outstanding and extremely responsible, Jerilyn adds. Everything is done thoroughly, and Taís follows instructions precisely. And smaller children like her. She delights in charming them.

When released from the institution a few months later, their mother exercised her visitation rights but acted crazily whenever she met with the children at the Social Services office. Because she habitually neglected taking her medication, Jerilyn says, their mom would embarrass Ana Paula and Taís with profanity and call them "ugly." That's why Taís would become extremely agitated whenever a visit was scheduled. Luis Paulo, who always thought of Iraci as his mother until informed that his real mom was the lady they had been visiting, thereafter complained of sickness and refused to go. Although Ana Paula eventually signed a paper that frees her from visiting her mother, her forgiveness is such now that she desires to visit with her occasionally, just to know how she's doing. They last met about three years ago when family members were legal witnesses to the adoption of Luis Paulo by José and Iraci, who had retired from *Lar Colméia* and moved to their newly purchased farm.

Are there any lingering regrets by Jerilyn about that missed thirty-seventh birthday celebration? Not a shred. Again, these were scars turned into stars, as Dr. Schuller says. Nightmarish, then, Jerilyn admits, but what an education! As she reflects, the lives of three children were restored, and that's everything to shout about in celebration. And wasn't her servanthood to the Lord on that birthday of January 26, 1996, just like her everyday ministry has been to this very moment at CHAIN of Love—stepping out of herself and into the shoes of another soul? Jerilyn is truly a summa-cum-laude grad of the university of relationships, sensitively tuning into everyone, praying daily for the welfare of all, just like Jesus does.

Furthermore, from this author's overview, it's absolutely mind-blowing how the Bayers have shaped the CHAIN into what could be a global role model, becoming even more lustrous as it grows, considering the array of barriers confronted daily from Brazil's social, economic, judicial, and political systems. But, before elaborating on the defect-ridden fabric of those systems, Sara and I must emphasize that the Bayers were grappling with far more urgent and pressing difficulties as this book was being updated in July 2006.

Construction of *Lar Colméia*'s eighth house (and tenth residence) was well under way. But the building pace had slowed markedly since financial constraints prevented Ken from keeping more than three men on the job. Devoted and determined servant of Jesus that he is, hard-driving Ken was being weighed down by a funding shortfall he feared could compel him to draw from reserves to cover the child-salvaging operation's monthly cost.

His and Jerilyn's divine lifeline for needy and tragically neglected Brazilian children was being heavily burdened by three hard and simultaneous realities: a) a continuing inflation level of 20 percent over the past three years; b) a 30 percent loss in the falling U.S. dollar—the benchmark by which Brazilian currency is measured; c) a hefty increase in ministry-administration service charges. As Ken points out, funds raised during the slow summer months are usually below the total needed to cover monthly costs; thus the reliance on reserves. "I have to use an iron hand with the reserves, so that we're not left without money. My faith is being tested—will we stay afloat?"[11]

Sara and I contend that this Jesus-like role model so worthy of being emulated by worship assemblies everywhere and so aptly entitled the CHAIN of Love must remain unbroken and vigorously sustained. After all, the CHAIN's success rate for restoration from hopelessness to salvation and growth is almost 100 percent! And children in desperate need of rescue are oblivious to the capricious swings of national and world economics. A growling stomach and an abandoned child's crying heart cannot patiently await monetary stability.

The dedicated Bayers soldier on with their ministry, its life preserver of hope and salvation hurled out in 2006 to bring in children like six-year-old Bruna Alexsandra da Silva Braz and eleven-year-old Lucas Coproski. Cost squeeze notwithstanding, desperate children of God *cannot,* in good conscience, be rejected. So, as Ken crunched the numbers, little Bruna was delighted to learn from house-mother Nair that she would be in the *Lar Colméia* family permanently. She would have her own bed and be fitted with some bright new clothes. For Lucas, as well, the CHAIN became an immediate haven of stability and security after being endlessly shuffled around among relatives. Reader, ask yourself what kind of hideous plight might have befallen Bruna and Lucas had the CHAIN not opened its doors! Abandoned by an impoverished mother, Bruna had twice thereafter been returned from adoptive homes. She remained in a halfway house until social workers arranged legal guardianship with the CHAIN, enabling her to be rejoined with older brother Guilherme, who had already been under its care for four years.

As for Lucas, would he have had a ghost of a chance had the courts not ruled family negligence and ordered placement with the CHAIN? Long ago abandoned by his mother, Lucas had been with an alcoholic father whose sole liquid provision to his son was *cachaca*, a strong Brazilian alcoholic beverage. As a result of this steady liquid diet, Lucas developed ulcers and had to be medicated. Fortunately, other kin temporarily took in Lucas, but that just set off a merry-go-round of being ricocheted from one impoverished family of relatives to another, all of whom claimed they couldn't afford to care for him. Thank God for the CHAIN's existence![12]

While the CHAIN's financial worries may well pass, remember, dear reader, that far more deeply embedded are those aforementioned barriers confronting the Bayers daily because of defects in Brazil's social, economic, judicial, and political systems. While surely unintentional, nevertheless, their structural deficiencies work against the CHAIN's outreach to God's kids. You may be dismayed, reading about the poverty from which the children interviewed in the next three chapters were extricated. Brazil's economic profile is a stacked deck against homeless street children. People everywhere, and North Americans especially, should thank God that missionaries like Ken and Jerilyn Bayer are so forbearing, enduring, and committed to victory for the love of God's kids.

Extremely frustrating, for example, is the disorganized social services system, Jerilyn emphasizes.

"Officials and workers don't seem to know the process required for legalizing the placement of children. You see this all over, and our hands are tied because of bureaucratic ignorance and red tape. At times we have been at a complete standstill because of elections and campaigning by government workers."

Ken points to an ongoing wrestling match with social services to make officials realize that CHAIN of Love is not a dumping ground.

"Our requirement is that they exhaust all options before coming to us. In that way, it becomes impossible for them to pull them out of here because some abusive parent suddenly decides to regain custody. And the kid becomes the victim."

Moreover, government-run halfway houses are pathetic. The old houses described by the Bayers are supposed to be temporary shelters for at-risk children, but some have remained there for as long as three years. That's because the system is stymied by overloaded courts deciding the children's futures. "Once a child is placed in a shelter, he is not allowed to be taken out until a judge makes a decision," Jerilyn notes. These children, she adds, are crammed into bedrooms with mattresses on the floor, and almost nothing is provided beyond their basic needs. It is all sterile, cold, impersonal. There is no male figure for the boys and girls, because only hired women cook and care for the children. Halfway-house residents can vary from a dozen to thirty or more children, Jerilyn says. Sometimes there are no infants, other times eight or more. Affection is almost non-existent from government workers committed only to a job. They will bathe the children and change their clothes, feed them, and usher them to bed. Play with them or teach them anything? No way! Even some older ones are not yet toilet trained, still in diapers simply because workers find it easier changing diapers than teaching them.

And what hope is there for young abandoned girls victimized sexually? Homes for girls must, by law, release them at age thirteen—either out onto the streets to fend for themselves or into a state institution, which is notorious for its record of introducing teenage girls to drugs while transforming virtually all into prostitutes. But there is now hope, genuine love, and a future for some of these vulnerable souls at CHAIN of Love.

Vigilant and protective fighter that he is, Ken has also been speaking out over the past few years against civic plans to establish paved roads in close proximity to the *Lar Colméia* complex. The increased traffic would endanger children walking or riding to and from school and disrupt family life generally at the site. So Ken has offered some alternative proposals.

Ken's cool and unrelenting determination never wavered under any problem or crisis during construction of the first six of *Lar Colméia*'s eight houses. With no money on hand, he and the crew just proceeded building the second home, Jerilyn recalls admiringly. "He just plowed ahead, making phone calls and writing letters to our mothers, fathers, aunts, uncles, friends, whomever. His attitude was 'whatever it takes.' The money and volunteers poured in."

As the fifth house reached a skeletal framework, news came again of no more funds available—and this from the headquarters of the North American Baptist Conference.

The message: better cancel the work; no money in the budget.

> "But that was like trying to stop a speeding train. You can't stop it on a dime. Our ceiling, house skeleton, and slabs had been poured. I advised the workers to find temporary jobs while we worked with the NAB in a fund-raising appeal. In six or seven weeks, we raised more than the $40,000, and all our workers returned."

Grief also intervened. One worker died of a heart attack while plastering in a home's second-floor bathroom. Work stopped for a few days of mourning for a fellow crewmate and friend, Nilci.

Occasionally, construction progress and the CHAIN of Love was harassed by followers of the so-called "spiritistic" movement in Brazil—but, judging by Pastor Ken's words, these irritations are as easily dismissed as swatting a mosquito on one's arm. Their mischievous aims are totally ineffective.

As explained to this author by Dr. Allan Effa, Jerilyn's brother and a professor of missions and cross-cultural studies at Taylor University College and Seminary in Edmonton, Canada, Brazil's spiritist movement took hold centuries ago with the settlement of African slaves. However, he strongly cautions that so-called "voodoo" and witchcraft should not be lumped in with spiritism since they are actually quite different. Referred to as *Umbanda* and *Candomblé,* "these forms originated with Nigerian (Yoruba) slaves brought into Brazil. They continued to practice their devotion to various indigenous gods and goddesses, as well as blood sacrifices to determine the sources of misfortunes and illnesses—practices that were frowned upon by Catholic officials. It was mostly an 'underground' religion of the lowest classes." Many, if not most, of these newcomers were baptized as Catholics and continued practicing both faiths, certainly a dichotomy in beliefs, it seems.

The problem is that people generally, and perhaps in Brazil, too, aren't informed enough to distinguish between various categories of spiritism and "voodoo"—thus the longtime and continuing public misperception. As Dr. Effa elaborates, the "world view" of those slaves, baptized and unbaptized, "was never greatly challenged because it was in their ancestral religions that they found power to overcome illnesses, misfortunes, etc. In this way, it acted much like many 'folk religions' act today around the world." That attraction continues powerfully through much of Brazilian society, he adds.

> "It is popularized by media figures, popular music (the samba), and the whole movement to assert cultural identity and traditional beliefs. It has never made a huge inroad among intellectuals or the upper classes because they already control power and don't feel the same needs to dabble in these matters."

Whatever the composition of spiritism and "voodoo" in Brazil, academic sources continue to emphasize that Brazil is simultaneously the world's largest Catholic and spiritist nation. One Internet source points out that many will worship at Mass on Sunday and then attend a spiritist meeting on Tuesday at one of more than 14,000 spiritist centers. A discrepancy between Dr. Effa's clarification on spiritism and another Internet source's explanation is highlighted by a statement from the latter that lumps spiritist worship into a whole with two distinct divisions: the lower variety that came with African slaves (voodoo, witchcraft, magic, etc.) and the popular upper-class New Age version (reincarnation and talking with the dead).[13]

All of this is cited here simply because during the course of researching *For the Love of God's Kids*, Dr. Herman Effa, father of both Jerilyn and Dr. Allan Effa, thought the presence of spiritism in Brazil to be a relevant and significant concern. He related incidents involving the killing of some poultry belonging to *Lar Colméia* that definitely revealed a ritualistic, spiritist message. Dead black kittens were also found under one of the homes being constructed. In the paragraphs following, Ken will outline what happened. But the senior Dr. Effa's interest is noteworthy since he was a missionary to Brazil for many years and is a former director of international missions for the North American Baptist Conference. As a research aid, he loaned this author a book on Brazilian spiritism entitled *Drum and Candle*, written by David St. Clair. That book, while it thoroughly covers all forms of voodoo and spiritism and the differences within them, puts everything under the umbrella of spiritism. As journalist St. Clair's book jacket states:

> "In Brazil, spiritism—or *voodoo* as we Americans might call it—permeates every aspect of life. In the remote villages of the vast interior and in the teeming cities along the coast, among both illiterate blacks and sophisticated whites, the power of unseen gods and spirits to heal or harm, to save lives or take them, is almost universally accepted."[14]

In contrast, Professor Allan Effa emphasizes that "spiritism," strictly defined, "is a highly intellectual form of religion, tracing its origins to France in the nineteenth century, primarily the writings of Allan Kardec. His form of spiritism is like a new-age spiritualism. It does not really attempt to blend itself with Catholicism, but sees itself as a superior form of religion. Where things get a bit messy is that spiritism also believes that spirits are present everywhere and that we can communicate with the spirits of the deceased. This, of course, lends it a bit of an occultist bend, but not in the direction of causing evil toward others, but of seeking guidance and direction for life."

From this author's reading of *Drum and Candle,* the beliefs and practices detailed by St. Clair constitute a mumbo-jumbo mishmash that, in their totality, rocket beyond even the most bizarre science fiction, in essence denigrating, demeaning, refuting, and making farcical the definition of genuine faith. St. Clair's account contains eight pages of photos, including scenes of a famous spirit healer shoving a kitchen knife into a patient's eye, a card-reading medium who "talks with the dead," and a man at a black-magic session kneeling in a circle drawn for "the devil, *Exu*" and tearing out the entrails of a live black chicken with his teeth. As the book jacket notes, St. Clair, fluent in both Portuguese and Spanish, had lived in Brazil and South America for the previous eleven years and had participated in ritual meetings, "seeing and feeling for himself the effects of the spirits—and gaining a new, often unsettling understanding of their power over the mortal world."[15]

Notably, the book's prediction of a "great spirit leader" coming to displace Jesus Christ in 1999, as the universe well knows now, did not come to pass. That prediction, made to St. Clair roughly thirty years earlier, came in an interview with the *Umbanda* medium Tancredo da Silva Pinto, known as the "Black Pope of Brazil," who asserted that Jesus wasn't the Son of God. As quoted by St. Clair, these were his words:

> "I am not a Christian," he told me, "but I admire Christ's intelligence and His ability to preach and reach the masses. He was not the Son of God, because God is the phenomena of nature and is not flesh and blood. He was a strong spirit medium, very strong, and the world is under his influence now. It will remain so until 1999; then another great spirit leader will come. I hope that I am still on this earth to greet him. There are many things I should like to tell him."[16]

Whatever orbits these voodoo or spiritist figures glide in, Ken is not in the least fazed or intimidated and will not be smashed off course from CHAIN of Love's mission of salvaging the lives of homeless children for someone truly divine—Jesus. "Their power is only a weak candle held up to the sun," Ken declares.

> "The majority of people come out of this. Their spiritual journey begins when shown they are no longer tied to the old powers that held them under their spell or possession. It's interesting that most of the people who abused their children and then subsequently lost them to the CHAIN of Love have tried through this spiritistic form to curse the homes and get their children back through this means. Of course none of this works, because of whom they are going up against. We have mentioned some experiences in the past to sponsors whenever we faced this kind of action. All of our chickens were

killed one night, their blood drained, and then placed in a circle around the dead rooster. The same day I found some black kittens in a home under construction with their heads cut off and the blood drained as well. We buried the animals and prayed that God's power would not let anything happen; then we returned to work. Our focus is not on the spectacular but the spiritual warfare. We dedicate these children to the Lord and imbue in them the desire to accept the Lord and see their entire past broken. We also have cast out dirty spirits from some children soon after they came to us. Once out of the children, many times the same filth tries to work through relatives or others in these movements who realize what has happened. We counter these attacks through daily prayer. The results speak for themselves. We are free."

Surely Ken's fearless words would have been resoundingly seconded by that illustrious eighteenth-century French author and philosopher Voltaire, whose own pearls of wisdom echo them: "As long as people believe in absurdities, they will continue to commit atrocities."[17] Uttered two centuries ago, those words are as relevant as ever in today's techno-wise but morally foolish world. And, to no lesser degree, they apply to all of humanity's yesterdays—not exempting the barbarism of those so-called Christians whose demonic acts during the Inquisition and other dark eras defiled the purity of true Christianity.

The CHAIN of Love, in contrast, is free, as Ken says, because its mission is purely on behalf of God's kids. And the results do speak for themselves, as this author observed in the sunny faces of children at CHAIN of Love and the warmth that exuded so spontaneously from their hearts. These are angels whose dirty faces have been shined to a lustrous glow by a devoted ministry of caring families. They thrive now, secure in the knowledge that some Jesus-driven people are finally looking after them. Never again will they be abused or abandoned. The next three chapters deal wholly with those children, who will tell you in their own enthusiastic words how being connected into a CHAIN of Love is divinely overhauling their lives from earlier histories of intolerable and hopeless abuse, neglect, and misery.

Then you will meet their housemothers and housefathers in the subsequent two chapters. These superstar houseparents will take you inside the day-to-day family lives and relate the powers used to nurture their children and how that consistently caring domestic atmosphere forges affectionate bonds among the children themselves. These housemoms and housedads are infused with the Spirit of God. Their magic flows entirely from that divine medicine called love.

7

FROM HORRID YESTERDAYS INTO HOMES OF HOPE AND LOVE

Many of the broken and homeless Brazilian children taken into the hearths and hearts of the CHAIN of Love are illiterate in areas of normal childhood beyond their country's native tongue of Portuguese. Tragically, they're illiterate in knowing care, compassion, affection, the warmth of a tender parental hug, the secure clasp of a mother's or father's hand, the security of a mother's or father's protective and encouraging love. They arrive as children deprived of a rudder for their lives, but that soon changes, thanks to a ministry that has been going all-out for the love of God's kids.

Besides the warmth of a full family—namely, devotedly loving parents intermingled with the camaraderie of other children received into their hearts as real brothers and sisters—these CHAIN of Love children benefit from a full range of programs and activities tailored to help them develop into fully rounded adults mentally, physically, emotionally, and spiritually. A boy or girl may go to school in the morning, for example, and spend the afternoon learning a trade or vocation taught by a volunteer at the technical-vocational center in the *Lar Colméia* complex. Or the daily schedule of school and vocational training could be reversed. Everything is flexible, with built-in supports. Private tutoring is available. Professionals, such as doctors, dentists, a speech therapist, and a psychologist, are on hand regularly. Volunteers offer morning, afternoon, and evening instruction in such diverse interests as shoe- and leather-making, dancing, playing a band instrument, sewing and quilting, baking and cooking, and using a computer. A high school physical education teacher drops by on Saturdays to engage the children in soccer playing and instruction. The list goes on and on. Volunteers and professionals alike speak glowingly of the amazingly positive changes they observe in the children. You will meet many of these dedicated adults in later chapters as they relate what's happening with God's kids.

At home the children are taught to pray regularly, share household chores, and participate in Bible-study discussions led by houseparents. On Sundays, the children and their housemoms and housedads are off to Good News Baptist Church in Novo Hamburgo for services and Sunday school. For those who don't go by car, there's the ministry bus driven by José, a housefather. Every Sunday morning that vehicle jammed with ninety children and adults makes an exciting journey of cheering, singing, games-playing in the seats, and nonstop high-spirited chatter. These children's lives are full.

Now contrast these blossoming lives of today to those dreadfully horrid lives prior to CHAIN of Love as we list a sampling of the situations from which they were rescued and then hear the children themselves elaborate about those terrible yesterdays and their hopes for today and tomorrow. Brazil's economic profile figures significantly in the misery from which these Brazilian children of God were extricated. The nation's economic system and all the other structural systems comprising the so-called foundation of Brazilian society are so unbalanced and defect-marred that, as a combined force, they unintentionally conspire against God's underprivileged children. "There is an enormous gap between the extremely rich and extremely poor," Ken explains.

> "About 19 million of Brazil's population of 176 million to 180 million exist on less than $100 a month. Three percent of the population controls 70 percent of the wealth, the middle class of 17 percent controls 20 percent of it, and for the bottom 80 percent it's a daily battle for survival grasping for a meager 10 percent."

As Jerilyn adds, this gross disparity in incomes is particularly spotlighted in a tax-dependent Brazilian healthcare system that suffers badly from a dearth of cash—a dearth especially seen in the drastic shortage of nurses. The government supports the system by taxing all financial transactions—and that "all" includes every bank deposit and bank withdrawal. But how can health care possibly be healthy with so many poor unable to pay into the system? Yet, Jerilyn points out, "Brazil is resource-rich and would be one of the best countries in the world if it were administered properly. The climate is great, and the people are friendly, but plain greed, pure and simple, is undermining the nation."

So, it's no wonder that virtually every child who has arrived at the CHAIN's doorway of hope and love had been impoverished on all counts—mentally, physically, emotionally, materially, educationally, and spiritually. Their lives had neither substance nor soul. Their world had been one of sinking sand—one so weakened that they couldn't manage the faintest cry for help. That help came to some only because a rescue-committed CHAIN of Love was out there to pull them in. Children, as the CHAIN staff knows from Psalm 127, are a gift of God, and it's morally intolerable that any child's life anywhere be fractured permanently by adult hands.

Consider the following children whose lives have been salvaged. A boy, now fifteen, whose real father is unknown, had two alcoholic stepfathers. The second, whom the boy says once tried to drown his now-deceased mother in a lake, was knifed and shot to death over a fuel-oil debt as he slept on a sofa in the family hovel.

A girl, the daughter of a prostitute, had been so violently raped as a seven-year-old that she arrived directly from hospital, where she had been taking the anti-AIDS cocktail until tests could determine whether or not she was infected.

A boy who cannot hear or speak, severely abused, was abandoned as a two-year-old by his seventeen-year-old single mother, who subsequently had three other children out of wedlock.

A girl of fourteen had been abandoned twice—first by her alcoholic mom, then two years later by her grandparents—followed by four years in a home for girls where she was not once visited by any family member.

Another girl of fourteen was atrociously neglected by two mentally deranged parents whose family shack had wall-to-wall human dung and garbage; when social workers took action, they commented that "not even a rat would live there."

A twelve-year-old boy was plagued with an "identity crisis" since his father was known only to be a nameless vagabond and his mother was brutally murdered before his eyes.

Two sisters have lifelong scars from beatings by their mother—in addition to the emotional scars of a revolving-door existence of living with first their mother, then their father, then an institution, and then through the cycle again.

An eight-year-old girl had been sexually abused by her uncle and grandfather. Her drug- and crime-ridden family included a father imprisoned for raping her older sister and a mother off wandering with her younger brothers as part of a nomadic political group seeking free land.

Now, dear reader, step into the shoes of the following children and imagine their feelings undergoing what they did prior to rescue by the CHAIN of Love. An abandoned six-year-old girl was scarred and left permanently bald on one side of her head when she accidentally tipped boiling oil from a pot on the stove as she reached up to it in a desperate grab for what she thought might be food.

An eight-year-old girl and two younger sisters arrived with lice-infested heads and worms invading their bodies. They had lived in a dilapidated hovel shared with other families and slept with their mother and baby brother—five in a single bed—because Mom, abandoned by an alcoholic husband during her last pregnancy, could earn, at best, twenty dollars a week scrounging for salable items in a garbage dump.

A six-year-old boy tried to awaken his mother, who had been slain with an ax swung into her head by a drunken and enraged husband she had kicked out earlier, a tragedy that brought the boy and his older brother and three older sisters into care.

A twelve-year-old girl at ten days old had been traded by her destitute mother for a liter of milk with which she could feed two older children. The exchange was with a trigger-tempered foster father whose batterings included one when she was eleven where he broke both of her arms pulling her back into the house while she was shielding her face from being smashed again.

Two brothers, ten and eight, sons of a father imprisoned for pimping, were in danger of descending into a childhood of crime on the streets because their grandmother could no longer afford to care for them.

Two brothers and two sisters, all under seven, were left by their drug-addicted aunt to fend for themselves in an abandoned shack for more than half a year before they were discovered—children whose hefty mother had borne nine children, all by different fathers, and was in jail awaiting prosecution on charges of drug trafficking.

A ten-year-old boy, whose scar-streaked face was the work of a knife-wielding father, was so hideously abused by a dad demanding that he stand motionless while enduring such torture that he futilely attempted to escape from CHAIN of Love on his very first day there, his mind having been fearfully ingrained with the notion that everyone, regardless of setting, would brutalize him.

Reflect as well, dear reader, on the revolting situations from which the following children were saved. Three brothers and a baby sister, born to drug-addicted parents, were taken along by their divorced mother to witness her alcohol-fueled promiscuity. She supplied condoms to the oldest and ultimately contracted AIDS while sharing a syringe with a transvestite.

A ten-year-old girl was ignorant of her own name when taken into care. She had been abandoned by her mother and her mentally-deranged father, who left to roam the streets following her birth, only to be taken in by a couple whose stepfather not only raped her but provided her body for erotic sexual exploitation and "entertainment" to neighborhood pals. She was later raped again by the new husband of her birth mother.

A four-year-old boy was so impoverished and uncivilized by a "bush" existence that his aunt, a brothel madam, labeled him a "bush rat." He was a freckle-faced red-haired kid with the wrinkled hands of an old man, the son of a mentally-challenged mother and the grandson of the man who is also his father, who had tried to kill his mom with a machete.

An eleven-year-old girl whose mother had tried to smother her to death at birth then lived peacefully for eight years with her maternal grandma. Immediately following the grandmother's death, her step-grandfather brought a new woman into the home, and both adults inflicted electrical-wire beatings on her until she ran away.

Finally, picture the helplessness of the following children before the Bayers' ministry pulled them into a world of loving care. A fourteen-year-old boy was so frequently bounced from one relative's home to another—some of whom believed they were ridding themselves of the "devil"—and into and out of halfway houses that he actually regarded himself as crazy.

Two brothers and a sister were first abandoned by their father, then beaten regularly by a prison escapee who had moved in with their mom, and finally were abandoned by both their mother and the fugitive.

A girl just shy of five when met by the Bayers was crying painfully from teeth that had decayed to the gums. She was the daughter of a prostitute who had repeatedly abandoned several children.

Two sisters, nine and seven, were adrift in a scenario of unending hope, which began when their mother died of leukemia three years earlier. Then neglect by an alcoholic father and beatings by a stepmother caused them to run away from home three times. Finally they had not a single place to turn, their most promising prospect among alcoholic, violent, or drug-addicted relatives being with a maternal aunt who suffered from both AIDS and spousal abuse and was thus totally incapable of responsibly meeting their needs.

An eight-year-old boy whose mother is unknown had been abused since infancy by an alcoholic father, evidence of which is a head scarred by some sharp object in several places under the hair.

One child was rumored to have been homosexually victimized for years in a children's shelter.

Two brothers, ten and four, and a baby sister, ten months, were offspring of a mentally-unbalanced mother away for treatment and a father who abandoned them to live with the daughter of his first partner—leaving all in a shack of indescribable filth and destitution. This forced the ten year old, much like that plucky hero Paulo Ricardo de Amaral de Assis of chapter three, to fetch food for his brother and sister, a responsibility that the boy strove admirably to fulfill by trying to cook, finding food in garbage mounds, by making certain his infant sister's stomach was filled regularly with baby beans, rice, stale bread, Coca-Cola, spoiled milk, whatever.

The foregoing digest of unbelievably deprived childhoods is merely a minuscule sampling of the horrendous degradation inflicted upon children, not only in that one small area of Brazil. It is a sampling that becomes infinitesimally smaller within the boundaries of the entire country and undoubtedly shrinks to a virtually invisible speck within the scope of helpless children crying out for preservation worldwide.

Individuals and worship assemblies everywhere might do well to consider the enormity of that challenge for just a moment. Perhaps you, dear reader, or your congregation might wish to build upon the role model progressing at the CHAIN of Love. You have a world of children to cultivate, and you have the potential to reap an enormously pleasing harvest of results from the seeds you help to plant.

In chapters eight and nine, you will read about the healthy growth that could sprout as Brazilian children themselves talk at length about how the hands of Jesus at the CHAIN of Love have gloriously reconstructed their lives.

8

JESUS AND COMPANY GIVE BIRTH TO JOY AND MIRACLES

The crowd of 300 could almost see and touch the presence of Jesus as the Most Honored Guest at the wedding of Adriane Ferreira Capeletti Moreira on November 23, 2002. There stood the bride, so elegant, so graceful, so radiant—especially in her brilliantly beaming smile toward one and all.

While walking out of Good News Baptist Church with her husband, twenty-one-year-old Adriane stopped and gifted Pastor Ken and Jerilyn Bayer with one of the most heartwarming moments of their ministry developing the CHAIN of Love. Only moments earlier, Ken had officiated as Adriane and Nei Moreira joined in wedlock. Bursting with joy, a tearfully smiling Adriane hugged and thanked the Bayers for having given her the opportunity for a changed life. She emphasized how so many of her dreams had materialized since the CHAIN of Love stepped in to rescue her as a thirteen year old—the victim of such consistent sexual abuse that her reproductive organs had atrophied.

Then, in April 2004, another heartwarming moment— a telephone call from Adriane to the Bayers with great news. She was in her first trimester of pregnancy, and they would be grandparents. Amazing how God and His servants can restore a girl spiritually and physically! Husband Nei, an English teacher, was then in seminary training at Porto Alegre, with a young man who subsequently became a son-in-law of the Bayers. In the meantime, Adriane and Nei assisted in starting a church at Sapacaia do Sul, where they head the children's ministry.

Jerilyn wondered in relating Adriane's story to this author: "To think of what she might have been, or probably would have been, had she not come here—dirt poor, no education, six children by now, and with no father around for the children. That pattern, which is so typical of girls like her, has been broken because of Christ, and Adriane's life has totally changed."

What an incredible growth journey from that first day of embrace by the CHAIN of Love eight years earlier on November 30, 1994. Ken's first view of Adriane in a social services office was that of a frightened thirteen-year-old, glaring down at the floor while huddled forlornly in a corner, a tattered old teddy bear nestled into her chest. Social Services had telephoned earlier that day, urgently requesting that the newly formed CHAIN of Love take the runaway into care. Otherwise, she almost definitely would wind up roaming the streets, a lost soul and extremely vulnerable. Whether Adriane was well mentally or physically was questionable as well, according to social workers, and no doubt the best medicine, whatever her condition, would be the loving warmth of caring people in a caring home. This was a child who stuttered so badly that even her few words were garbled. She had testified against her father for having raped her over several years, beginning at age seven. Sexual abuse had continued after Adriane had been placed with a foster family. Recently, Adriane had been virtually invisible to another set of foster parents—all attention was focused on their own two young children. After a year, Adriane ran away, but she was quickly found by social workers.

Her plight was so desperate that the Bayers decided to reverse their original decision to only accept children under seven and to broaden their intake mandate to include older children, even teens such as Adriane. For her, the Bayers enlisted Eronilda (Grandma Vó Nida) as a housemother. When approached by the Bayers, Grandma Nida, a widow and a member of Good News Baptist Church who had come into Christianity as an adult, delayed her decision because of a recent heart-splitting experience involving a little girl. But, happily, she did open her own home and heart to the broken and confused young Adriane (land clearance and site preparation had just gotten underway for the *Lar Colméia* complex). As the future would prove, Grandma Nida was the perfect person to oversee Adriane's upbringing. Adriane was the third child taken in by the new ministry, and because of her age, she would represent the first hard trial of the CHAIN's legal guardianship approach toward preparing children for adulthood.

As it happens, the Lord had another angel on duty besides Grandma Nida for that fateful November day in 1994—the Bayers' daughter Jessica, who accompanied her dad to the social services office. Jessica, then just eight, took two Barbie dolls with her. She asked Adriane which one she preferred and gave it to her. Then they played with the Barbies while the paperwork transferring legal custody was being completed. Playing with the dolls immediately bonded the girls as friends in the office and later during the car ride to Grandma Nida's. As mother Jerilyn says, "Jessica's compassion conquers people right away. She is so loving. She even comes home with wayward mongrels— that's how big her heart is."

Meanwhile, social workers handling custody documents at the office filled Ken in on what a gynecologist's tests had determined. Damage to Adriane's sexual organs had been severe. "She may never develop normally," a worker said.

Grandma Nida was also undergoing some heart-breaking times of her own during the weeks leading up to the linkup with Adriane. In fact, she had told herself to never become involved emotionally with any child after the bitter loss earlier of a girl who had captured her heart. Her first experience with child care unfolded this way: a mother in her neighborhood had been consistently leaving her little daughter behind at a corner tavern, disappearing frequently for weeks before returning to reclaim her from the bar owner. Finally, the frustrated proprietor told Grandma Nida that he was not obliged to keep looking after the little one. Grandma Nida could not bear continuing to witness a child of God habitually forsaken by a neglectful mother, so she took the girl into her own home.

For nine months, this servant of Jesus looked after the girl, finally requesting the mother's permission to adopt. The mom refused, and the case went to a judge who advised Grandma Nida to confront the wayward mom with an ultimatum. "Either you sign the adoption papers," she told the negligent mother, "or you take your daughter and care for her." The mother brusquely snatched her daughter's hand and marched off scowling, leaving Grandma Nida tearful with heartbreak. For her own emotional equilibrium, she prayed, "Lord, I never, ever, want to get attached to a child again."

But two weeks later, Ken was at Grandma Nida's door telling the story of Adriane and requesting that she take in this girl so desperately in need of a safe harbor with a loving anchor. She promised to seek guidance in prayer, and that she did. That entire night was sleepless as she prayed and wrestled with whether she could possibly risk more heartbreak "Lord, is this really for me? Am I able to do this? What are you doing, sending me another child?"

Three people arrived the next day at Grandma Nida's door—Ken, the social worker, and Adriane. In Ken's car were Adriane's clothes—that's how certain he was that a "yes" was forthcoming. Everyone reviewed the situation, including Adriane. Then Grandma Nida questioned Adriane, "Do you want to live here with me? I'll take good care of you."

More discussion followed, and Grandma Nida saw how much Adriane wanted to stay. Everyone agreed that this was the solution. "Oh, by the way," Ken smiled, "all of her clothes are in the car."

Thus began the formation of a heart-stirring bond of mother-daughter devotion. Actually, their linkup was so successful that soon Grandma Nida's home became the CHAIN of Love healing center for other adolescent girls gruesomely victimized by sexual predators. Adriane and Grandma Nida had blazed the way.

As she matured, Adriane became a cheerful and responsible domestic helper to Grandma Nida. She held her head high and worked enthusiastically at home, and, while not excelling at school, Adriane always studied hard. At one point, she dreamed of working in a day-care center—an ambition spurred by an after-school job caring for small children.

That steady growth with Grandma Nida at the CHAIN of Love magnifies all the more the depths from which Adriane had been rescued. Those gruesome earlier years of Adriane's story, in fact, are as dramatic a demonstration as any of Pastor Ken's observation that God even collects the "garbage" of people's lives and "recycles it for His purposes."

Indeed, from Adriane's own description of events, her childhood had been unbelievably miserable. Never had she been given a choice in anything. Her father began pouncing on her sexually, almost nightly, starting at age seven. Meanwhile, her mother slept, unaware. Her younger brothers, though, heard and listened in fearful silence to the evil racket that was seeping through the wall cracks of their rickety hovel. They also heard their terrorized sister cry herself to sleep nightly. As for Adriane's mother, ignorance was more blissful. "When I tried to tell her, she didn't believe me and warned that I be quiet and not talk to anyone."

Thanks to a concerned neighbor a few years later, the truth finally came to light. This was in Porto Alegre, where the family had moved from Campo Bom and, in God's grace, settled in the neighborhood of a woman who befriended both nine-year-old Adriane and her mother. Once her trust deepened, Adriane revealed to the good lady how she was being wickedly defiled by her father. That kind neighbor seized the initiative, escorting both Adriane and her mother to the government commission of children's rights, where a counselor recorded her story in preparation for legal action. Results of a physical exam corroborated Adriane's allegations. Later at home, her infuriated mother defiantly faced down her husband and, as Adriane recalls that confrontation, declared, "I didn't want to believe Adriane, but here's proof. Now I want you to say something about it." As might be expected from any wounded wild animal, Adriane's father fumed crazily.

Adriane fled to her trusted neighbor's house, where she lived until her mother and brothers moved back to Campo Bom. "The counselor in Campo Bom placed me with my grandparents, but when my grandfather started touching me sexually, I froze in fear." Social Services, acting on her accusations, then placed her with a family that was simply incapable of reaching out responsively with the attention Adriane hungered for. So she ran away and, once returned, asked her counselor whether there was indeed any place suitable for her. Thus CHAIN of Love came into the picture, along with a small army of human angels, particularly the widow Grandma Nida, who would guide this wretchedly deprived girl into a life-changing relationship with Christ.

"I had mixed emotions going where I didn't know anyone," Adriane confesses. "It would be scary starting a new life, but I also knew I was going someplace where I would never again have to face the abuses I had endured before." Her happy feelings alternated with dreadful questioning. "It was hard to be placed with a new family where I had to learn a whole new way of life and adapt to doing things their way."

Adriane's questioning of God at that point and her security in the Lord now are remarkably contrasting. She asked why God had permitted everything that happened to her. Why all the sadness? "Now I have come to know that all things really do work together for our good for those of us who love God."

Two years after her arrival, the divine artistry of love was especially aglow at Adriane's fifteenth birthday party. There stood an excited princess in a frilly blue dress, stuttering much less and elegantly greeting fifteen girls, who each presented a rose to her and read a specially composed poem of tribute.

Jerilyn Bayer had been teaching her about Jesus since soon after she arrived, and not long after that fifteenth birthday, Adriane fully accepted Jesus into her heart and was baptized by Pastor Ken. Thereafter she became actively involved in many youth activities at Good News Baptist Church, took a junior evangelism course, and then co-taught that course with Jerilyn.

"We were thrilled watching her grow in every area," Jerilyn says. "That fifteenth year of hers also brought another reason to celebrate. Adriane began menstruating and developing normally."

Meanwhile, Adriane had been working hard to stop stuttering. Her efforts were recognized when Ken confidently asked her to read the Christmas story from Luke 1 for the church Christmas program. She vowed to practice diligently. Then on that big day, Jerilyn, more skeptical than Ken, held her breath and prayed. "I finally relaxed as Adriane spoke into the mike without a problem."

Her education also improved, with admirable milestones. Having arrived with a third-grade-level education, Adriane completed the eighth grade by 2001.

Through the years, Adriane occasionally agonized through terrifying nightmares in which her father was charging to grab her. She admits that in those first years her own conscience had been tortuous. She had been convincing herself that she was guilty for what had happened to her father, then imprisoned for his depraved brutality. "But as the years passed, I realized the problem was his. I learned he had black magic books under his mattress, and that tells me he was possessed by something evil."

Much of Adriane's conquest of this mental torment is attributable to therapy by the CHAIN's psychologist, Mariene Tammerik, whom you will meet and hear from in chapter fifteen. "But God has been my biggest help, and it was at the CHAIN of Love that I came to know Him." She has forgiven her father and continues to pray that God will penetrate his soul so that he is transformed totally. "I want to believe that he didn't realize how horrible this had been for me—that alcohol and whatever possessed him caused him to behave as he did. I no longer hate him, but I regret that he was that kind of father. Knowing other children have fathers like him troubles me. It is only because God stepped in that I have the life I have today and the happiness I feel."

During those years at the CHAIN of Love, Adriane drew on her own experiences to counsel other girls who had undergone similar abuse and to lead them in prayers to God for the strength to forgive and leave their past behind. As she gratefully emphasizes, "I got to know the love of people who were always there for me, like Pastor Ken and Jerilyn and others. When my own relatives did not care for me, I came to know that people can love and care for strangers—not just their own families."

There is a sequel to this amazing tale of God's redesign of a once-lost soul. As we write this, news has just arrived from Pastor Ken by e-mail that on October 6, 2004, Adriane and Nei welcomed their daughter Ana Raquel into the world. Remember those terribly discouraging words more than eleven years earlier from a social worker reporting the conclusions of a gynecologist's tests of Adriane? Her sexual organs had atrophied so severely that she might never develop normally. Well, under the healing touch of God, as the Bible stresses repeatedly, all things are possible to those who believe in Him (Matthew 19:26; Mark 10:27).

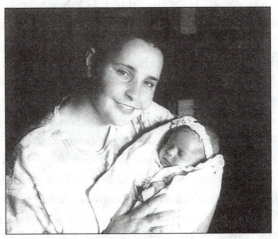

Adriane Capeletti Moreira nestles daughter.

And so Adriane, tiny Ana Raquel Moreira nestled into her chest, and husband Nei walk into the sunset clasping each other's hands, Jesus beside them, a remarkable and continuing story of Christ's love and rescue. But the book of Author Jesus is never-ending. So long as there is one lost, homeless kid wandering loveless and in darkness anywhere on this planet, there is more restoration and reconstruction of lives to be undertaken, another chapter to be written, another story of a hopeless life to be told, another book to be penned by the Supreme Author. The work goes on.

And the work went on, for example, with sisters Ana Paula and Taís de Oliveira, whose early childhood stories of violent sexual abuse are strikingly similar to that of Adriane. Remember them from chapter six, the lice-infested offspring of a mentally unbalanced mother? Those raggedy urchins of eight and six were scavenging like dogs for food scraps atop a garbage mound at the municipal dump when found on January 26, 1996, by a social worker and Jerilyn. That day, you recall, was Jerilyn's birthday, and on that long day she sacrificed a family dinner celebration that today, in retrospect, seems trivial in light of the enormous life changes that more than ten years of nourishment at CHAIN of Love have produced for Ana Paula, nineteen, and Taís, seventeen. All the birthday cakes ever baked couldn't buy what has transpired in the lives of these sisters through the ingredients of love and care by Jesus-guided servants. They have been infused by the Heart of God.

(In fact, shortly before *For the Love of God's Kids* went to press in January 2007, word arrived of radiant Ana Paula's glorious wedding. A beaming pastor Ken escorted her down the aisle to unite at the altar with now husband Marcio. By God's grace on October 21, 2006 the newlyweds strode out arm in arm, committed to establishing a dynamic, new Christian home and family. But, to illustrate Ana Paula's astounding Christian growth, let's backtrack for a few pages to our interview of Ana Paula in May of 2004.)

Today, pretty Ana Paula stands tall with pride, strides confidently, and dresses smartly with the striking poise of a young fashion model, far removed from the mousy figure of that January day in 1996 when she and Taís arrived at the home of their first houseparents, José and Iraci. "I was too embarrassed to get out of the car with Jerilyn and the social worker," she says.

> "I just wanted to stay hidden in the car. My dress was dirty, raggedy, and smelly, and the flip-flops on my feet were too small. I felt the other children would be all so clean and nicely dressed. But Jerilyn said not to worry as she brought me out to meet the other children."

Ana Paula went on to note that she couldn't recall the last time she had seen her mother, although she believed it had been at least several years. She said she would like to see her someday, just to know how she is faring. The last word about Ana Paula's mom was in 2003, when the mother was present for the legal adoption proceedings of brother Luis Paulo by José and Iraci, the houseparents who had cared for the three de Oliveira children for seven years before leaving CHAIN of Love to buy a farm. Luis Paulo was that seven-month-old brother whose reflexes were virtually nonfunctioning when he arrived to join his sisters. Like speechless Taís, he would, as he grew older, babble helplessly and lag in learning because of toxoplasmosis, which the two had been infected prenatally because their mother had eaten food contaminated by animal waste. As with Taís, a family circle of love plus the CHAIN's psychologist and speech therapist have performed wonders with Luis Paulo. He now understands others, and they understand him.

In reviewing her horrific childhood Ana Paula recounted a tale of ongoing rape by various men in a divided ramshackle house jammed with several families. It was truly a house of horrors in Campo Bom. Her stepfather was an intercity bus driver with lovers everywhere, and he brought little money home to support them. An uncle was among those who did the raping, she said, and there were whippings and beatings by someone who chained the children.

But now, in a warm, safe environment peopled with devoted servants of Jesus, Ana Paula feels the power of prayer—hers and theirs—is working in all areas of her life, for example, in her studies. Before she arrived there, she had already repeated grades one and two at school, and she began in grade one again at CHAIN of Love. She later failed grade five, and that set her back temporarily. But, when interviewed by the co-authors, Ana Paula was whizzing along and achieving good marks in grade eight, thanks to intensive studying and some encouraging and persuasive nudging by her houseparents, Cida and Renato. Her progress in the Portuguese language class was especially noteworthy. She said,

> "I had been poor in that subject but my mother [Cida] offered some sound advice. She suggested I try memorizing from the book, do that by memorizing one paragraph at a time, and then, when taking a test, to complete it by writing each paragraph separately. Did I surprise myself! Seventy percent on the last test, which is great for me in that subject."

Preparing for that test, Ana Paula had been the profile of determined stick-to-it-ness, spending hours and hours memorizing and verbalizing book passages at the kitchen table and strolling through every room with her nose into the text. "I had never prayed before taking any test, but for this one I did—just as mom advised."

Housefather Renato, an engineer, was also tremendously supportive. He coached her in various studies, notably mathematics.

Like Taís, Ana Paula is innately shy, but she became far more talkative at school and among her friends, as Cida pointed out. In addition, she's gifted in drawing, and that was obvious from the A marks at school and her polished creations so prominently displayed at home.

Singing is also one of her passions, an interest sparked from hearing songs on the radio since early childhood. Ana Paula was thrilled from the start to be included in the church ministry's morning-worship team and was particularly inspired by one of the lead female singers to undertake voice training. That singer happened to be Luciana, daughter of José and Iraci, Ana Paula's first houseparents. Now she practices once weekly for Sunday school openings and as part of the congregational worship team. Jerilyn, who is coached her, says, "She loves to sing, but she does have a good voice that requires a lot of training."

Who knows? Ana Paula may just achieve her goal of becoming a gospel singer and combine that career with marriage and a family. The drive she displayed in nailing a good mark on that Portuguese test could be just the ticket. But she did confess that she had stumbled occasionally. For example, for a time she had dated a boy Cida and Renato disapproved of and distrusted. So her houseparents inserted a tape recorder into her school backpack and confronted her with the recorded evidence of a liaison with the boy. They warned Ana Paula that she would be prohibited from singing on stage at church Sunday mornings if her disobedience continued—disobedience, they stressed, that conflicted with the teachings of Jesus. Wise, caring, loving, and responsible parents indeed! "So, I made a decision," Ana Paula said. "Either I continue as I had, or turn back to God. So I obeyed. And I do want to become a gospel singer."

Cida, she added, has been very good to her, not only counseling her on worldly realities but reading and interpreting
the Bible regularly to her. "Jesus is everything in my life, and
I can't do anything without Him."

As for younger sister Taís, that poor child so viciously
skewered with barbecue spears by rapist relatives—well, her
speech and confidence are clear and soaring. Observing her
over twenty-five days tells you she is a stickler for precision
and top-flight performance. She dazzles everyone with her
work as a paid housekeeper in *Lar Colméia*'s technical-
vocational center. Even Mr. Clean would cheer!

9

GOD'S GLORIOUS CHILDREN OF ENDEARING CHARMS

They're all such charmers, God! Every one of Your children at the CHAIN of Love, Lord! They steal a guy's heart away! Especially when they switch on those captivating smiles, transmitting joy throughout the day. Those cherubic smiles are as automatic and predictable daily as Your unfailing love for them and all of us mortals. That's what Your faithful adult servants generate with their love for God's kids. They're just downright amazing, this playful Jesus-loving gang—so incredibly happy and so totally transfigured from the wretchedly downcast souls they had been before being pulled out of the darkness by this unique ministry of Ken and Jerilyn Bayer!

No doubt about it, to this point, almost every story has been one of from rags to riches: from the rags of misery, fear, despair, destitution, abandonment, abusive cruelty, and hopelessness to the riches of love, security, encouragement, faith, hope, education, recognition, and dreams of successful futures as Christian adults. The world being constructed for them currently tunes this author's ears into a congregational song often sung in his church, Trinity Baptist, in Kelowna, Canada: "This Is a Church on Fire." Well, the CHAIN founded by the Bayers is a ministry on fire with and for the love of God's kids, children such as Alexandre, Graciele, Paulo, Patricia, Deise, Altamir, Linda, Deneclei, Cristiano, Amanda, and Norli.

Take Alexandre, for example. He's that unnamed boy in chapter seven whose real father is unknown and whose alcoholic stepfather was knifed and shot to death over a fuel-oil debt as he slept on a sofa in the family hovel. Well, as the dear Lord knows, and now you as well, dear reader, he is Alexandre da Silva Fonseca, and this seventy-three-year-old author is very proud of him, just as he is of his own son, Steve, and grandchildren, Jessica and Nicky.

I am one of Alexandre's North American sponsors, and the two of us, language barrier notwithstanding, had a glorious time talking, playing, laughing, and becoming friends during my twenty-five days observing and interviewing with teammate and translator Sara Esther Luna Cezar at the CHAIN's *Lar Colméia* community complex in May 2004. I went shopping in Novo Hamburgo with my pal and Sally Antholzner, then an office assistant with the CHAIN. And what an adventure that was! We were selecting and purchasing gifts in advance for his thirteenth birthday in July 2004.

Besides some needed school clothes, we picked up a remote-control, battery-run toy race car, which for at least the next week was the playtime hit with other children around the *Lar Colméia* complex. How coincidental, by the way, that a toy car Alexandre found as an eight-year-old was discarded by a mean neighbor whose spiteful action was motivated wholly by dislike of Alexandre's mother! Such is the kind of malicious behavior bred where neighborly love is lacking amid an environment of destitution and hopelessness.

As for today, Alexandre says he loves living among the CHAIN of Love gang with such affectionate and devoted houseparents as Tadeu and Deny, one of ten committed houseparent couples in the ministry. That has been home since August 2000, when he reunited with younger brother Regis Fonseca de Lima, now fourteen, who had arrived there two months earlier. Their sister, Taiara Fonseca de Lima, twelve, lives in the home next door with houseparents Sérgio and Romilda, having joined her brothers in May 2001. Together, they are such riotous fun!

"I love my mother Deny very much," Alexandre smiles, answering questions for translator Sara and myself. "She makes me so happy, giving me hugs when I return from school and asking if I'm hungry. It's so good here because I now have a bed. Before coming here, the floor was my bed." (The eleven children being cared for and the three children of Tadeu and Deny sleep in upper and lower bunk beds built by North American volunteers.)

What a contrast to the earlier lives of Alexandre, Regis, and Taiara! Their first home was a weather-beaten shack near a sewage canal in a beachfront city. There, Alexandre notes, is where their alcohol-stupefied stepdad had clumsily tried to drown their mother in the lake until she wriggled out of his fumbling arms and swam ashore. An older brother was then living with them, but Alexandre no longer knows his whereabouts. As for their real father, Alexandre doesn't know whether he is even alive. But he does fondly remember his older brother and himself as little ones helping each other with their school homework. "It would sure be nice to have him here now, so that we could do our homework together again. It was so nice, too, when all four of us and our mother walked to the small lake nearby and played together in the water."

Later, minus the older brother, the family moved into a tiny divided two-family shack in a slum close to a stinking dike near the old Good News Baptist Church. There is where Mom, Stepdad, and the three children shared the floor in the same room.

> "Whenever I walked to our grandfather's house, I would see people fighting, taking dope, and picking out stuff from the garbage piles, and the whole neighborhood stunk. It was awful. I would always get an irritating itch, which my grandfather would treat. He would ride me on his bicycle to the dump, where he would pick out bones with which to make soup."

During those years, Alexandre was forced to drop out of school for a year to help care for his mother, then ill with a respiratory infection. The small change he earned assisting a man cleaning houses would help sustain the family. And soon after his stepfather was murdered, his mother died of pneumonia. Orphaned, Alexandre and Regis then lived briefly with a neighbor, whose beatings forced Social Services to remove them to the city's halfway shelter until the CHAIN of Love was awarded legal guardianship. Taiara, meanwhile, had lived with a family friend until being warmly reunited with her brothers.

With supplementary instruction by the CHAIN's private tutor, Isabel, Alexandre advanced quickly in school, catching up on the education missed during his mother's pre-death illness. A quiet and slightly built young man, Alexandre is now an eleventh grader who enjoys studying and emphasizes that he intends to keep cracking the books intensively so that he can go to university. He evens helps Regis with his homework. Moreover, Alexandre is one of the top students in his English-language class at Campo Bom's Fernando Ferrari School. One test dealing with personal pronouns particularly spotlighted his potential. He scored highly in smoothly translating and answering English-language questions in Portuguese.

"Classmates call me 'Canada,'" Alexandre grins proudly, referring to his sponsorship by Canadians and shirts received from them bearing Canadian logos and scenes. His favorite subjects are history and religion, and he likes his two teachers. Greek myths and heroes especially intrigued him in one class and so did the explanation of the origins of Mother's Day. Besides his houseparents, Alexandre's personal hero is the late Aírton Senna, a Brazilian Formula One race-car driver; the anniversary of his death in a racetrack crash was commemorated the week of our interview.

Meanwhile, Alexandre's youthful zest spills over daily around the complex. Mornings at the technical-vocational center, I looked down from the first-floor banister railing into the basement shop where he was diligently and meticulously fashioning shoes, belts, and women's handbags as part of leather-trades training. Another time he was ducking around a doorway in the center's laundry room, a beaming smile across his face and fingers touched to his lips since he was hiding from a buddy. Still another time, he was behind a playful ruse—a pal, Isaac, knocked at the door of my dorm room in the vocational center with instructions that I was wanted at an office in the building, which turned out to be empty. When I returned, puzzled, I found an envelope on my bunk bed bearing a penned greeting in English and yellow-outlined words underlined: *"Friendship. By order of correio!!!"* (postman, in English) On the back of the envelope were the words, centered in the penned drawing of a heart, "I love you Wally!!!" with the letter *W* centered in five penned illustrations of yellow-outlined sun rays. Beneath the greeting was a white T-shirt with "CANADA" in pink-striped, capitalized block lettering imprinted through a sailboat sketch. It was enough to melt anyone's heart! The next day, I present Alexandre a sweater with maple leaves across each bicep, a sweater I intended to leave with him anyway as a parting gift. There was also a Canada baseball cap for him, and one each for Regis and Taiara. All the children do cherish ball caps, as I soon discovered in trades among a couple of boys.

Flash ahead to June 2006, and imagine the explosion of smiles from the entire lot of those young athletes as they cheered on soccer-crazy Brazil's winning start in the World Cup tournament. Many of the cheering boys watching games after Sunday school in Good News Baptist Church had their faces painted with the Brazilian flag, and some wound the patio pillars of their homes at *Lar Colméia* with yellow and green streamers. This was followed by heartbreak later when France ousted Brazil 1-0 in the quarterfinals on July 1, 2006.[18]

Long before I arrived at the *Lar Colméia* campus, Alexandre had sent a written illustration thanking me in

Portuguese for holiday gift money with which to purchase Christmas gifts there. Alexandre reported having bought a shirt, pants, and sunglasses, and that he had passed into the sixth grade. He expressed love to myself and family, and *"Feliz ano novo novo! para você e sua FAMILÍA"* ("Happy New Year to you and your family"). Besides many other multicolored words of gratitude is Alexandre's cartoonish yellow-highlighted pencil drawing of a smiling bear cub with outstretched arms, bearing the caption, *"Eu quero um abraço!"* ("I want a hug!").

Alexandre's brother and sister, Regis and Taiara, both flash such toothy and winsome smiles that they would be endeared to even the grimmest grump. Each is a carbon copy of the other. Regis loves helping Deny clean dishes after the children's meals, and he proudly shows the belt he wears to everyone—because he had never owned one until recently. Taiara is a born little performer with a bubbly personality and makes friends easily. She fancies herself as a comedienne and is indeed a hoot, making everyone chuckle when she launches into her "hillbilly" speaking act. And she loves scampering about barefoot.

And could there have been a more luminous smile on the Sunday evening of May 16, 2004, than that on fourteen-year-old Patrícia Catile Viana's face as her head bobbed up from the water in a basin on the stage of Good News Baptist Church? She had just been baptized by Pastor Ken. That spectacle of celebratory rebirth also included about thirty other baptisms of children and adults by Pastor Ken and his assistants.

It's nothing short of incredible that Patrícia is one of those two sisters cited but not named in chapter seven. The other is Aline, now eighteen, who has since been transferred to one of the CHAIN's private homes off the *Lar Colméia* complex. The two bear lifelong scars from beatings by their mother, plus all the emotional scars of having been consistently subjected to a revolving-door early childhood, living first with their mother, then with their stepfather, then in an institution, then back with their mother, and so on.

What a difference there is from that first day at the CHAIN of Love on February 17, 1997, for Patrícia, then seven, and Aline, almost nine! After the first twenty-four hours with houseparents Ademar and Marlene, they wanted to leave because they objected to having been assigned daily housekeeping jobs like the other children there were. So drastic had been their damage that they had come with absolutely no sense of family and sharing. Only a few days of experiencing familial teamwork and caring unity remedied that. By contrast, those false "family settings" of pre-CHAIN years must seem to the sisters now as having been on some ungodly, nightmarish planet. Interviewed two days before that heavenly baptismal ceremony, Patrícia recalled how her viciously tempered mother would strike her with anything near at hand—once with a garden hose, another time with a belt buckle that left a small scar under her right eye. Other times the mom would force her and Aline to stand barefoot on open pop caps or small pebbles or rocks, or else to kneel for an hour. "That was even more excruciating than standing on them." So-called offenses as trivial as awakening their mother would ignite such bestiality. Two older sisters, meanwhile, had run away and were eventually taken in by concerned relatives. With no food in their shack, Patrícia said, she and Aline would shoplift from a neighborhood supermarket, beg on the streets, or scavenge for leftovers amid trash piles.

Today, with Jesus implanted in her heart, Patrícia views their mother with understanding, compassion, and forgiveness, since she never could scrimp up enough money to care for them properly. Echoing their mom's words, Patrícia claims she had not been solely guilty, since the family had been abandoned by their birth father when Patrícia was just two years old. Before his exit, their mother had been beaten consistently for years during his drunken rages. Now stripped permanently of legal guardianship, Patrícia's mother brings cookies, presents, and other goodies to her daughter during their visitations as tokens of reparation, care, and goodwill.

Most gratifying about her life now is the close camaraderie, fostered by talking with the children next door and going to church on Sunday with everyone, and the loving maternal concern of housemom Marlene, who not only does innumerable little things for Patrícia and the other children but whose ears are always ready to listen understandingly when they wish to confide and need guidance. Sunday school over the past nine years, meanwhile, has broadened Patrícia's faith enormously. And she says it's delightful to express it weekly in song during Sunday school worship services. At summer Bible camp in early 2004, Patrícia was thrilled to act in the role of a spy from the tribe of Levi during reenactments of the Old Testament Book of Joshua.

Early February at summer camp in 2004 also saw Patrícia connect passionately with Jesus. One speaker there drove her to tears by describing the suffering Christ endured in dying for her sins. His heart-gripping words were thunderously reinforced by R.R. Soares, a famous Brazilian televangelist and missionary, whose prime-time TV speech stressed the need for viewers to accept Jesus before His second coming. That message kicked off a seven-week series that Patrícia continued watching faithfully to conclusion when she returned home from summer Bible camp. "I was touched by God."

Following the last televised evangelistic church service, Patrícia erupted tearfully and asked Marlene and housefather Ademar to pray with her. They went to the kitchen table and repeated together the words of "Come and Live in My Life." Then she prayed it alone, declaring acceptance of Jesus as her Redeemer.

Her growth in both academics and life skills has also been outstanding. Math and art in 2004 were her strengths as a seventh-grader in Campo Bom's LaSalle Middle School. Meanwhile, Patrícia was taking weekly dance lessons from a volunteer at *Lar Colméia*'s technical-vocational center, an interest sparked earlier at camp by choreography instruction in religious dance. She has also benefited from cooking and computer literacy classes in the CHAIN's volunteer-taught vocational trades program. Patrícia smiles appreciatively for having had those opportunities.

Considering smile power, you would be hard-pressed to match the duo of Altamir and Linda for super smileage. These two seemingly are always on the dash for fun, or at least they were with this writer every evening in May 2004 when he arrived, as scheduled, for dinner from Romilda, their housemother and the CHAIN's mom specializing in children with special needs. Endearing indeed was their affectionate assault with bear hugs and chatter as I sat at the kitchen table, Altamir wrapping himself around my knee just as he did five years earlier whenever Pastor Ken's assistant, Clovis, turned up at the children's shelter. That's how desperately Altamir, then three and now ten, wanted to leave with Clovis for the CHAIN of Love after more than a year in the halfway house.

Altamir is Altamir Matias, the boy referred to in chapter seven, who cannot hear or speak, neglected and abandoned several times by a seventeen-year-old mother who never wanted him and whose severe beatings ultimately compelled civic authorities to take him away and shelter him until the CHAIN of Love became his legal guardian in March 2000. Linda is Linda Débora de Lima, a twelve-year-old afflicted with a neurological disorder. Considering the ugliness of Linda's treatment by her parents, it seems ironic that her given name means "beautiful" in Portuguese. Beautiful though she is, Linda never learned how to talk because, as the neglected daughter of two alcoholics and especially after her boozing mom's death, she roamed the streets much like a wild animal, fending for herself for months before the Bayers' ministry was awarded guardianship in March 2000. As her soused father drifted in alcoholic oblivion at home, Linda taught herself how to walk by hanging on to the tail of a neighborhood dog. Her father ultimately lost parental rights and eventually died of cirrhosis of the liver.

Altamir and Linda crowded around me at Romilda's kitchen table amid the hubbub of their family flock of "brothers" and "sisters." They were virtually glued to me as I penciled a drawing from my T-shirt on a table serviette and then nestled them, each in one arm, as they read in Portuguese from illustrated children's Bible storybooks on the table. Stories about David and Goliath, Jonah and the whale, and the Jesus child with Mary and Joseph in the stable warmed my heart as they pointed to the color drawings illustrating the narrative. It was just a tiny manifestation of the Holy Spirit working through the CHAIN of Love.

Altamir and Linda seem to pal around together constantly, and it struck me that each probably strengthens the other, and they thereby share a bond built out of their speech handicaps. Altamir, for example, first found a communication link with Clovis at the shelter because Ken's assistant knew a little lip-reading. It's terribly frustrating for a kid like Altamir, who so desperately yearns love and attention, to convey his ideas effectively. Except for lip reading, his only tool is facial and body expression. That's why he occasionally lashes out at other children physically. However, Altamir is advancing socially in many areas now that he is in a special-needs schoolroom. He is being helped by the CHAIN's speech therapist and psychologist and receives generous doses of genuine care, attention, and loving discipline from his mom, Romilda, who has learned sign language and is abundantly gifted in parceling out exactly what's required for children with special needs.

As for Linda, visits by the Bayers and Romilda to both the halfway house and special-needs school into which she had been immediately enrolled by government social workers showed clearly that Linda suffered from an extreme case of social retardation. Then five years old, she had learned neither basic hygiene nor how to control her bowels. Thanks to that dog, Linda had at least discovered how to travel on her two legs. Her body was a mass of scrapes and bruises, her teeth totally rotten from never having felt a toothbrush across them, and the Bayers say they had never seen so many lice infesting any kid. As Romilda recalls, "There was a layer of encrusted drool under her mouth and down her chest; when we removed it, we could see worms eating away her skin. Medication cured the condition." Forced to look after herself, Linda had survived while biting at rocks, consuming dog feces, and eating vegetables dug out of people's gardens. To this day, she prefers a salad to candy or ice cream.

With the start of speech therapy at the school, however, Linda began learning some words. Over the next several weeks, Romilda visited her regularly, both in school and at the halfway house, so that the two could become connected as mother and daughter and thereby ease transition into the CHAIN of Love family.

Brought into care in September 1999, Linda's toothless grin and always happy spontaneity has a positive impact on everyone, especially the smaller children, who obviously love her as much as she loves them. Romilda says she is actually extremely bright and can now talk understandably, albeit with a limited vocabulary. Before that, gesturing and sometimes salivating had been Linda's means of communicating her wishes. At first she slept wearing a diaper because of that bowel problem. But all that is now under control. Not so Linda's adventurous streak, however. The home's outside front gate must be always closed; otherwise this born explorer previously unaccustomed to physical boundaries would be off to who knows where. Once, her disappearance sparked some fretting—until she crawled out, toothlessly smiling, from the crawl space under Romilda and Sérgio's house.

Delightfully unpredictable and always expressive, Linda's first experience in church is fondly remembered by Jerilyn. When Jerilyn began strumming the guitar in worshipful praise at Sunday school, the music struck a dynamic chord with ebullient Linda. Romilda dashed to snatch the speedy Linda away before she could barrel into Jerilyn.

Today, Jesus is very much at the heart of Linda's now-civilized life, and that's dramatized by how excitedly she anticipates going to church. Her gallop early Sunday morning to the CHAIN of Love bus is very much in the running as children barge ahead at various intervals for the vehicle, waiting in the driveway beside the technical-vocational center with engine running and José, a housefather, at the wheel, blaring the horn repeatedly.

During my visit, Sunday morning at eight brought a cacophony of competing sounds with up to ninety children scrambling aboard (along with a few adults) for the twenty-minute bus ride to Sunday school classes and services at Good News Baptist Church. There were dozens of yelled conversations cross the bus from front to rear, children hanging out of windows, everybody either smiling or laughing. His head poking out an open window, Alexandre waved me aboard and shouted, asking whether I was going. Nope, I yelled back, saying I'd be at the services that evening and promising that *"Vou à escola Dominical a semana que vem."* ("I am going to Sunday school next week.")

Same time, same station the next Sunday, and it was the same scene of escalating exuberance piling aboard and riding away. Seated on my knees were Altamir and Taiara, and the three of us were having a hand-slapping ol' time loudly playing patty-cake. Meanwhile, everyone was riding high as they joined a chorus of church hymns initiated by children in the rear seats. Believe me, if the energy aboard José's bus could be recycled for gasoline, there would be fuel enough for traversing the length of South America. Riding back from church, Linda, seated on my lap, charmed everyone, turning in all directions with her toothless smile.

As I jogged one morning through the *Lar Colméia* complex, lovely lyrics floated down from a second-floor window. His head out the open window, the boy's face was a gigantic, luminous smile, his voice repeatedly caressing the words, "Jesus loves me, this I know, for the Bible tells me so." And, wham, it hit me: what the Bayers and the entire CHAIN of Love ministry are cultivating in the fertile minds and hearts of these children is friendship packaged in love—friendship eternally with Jesus and friendship eternally with their brothers and sisters as they share and participate in God's love.

One example of friendship is that showered upon buddy Diego by nineteen-year-old Dionatan Geraldo da Silva, who has been showered with four years of Christian love since he came into the CHAIN's embrace in 2002. Diego was baptized in June 2006 in Good News Baptist Church, a conversion directly attributable to the friendship developed over several years with Dionatan and steady, persuasive evangelization from a trustworthy friend.[19] Dionatan is that boy from chapter three who came to the CHAIN with four younger siblings after the grisly tragedy of a drunken father axing their mother to death. Yes, wounds heal and love and friendship grow in Christ's healing circle of servants!

Another friendship is being shaped by Cristiano Aparecido Lessa and Norli de Souza. That friendship has been more than nine years in the making, rooted in March 1997 when Cristiano, then ten, came into the CHAIN of Love. He joined Norli, then eleven, and Norli's younger brother, Ângelo, nine, who had already been with the ministry for almost two years. However, all three were then with different houseparents in different homes. For the past three years, though, they have been together as house brothers with five other children in the off-campus private home of houseparents Lauri and Áurea. And surely it's the parental examples of both Áurea and husband Lauri, an elder at Good News Baptist Church and the CHAIN's volunteer shoe- and leather-making instructor, that have figured in Cristiano and Norli's bonding as buddies—a closeness that has each routinely borrowing the other's T-shirts and other clothes. The two thrive, thanks to role models Lauri and Áurea, who exemplify the finest qualities of family unity as father and mother to two children of their own as well as to their foster children.

When interviewed, Norli was wearing Cristiano's soccer jacket. "I consider him like a blood brother—we help each other and confide in each other," says Norli, who turned twenty in April 2006. "We have a strong and deep relationship." Having played together for years as soccer teammates has also strengthened their ties. These buddies, in fact, are proof of the heights children are capable of scaling when they are nourished in a loving, Jesus-focused environment that both encourages and provides the opportunities for their God-given giftedness to blossom.

Such potential almost inevitably would have been hopelessly crushed had they continued floundering without an anchor for their lives. Consider their lives before the CHAIN of Love. Just a year before Norli came into the ministry's legal guardianship as a nine-year-old, his mother, a diabetic, had died of internal hemorrhaging following surgery. Soon afterward, his father, a shoe-factory worker, came down with a severe heart condition, for which he wears a pacemaker, and he was battling terminal cancer in 2004 when Norli spoke with us.

As Norli says, although his father occasionally beat him and brother Ângelo with belts, garden hose, and sewing-machine straps, he did attempt to look after them. But failing health landed his father in hospital for extended stays of two weeks to a month for almost a year. During that year, a neighbor would feed Norli and Ângelo in her home, but otherwise they would fend for themselves. Pretty much on their own, Norli and Ângelo were being beaten and harassed by older children in street gangs. Fearing that his two sons would soon be into drugs and become gang members themselves, the hospitalized father asked Social Services to place them someplace where they could receive proper care.

Taken in by the Bayers in 1995, the brothers were at first in different homes simply because the available space for children at that time could not accommodate both in the same home. For Ângelo, then seven, life still remained traumatic. At school, he resorted to the con tricks he had learned as a street kid to manipulate his teachers. Although bright, Ângelo didn't study and was eventually suspended from school for troublemaking. At home, he beat up other children, neglected to do assigned chores, and then ran away.

For almost three years, Ângelo was part of a gang in the de Souza family's old neighborhood, living again with no restrictions or guidelines. Prayer from the entire CHAIN of Love ministry surely prodded Ângelo to return voluntarily and not follow in the pattern of an older sister, a prostitute, and an older brother, an imprisoned criminal. So, the CHAIN gave him another chance, knowing he hadn't done drugs while footloose and continued going to school without any adult's persuasion. There's a momentous difference in Ângelo's attitude now that this eighteen-year-old is with brother Norli in Lauri and Áurea's home, where all the boys are teenagers.

As for Cristiano, perhaps the greatest birthday present he may ever receive on earth came belatedly on March 13, 1997, when he came into the caring embrace of the CHAIN of Love, just one day after he had turned ten. Until then, his upbringing was fully that of a kid who was "unwanted," not only by his mother and father, who had been separated for many years and lived in different states, but also by various and sundry relatives. At first, the infant Cristiano remained with his mother when his parents separated. Soon a stepfather came into the picture—a brute who pushed a two-year-old Cristiano down five stairs for the "crime" of having tied a piece of cloth around a pet cat's tail. A lifelong scar on Cristiano's knee is the legacy of that "punishment"—an incident, Cristiano says, that was witnessed by his own mother yet excused as inconsequential. Later, each of his grandmothers housed him, plus other relatives who remain unidentifiable even in Cristiano's memory, and lastly an aunt. In all of these settings, Cristiano was practically reduced to "child-slave labor," the Bayers point out, particularly with the aunt, who was separated from her husband and would have continued exploiting Cristiano to support her and her several children. Cristiano's schooling would have ended in favor of menial-paying jobs outside the home and additional household labor after work. Abhorring that possibility, a grandmother planning to move shortly to another state urged the CHAIN to accept him. As that grandmother stressed, she had until then been caring for Cristiano as best she could but was already overburdened with the care of many younger grandchildren.

Before his transfer to Lauri and Áurea's home and the fostering of even closer companionship with Norli, Cristiano had been looked after for five years by houseparents Eva and Antônio, until they moved. The pain carried over from Cristiano's upbringing was of such severity that he endured fully three years of nightmares every night. The predominant one of the two versions had him walking haphazardly with closed eyes, then knocking on his mother's door and crying, "I don't want to die! I don't want to die!" Once, while Cristiano was suffering from a fever, Antônio says, he repeated those words in the same nightmare. The second nightmare, which was only occasional, had Cristiano being crushed within a truck whose top, sides, and bottom were being folded inward.

Cristiano fondly recalls how during those first five years Eva and Antônio worshipfully guided the flock of children in morning prayer sessions kicking off each new day. "A different kid would lead us in prayer each morning. And we learned from each other through prayer." Being educated spiritually through prayer, Cristiano explains, enabled him to flush out the bile of bitterness that had ravaged his gut for years.

"It took years to forgive others and myself, but praying daily did it. I came here really angry with my parents, but now I understand why everything happened as it did. I have learned to let go and let God."

In retrospect, Cristiano likens his arrival at CHAIN of Love to turning over a new leaf. He loves church and is grateful to the Bayers for having given him the Bible he requested as an aide for a youth-study group and Sunday school. In fact, Cristiano's growing friendship with Jesus was the dynamic that thrust him into church youth leadership as one of five teens who organized and now run weekly

Saturday night Bible study sessions in the *Lar Colméia* campus gymnasium.

Likewise, buddy Norli values the worship so ingrained into his family and community life and the fellowship it produces. Norli's gratitude is obvious in how devotedly he runs the overhead projector at Good News Baptist Church. "It would be terrible to live in this world without God." Having been rescued from an area where neighbors were ungodly, Norli also points out that the attitudes governing the CHAIN of Love have taught him and brother Ângelo "to respect other people's opinions and others as brother and sister human beings."

Meanwhile, buddies Cristiano and Norli outdo each other in praising "father" Lauri and "mother" Áurea." They love us, and they care for us," Norli says, "We didn't even know there was any such quality as love until we came here. Lauri will talk to us about the attitudes we should have as Christians, and to us he's all that a father should be. He's an excellent role model." Áurea, he adds, demonstrates motherly devotion by patiently talking with him at length about such intense subjects as dating. Cristiano points out that Áurea is contributing largely to the growth of a downtown clothing shop as a hard-working and top-flight saleswoman. Lauri, he adds, is a calm and patient man, always offering wise counsel. "His advice always proves good. His two major suggestions are to be right with God first and to study for a good future."

Cristiano says the entire CHAIN of Love approach has shown him that he isn't required to do everything on his own—the mindset carried over from his earlier life. "I know now that my parents are responsible for me. And I have learned from them to always give people second chances, just as God does, and to help others with a generous spirit."

In the meantime, as classmates at Wolfram Metzler School in Novo Hamburgo, Cristiano and Norli are solidifying both their friendship and their potential futures. When interviewed in 2004, they were both ninth graders. Cristiano envisioned university studies in physical education or electrical engineering. Norli was already registered with the Brazilian army, intent on making the military a career. "I dream of becoming an army officer."

In fact, these buddies are blessed with a dazzling array of talents. Cristiano is a born thespian who is an excellent public speaker and demonstrates skillful versatility in a variety of character portrayals. He almost always has the lead role in any household drama. In addition, he has a natural mechanical aptitude. "I love experimenting with things. I have repaired motors, fans, television sets, vacuum cleaners—you name it." Cristiano is also an incredibly gifted athlete. He believes his innate athleticism is flourishing because "there's a lot of space to play here—we have a huge playground and gymnasium at *Lar Colméia*." He loves soccer, Portuguese rugby, and American football. Football is especially appealing, he says, noting that he had played quarterback in a game organized by him at youth Bible camp. "I'm fascinated with the technical training, the strategies, and the mental challenges that sports offer." Fortunately, Cristiano is unbelievably energetic. He points out that at nine years old he walked the twelve-and-a-half miles into downtown Novo Hamburgo with a friend. "I only sleep because I have to," he chuckles.

Norli, too, is incredibly energetic and works hard helping volunteers and staff in virtually any facet of repair or construction proceeding at the *Lar Colméia* complex. He will tag along often from their off-campus home with house-father Lauri, whom he emulates, whenever Lauri is headed there to instruct children in shoe- and leather-making. Norli's carpentry skills are masterful—a gift honed through years of assisting and observing workers in building the houses and other structures on the site. Besides the exteriors and interiors, Norli has also helped craft furniture for the dwellings. Four years ago he helped volunteers construct the bunk beds for dormitories in *Lar Colméia*'s technical-vocational center. Three years ago, he completed a year-long, government-funded building-trades course in Novo Hamburgo. His long-range plans, complementing an army career, include owning a carpentry business. "It would be great if Cristiano and I could set up shop together."

As this book was being updated in July 2006, word came that Cristiano, now nineteen, was being trained in the Brazilian army and was to enlist in officer training in December, at which point he would be earning enough to move out of the CHAIN's youth home and live independently.

In the same ambitious vein as pals Cristiano and Norli, there's jolly, stocky Paulo Ricardo do Amaral de Assis, who, as a four-year-old left to his own wits, somehow looked after both himself and a younger brother and sister for more than a year before being discovered in a hovel by social workers. Well, plucky Paulo, who turned fifteen on October 21, 2006, is playing as industriously as ever to become a professional musician. He wants to strum the guitar, but for now, his fingers are too small and stubby. So Paulo has learned and is playing the keyboard. At the moment, piano lessons are simply too expensive. In any case, Paulo's life is reaching ever-higher notes, and the ongoing transformation in him is music to everyone's ears at the CHAIN of Love.

Joyous pride rang in the hearts of adults touched at the CHAIN at the eighteenth birthday party of Daniel Lopes da Silva on April 12, 2006, as Daniel handed a book to house-mother Alzira Tavares. Hand-written in pencil and stylishly composed and designed, it is the product of several years' labor by Daniel and relates gratefully how his life has been transformed since coming into the ministry's loving arms just three days after his eleventh birthday in 1999. He arrived there, with three younger brothers and a sister, from a hovel so filthy that shocked social workers claimed not even a rat would tolerate it. Human dung and food were strewn everywhere. Daniel and his four siblings had been abandoned by a delusional father to be "cared for" by a mother later institutionalized with mental problems. As Daniel writes, "God took me out of a very difficult situation and placed me at the CHAIN of Love. Because of my love for Him and my desire to say 'thank you,' I have written this book. It is dedicated to God, to the Bayer family, and to those who support CHAIN of Love." Daniel then relates the purpose and history of the homes and tells about the current families residing in them. "CHAIN of Love was something that moved me," he writes.

> "It is a place that surprised me with its love and dedication to the family. I am grateful to the Bayer family for spearheading this in order to give a home to children who needed someone to love them and for giving of themselves to see that the children grow in the Lord's paths."[20]

Meanwhile, marvel, dear reader, at the career goals of these other amazing children loved by God. Deneclei Calderini: a professional soccer player or teacher of English.

Amanda Pricila Veira Ogando: veterinarian. Deise Graziele Pinto Ribeiro: nurse or computer science specialist and programmer. Aline Correia, the biological daughter of houseparents Marlene and Ademar: fashion designer.

Deneclei's upbeat smile seems as perpetual as his breathing. See him anytime, anywhere, and it's always there. This seventeen-year-old's story is a shining illustration of a child of God now thriving in the warmth of a family circle because of his rescue from potential street destitution. Until Deneclei's arrival at the CHAIN of Love with younger brother Edinei in May 1999, smiles were about as probable as frost on the Sahara. Their father was in prison for pimping, their mother didn't want them because of the large family into which she had remarried, and their poverty-stricken grandmother could no longer afford to look after them. So, only hours after Deneclei and Edinei, then ten and eight, were fastened into the CHAIN's care on that life-changing day of May 4, 1999, the two brothers were joyfully calling houseparents Alzira and José "Mom" and "Dad." Once they spotted the large playground, they immediately dashed to it and onto the forty-foot-long slide. It took just minutes before the two learned that sliding is faster when water is poured down the chute. Deneclei and Edinei's elation and resultant smearing from sliding wet into the red soil would replicate the happiest pig herd anywhere.

From this author's first meeting with Deneclei it was clear that joviality and joking are as integral to his persona as the various baseball hats he wears. We hit it off by trading ball caps. He's a delight, singing with the youth band at Good News Baptist Church. This bright kid himself delights in everything undertaken. He even loves studying and doing homework for classes at LaSalle Middle School in Campo Bom. Leading the list of delights, however, are the nightly family Bible studies led by houseparents José and Alzira following the evening meal. They last for an hour or more, and Deneclei notes that those sessions furnish thought-provoking reinforcement to classes at Good News Baptist Church. In fact, he's so versed in biblical teachings that he often questions Sunday school teachers when he wonders if they have erred on biblical passages. It seems that the Bible Pastor Ken gave Deneclei the day after arrival into care from a boys' shelter gets a strenuous daily workout. The album Ken gave him that same day illuminates his face with pride as he turns the pages, explaining to me the photos tracing his personal history over the years.

"I like everything here," he says, recalling fondly how he and Edinei were warmly welcomed on the first day with the gift of a pet cocker spaniel named Princess. School, too, has been tremendously rewarding from the start, Deneclei adds, citing physical education and English as his favorite subjects. "I have even learned to like math. Just started studying harder, and the teacher was surprised when I suddenly began averaging 80 to 90 on tests." In phys ed, Deneclei is the school soccer team captain and has even refereed matches in municipal league competition.

Driving all of his many interests is a devotion to Jesus so committed that Deneclei relishes every opportunity to spread Christ's message of salvation—such as missions to town where he distributes tracts to pedestrians. On one such outing, he and Edinei bumped into their mom, who expressed the desire to have both sons back with her. However, the brothers, being neither unloving nor resentful, tenderly refused their mom's offer and pointed out how much more positively they were progressing in all areas of their lives. As they so sensitively explained to their mother, all this would be lost, since it was very likely that reuniting with her would only repeat the in-and-out-of-home pattern of their childhoods.

Deneclei adds that he learns a lot from and thrives on all the action generated at the *Lar Colméia* campus by visiting volunteer church groups from North America and elsewhere. He says it really pumps him up, observing how these servants of Jesus donate their time and talents not only to housing construction but also to teaching the children many special skills. Deneclei points out proudly, for example, that he was the first kid in José and Alzira's house to complete a three-week auto mechanics and repairs course taught on campus by two volunteers from the author's own church, Trinity Baptist in Kelowna, Canada. Caleb Peckham taught and Art Isaak translated as the children and the volunteer instructors completely overhauled a 1984 Volkswagen van. Noting Deneclei's consuming interest in the English language, another volunteer later wrote from Canada detailing possible employment opportunities for Brazilians conversant in English. "One day maybe I can work at some airport using the English language to help passengers."

Last year, several of the eleven Americans and Canadians who sponsor Deneclei played soccer daily with him and his CHAIN of Love pals. "I would really love to play that sport professionally in the United States, and as I learn more English, I know that could help me become a pro." He also struck up a friendship with a teenage girl from Edmonton, Canada, whose stories of Canada's scenic wonders have Deneclei keen on undertaking a cross-continent North American journey someday. His friend, incidentally, is the daughter of one of several

Canadian dentists volunteering their skills without charge to repair the children's teeth.

As for his houseparents, Deneclei describes them as absolutely super. "All the time our mother [Alzira] comes up with surprises. For example, Mom will bake a cake for no special reason—just to treat us. "And Dad [José, the CHAIN's bus driver], he's always kidding and goofing around." Then, grabbing a framed picture from the living room mantel, Deneclei shows it to me, grinning, "This is why I like him." In it, a laughing José is wearing a candy-striped red-and-white shirt and his arm encircles Deneclei's shoulder, Dad and son together.

In an environment so continuously overflowing with affection as that between Deneclei and José, it's understandable why the children heap affection so generously upon each other, upon their houseparents, and, in fact, upon all of God's creatures. Eighteen-year-old Amanda Pricila Veira Ogando lavishes love upon Tuca, the boxer dog that is the pet of the children in the *Lar Colméia* home of houseparents Sérgio and Romilda. Little wonder that affectionate Amanda has her sights on becoming a veterinarian. She's the child charged with Tuca's care, and when interviewed in May 2004, Amanda politely cautioned everyone to treat Tuca tenderly, since the mutt would be delivering a litter any time. A few days later the home rocked with laughter as Tuca's pups slurped the cheeks of one hugging kid after another.

Given her atrociously abusive upbringing, one could almost excuse Amanda if she behaved as a callous, insensitive, and defiant teenager. Yet today everyone basks in this girl's warmth. That warmth, suppressed for many years by fear, beatings, and neglect, is fully aflame now, Amanda explains, because she "loves having a father and a mother in Christian home." In the jargon of social workers who dealt with Amanda before the CHAIN of Love, hers was a "dysfunctional family." That seems a mild description. First, she never knew her father, said by her mother to have been a philandering lout, filthy in his personal and domestic habits, who beat her while keeping her as a fearful household slave before he abandoned them. Her mom, Amanda says, was an alcoholic but was neither a prostitute nor a drug addict as believed by social workers. She had been dating men, but she was employed in a shoe factory.

Amanda's mom abandoned her as a four-year-old, leaving her with her grandparents. Amanda says those grandparents never mistreated her during the four years she was with them. In fact, they loved her. But Amanda can't fathom why her mother deserted her at that tender age. The domestic setting with the grandparents, while caring, wasn't the least conducive to a young girl's learning development— her grandfather, for example, was blind and confined to a wheelchair. When she was six years old, school tests showed Amanda to be cognitively slow, according to a teacher who is a member of Pastor Ken's Good News Baptist Church.

After four years, the grandparents were no longer physically capable of looking after Amanda, so her mother reclaimed her, and the two moved into another relative's home on the outskirts of Estância Velha, a city in Rio do Grande Sul province. Now there was a man in the picture as well—a stepfather. Here the horror begins. One evening toward dusk, while her mother was working at a shoe factory, the stepfather, intending rape, suddenly thrust himself at Amanda while they walked toward the woods close to their home. But she broke free, outrunning the stepdad to home, where she locked herself in alone until her mother's arrival four hours later. Her mother didn't act upon Amanda's complaint, and the stepdad grabbed her a second time several weeks later as she entered an outhouse. Again she escaped. Again, no action by Mom.

But her mother, when drunk and upset, would occasionally lock Amanda into a room for several hours. On one occasion, Amanda began screaming in objection to another lock-in. Then her drunken, enraged mother whipped her unmercifully with an electrical wire for twenty minutes. Shocked neighbors telephoned police, who rushed her to a girls' shelter in Novo Hamburgo, where an examination showed Amanda's thighs sickeningly discolored by the wire blows. Two months later, her mother visited the shelter, but Amanda was too terrified to go to the reception area and meet her. A month and a half later, the mother again turned up and Amanda did talk briefly with her. For the next three-and-a-half years, neither her mother nor any of Amanda's relatives dropped by.

Upon being taken in by the CHAIN of Love in February 2001, Amanda was told she would have to appear before a child-custody hearing to be attended by her mother, stepfather, and godparents. "I freaked out hearing this, but good thing Ken, Romilda, and Clovis [one of the housefathers] accompanied me," she recalls. "Thankfully, my mother and the others didn't turn up. And I heard that my stepfather had disappeared. Good riddance."

From the very moment of her arrival at the *Lar Colméia* campus on February 16, 2001, Amanda's life has been one of promising and continuing Christian growth. Then a twelve-year-old, she immediately found houseparents Sérgio and Romilda attentive, tenderly concerned, and always ready to offer sound counsel whenever asked. Two incidents stand out in Amanda's mind as illustrative of their love.

"Dad is always patient and calm. After I slapped one of the smaller boys here for taking an extra portion of yogurt, Dad took me aside and told me nicely not to get stressed and worried about such a minor thing. I'm responsible for helping Mom by setting out the food for the children, and I knew this boy had already eaten a yogurt beforehand. Anyway, it was no big deal, as Dad said, so I smiled and gave that hungry boy the yogurt I had taken away. Mom, too—she's so good in dealing with all the children's questions. She's always ready to listen. Once after I had kissed a boy at summer Bible camp, I felt I had better tell Mom before others did so that the story wouldn't get out of hand. So I asked her whether it had been right to kiss the boy. She said kindly that a kiss is all right but that I should reserve it 'for the right boy.'"

Meanwhile, if any child is the picture of that famous song line "whistle while you work," smiling Amanda is. The author observed that while seated at Romilda's kitchen table for supper. Beaming Amanda would be the ideal actress for any TV commercial pitching housework products. She delights in helping Romilda prepare meals for the younger children and washing dishes afterward. And her gusto in sweeping and mopping floors is a sight to behold!

No doubt, that sunshiny energy and disposition are ignited by Jesus living in her heart. Group Bible studies in the home grabbed her interest from day one. But Amanda wanted her own Bible for independent study rather than having to share the family's edition with all the other children. So, she asked Romilda to buy her one. Good idea, Romilda figured. On her third Sunday morning at the CHAIN of Love, Romilda tapped Amanda, seated next to her in Good News Baptist Church, and surprised that excited young lady by handing over a Bible to be cherished as hers forever. Romilda had also bought Bibles for the dozen other children in her household flock. "I pray with it nightly after reading a verse or two," Amanda says.

Among all the happy moments derived from living in the Lord's Word, one stands out for Amanda as the most thrilling. That occurred at a Sunday morning mini-service at Good News Baptist in February 2004, when she sang on stage with Jerilyn Bayer, Sally Antholzner—then an office assistant with the CHAIN, and Ana Paula de Oliveira—the aspiring gospel singer whose heart-rending story was told in chapters six and eight.

> "I had asked Jerilyn if I could sing with them. Wow! Was I nervous at first—my voice was cracking in the first few lines. But then everything was okay. The words began coming out clearly. That was my happiest moment ever, and I sang my heart out after that".

As for smiles and happiness, what splendid medicine awaits patients if twenty-year-old Deise Graciele Pinto Ribeiro undertakes her primary career goal of becoming a nurse and eases their pain or discomfort by flashing on her magnetic smile! If she opts for her second choice of computer science specialist and programmer, Deise can plug her innate artistic talent into the design of computer programs. Art had been her favorite subject at LaSalle Middle School, and her creativity is evident in drawings displayed around the home of houseparents Sérgio and Romilda.

One evening, when I sat for dinner at Romilda's kitchen table, Deise came to my chair. There she stood aglow with pride and pointed to the thumbnail-sized color photo of herself as a twelve-year-old along, with photos of four other children, on the cover of *Links in the CHAIN of Love,* a small booklet on the ministry authored in 2002 by Mary Jo Stockdale, an American from Phoenix, Arizona, who had been on a mission to the *Lar Colméia* complex with husband Gene a year earlier. For Deise, the years since her arrival at the CHAIN of Love on December 17, 1998, have all been two thumbs up, just as they have for the beaming boy displaying that signal in a photo adorning a leaflet from the North American Baptist Conference advertising the Bayers' ministry.

In contrast, the years before the ministry assumed Deise's legal guardianship were ugly. Deise is the girl cited in chapter seven as the ten-day-old infant traded by her destitute mother in exchange for a liter of milk with which she could feed two older children. From Deise's perspective, the next twelve years contained spurts of pure hell. Certainly her first days were an ominous prelude to the subsequent horror unleashed upon her by the trigger-tempered foster father to whom she had been traded. Ten-day-old Deise was so dehydrated when traded that she required two months of hospitalization before her step-parents could take her home. Upon Deise's release from hospital, her birth mother signed adoption documents surrendering Deise to the foster parents. But shortly thereafter, her new foster mother died, and with that death began the ongoing tragedy of a terrifying "family" life for

Deise and the other children, all older. Her foster father was responsible only insofar as providing food for the table. Much of his time and earnings as a construction worker were used up boozing at the neighborhood bar. The children all hid whenever he staggered in drunk, which was often. "If we said anything, he would fly into a rage and beat anyone he could grab quickest," Deise says. "He was always irritated with everybody, screaming and yelling a lot, and he never explained why we were being abused and punished."

For Deise and her foster brothers and sisters, home was virtually a prison ruled by an alcoholic monster whose outrageous temper caused one live-in woman after another to flee. None stayed more than a year.

One Friday night as an eleven-year-old was especially horrific for Deise. Her creepy foster father ordered her home from a first communion party honoring a girlfriend. He had gone there and dragged her outside, where he bashed her head against the corner of the house. Still dizzy, Deise sat in the doorway when she arrived home with him, fearful of going any further. Her foster father yelled not to go out, but a scared and bewildered Deise began walking toward the gate. Then—bam!—the beast knocked her down. She covered her face with both arms before he kicked her in the face and then pounced on her, attempting to crush her face with her own arms. Both of Deise's arms broke lengthwise. The brute refused to take her to a doctor.

Deise's arms swelled up that Saturday and Sunday, and by Monday they were a hideous mass of black and blue. Her foster father demanded that she not leave for school that day because the ugly discoloration would raise questions that could expose his cruelty. "But I had stood all I could take," Deise says,

> "...and I did manage to sneak out after he went to work. I went with the same dirty, blood-stained dress I had worn to the party, so that I could reveal what had happened. My girlfriend loaned me a blouse to wear. Still, I was too ashamed to go inside the school, so my girlfriend went in and brought the teacher outside. The teacher was shocked seeing me so swollen, bruised, and so much of the pain showing in my face. I described my foster father's beating, and my teacher became very angry with concern and immediately took me to the principal's office to report what had happened. Then she telephoned the city's Board for the Rights of Children."

The board took Deise into care and arranged for X-rays of her arms. In addition to two broken arms, the doctor's report also listed body marks unhealed from earlier beatings. Later the board learned that on least three earlier occasions one of the foster dad's married sons had reported being beaten by him. So, for Deise's protection, the board moved her into a halfway house pending a court decision on future care.

A halfway house, as Jerilyn Bayer points out, isn't exactly the most productive environment either for children pulled out of traumatic situations. Operated by the government, they are old houses supposedly designed to shelter children temporarily until their future is legally determined. At the most, temporary should mean three months, Jerilyn says. But all too often, children stay for years. "The children are crammed into bedrooms with mattresses on the floor."

Everyone follows a timetable as rigid as the military's:

when to get up, to eat, to play. It is impersonal, and affection is almost nonexistent, since most government workers look upon their duties as nothing more than jobs. Children are bathed, changed, fed, and put to bed. They are not taught or played with, and Jerilyn says some of the older children who should have been toilet trained are still in diapers because the workers find it easier to change them than train them. There are no men around. Little more than the children's basic needs are met by the women hired to cook and care for them. House numbers can vary from a dozen to thirty or more children, Jerilyn notes. "Sometimes there are no babies there, other times eight or more infants."

Meanwhile, Brazil's creaky justice system is so overloaded, Jerilyn says, that some children remain in a halfway home for as long as three years before a judge decides on their futures. He or she cannot be taken out until that decision is rendered. Deise had been sheltered for five months when social workers—not the snail-like court system—reached a decision. They had futilely tried to track down Deise's birth mother or other family members willing to take her in, but none was found. So, stymied, officials gave her this news: "We are giving your foster father a strict warning and sending you back home."

That arrangement lasted no more than half a day. That night, a frightened Deise overheard the beast telling his live-in woman in the next room of the small, thin-walled house: "This time, I won't beat her. I'll kill her, so she will have nothing to say."

Deise recalls, "I was so terrorized I dashed out to a friend's house, and in school the next morning I told my teacher about that vicious death threat." Back she went to the halfway house a second time, again for several months, until the court requested that the CHAIN of Love undertake legal guardianship.

Again, fear drove Deise to tears. She knew zilch about the Bayers' ministry, and she cried, pleading to shelter workers to stay there where at least she felt safe. But on that life-changing day of December 17, 1998, Pastor Ken, at the shelter to pick Deise up, assured her that she would thereafter not only be loved and cared for but also no longer abused by anyone. "When I arrived at my new home, Jerilyn was there and hugged and kissed me, saying there was no need to be afraid—that she loved all the children at CHAIN of Love as if they were her own. And Jerilyn said I could come to her any time for help or advice." Deise's new houseparents in a rented home in Novo Hamburgo were Pastor Carlos Valentin, a Baptist minister temporarily on leave from the ministry, and his wife, Angelina. They were also members of Good News Baptist Church, and Deise quickly came to love going to church with them and the other house children.

As the Valentins prepared to leave in 2000 for another ministry assignment, Deise again fell into nervous uncertainty. But new housemother Romilda swiftly erased it with her engaging warmth as Deise moved into her *Lar Colméia* campus home with twelve new brothers and sisters and housefather Sérgio. To Deise, Romilda is the absolute embodiment of the nurturing mother. (Incidentally, dear reader, Romilda will tell you her story in chapter eleven.)

Deise, wearing a necklace centered with a cross that was donated by one of her sponsors, credits her nurturing housemother for instilling and building faith and forgiveness in her. "Mom [Romilda] taught me that I must learn to forgive by pointing out how the Bible teaches everyone to pray and ask God to plant forgiveness in them."

Deise hasn't seen her birth mother since her departure twenty years ago. When her mom moved back to Novo Hamburgo from parts unknown seven years ago, she asked to see Deise, but Deise refused, asking, "Why should I meet with someone who sold me for a bottle of milk?" But she says, "I had hated my mother and now, thanks to Romilda's words, at least in my heart, I have forgiven her and even my foster father. Now, it seems as if they never existed."

One evening particularly flashes vividly into Deise's mind as an outstanding illustration of Romilda's nurturing. The entire family was watching television when Deise erupted into tears at the start of a program detailing the abuse and violence inflicted on Brazilian street kids. The program was an in-depth look into the problem, as well as how children suffered in unhappy families. Romilda switched off the TV and sat down beside Deise. "What's on your heart, Deise?" she asked. Deise says, "A great burden lifted as I poured out my heart about my past." As she told Romilda, the flood of tears served to vent her seething anger at adults who hurt children. Still, Romilda softly and kindly urged Deise to pray not only for the children violated but also for the violators, plus those now entrusted with the care of abused children rescued from the streets, including her own houseparents.

At the youth summer Bible camp later in that year of 2000, Deise walked to the front stage, knelt, and prayed, forgiving her mother and other family members who had beaten and abused her. As Deise walked away, she was handed a small leaflet containing a biblical verse. At home Romilda read and explained the passage, Ephesians 1:10.

As Romilda told Deise, God's purpose was set forth by His Son, Jesus, "as a plan for the fullness of time, to unite all things in him, things in heaven and things on earth" (ESV). The two then prayed, and a few weeks later Pastor Ken baptized Deise.

The transformation in Deise over the past nine years borders on miraculous, based on what this author observed during both our interview and nightly dinner visits to Romilda's kitchen. There was mild-mannered Deise, aglow with her Mona Lisa smile as she swept, set out dinner for the children and guest, and later cleared the table and washed dishes. The other house children looked to her as the center of sibling love. "They all confide in me," she smiles.

Still, Deise can become exasperated—occasionally and understandably. But here again she is astounded by housemom Romilda's seemingly inexhaustible patience. The high jinks of the fun-loving pair Altamir and Linda can bug anyone ultimately—except Romilda. Indeed, even toward them, Romilda's disposition appears to harmonize perfectly with the wisdom of Ephesians 4:2: "Be humble and gentle. Be patient with each other, making allowance for each other's faults because of your love" (NLT). Deise points out that soon after Altamir and Linda arrived, for example, the two dragged around their diapers and laughingly ran around wiping those soiled diapers on walls throughout the house.

"They kept everyone awake. And they both flooded the floors by turning on the kitchen sink faucet full blast and allowing the water to overflow the basin onto all floors throughout the house. Another time Altamir switched on lights in all our bedrooms after we had fallen asleep. Romilda cleaned all the smeared walls and everything else, never once screaming or yelling at them. But I was ticked off, thought that Mom was maybe being too lenient, and told her so."

Not to worry, Romilda assured her, they would change; for now, just pray for them. "And here I am, frustrated and thinking, 'Do I have to pray for everything?'" Deise smiles. Patient Romilda had a punitive-and-curative solution in mind: thereafter, Altamir and Linda would have to stay put on their respective toilets until all their business was completed. To be sure, family togetherness does have its fluctuations, as Deise observes, but "my hope is that more children like myself can find the love I have experienced here."

So infectious is that love at the CHAIN of Love that it not only flourishes in the hearts of the children taken into guardianship but also tenderly imprints the biological children who share in their care along with their parents. Lifelong bonds of camaraderie and friendship are forged as they work and play side by side with boys and girls of their own generation.

Twenty-year-old Aline Correia, for example, thanks God that her mother, Marlene, and father, Ademar, accepted the Bayers' offer to become houseparents in July 2001. "I felt God had been moving in my parents' hearts, and that's why they took Pastor Ken's offer." Before becoming full-time houseparents on the *Lar Colméia* campus, Aline's parents had already accumulated extensive know-how as houseparents looking after children legally entrusted to guardianship by the CHAIN of Love. That transpired over three years in the Correias' home in Novo Hamburgo, where Marlene and Ademar, as members of

Good News Baptist Church, had initially responded on October 30, 1997, to Pastor Ken's emergency plea to take in Levi Josué da Silva, then twelve and the eldest of three sons of Sérgio Luis da Silva, who is now a fantastic house-father but was then a recovering drug addict camping out in hospital for most of the next two-and-a-half years at the bedside of his dying little daughter, Kaiane. (The coura-geous and heart-rending story of Kaiane, who died just short of six years old in 2000, will be told in chapter eleven, along with that of her heroic and compassionate house-mother, Romilda; in chapter twelve, Sérgio will tell of his spectacular triumph after long years of severe addiction as he journeyed into a loving partnership with Jesus.)

The Correias looked after Levi, now twenty-one, for about three of his years with the CHAIN of Love. (Now an adult, Levi is residing with friends.) "At first, my brother Emerson and I did feel a different mood through our home after he and other children settled in, but it wasn't long before we all adapted," Aline recalls. "We felt sorry for Levi, knowing that both his mother and father were drug addicts and that his mother had recently died of a drug overdose. We knew we were lucky because our parents had always been good and loving." Levi, in fact, had run away from one of the homes on the *Lar Colméia* campus just before Pastor Ken asked the Correias to accept him into their home from Novo Hamburgo's children's shelter. They did so because son Emerson and Levi were already friends, a bond forged from participating together in activities at Good News Baptist Church.

Again, Aline and Emerson underwent a difficult but short adjustment when their parents moved into a home on the *Lar Colméia* campus in July 2001, succeeding a couple who had left the ministry. That brought nine additional children into their lives. "We just didn't know them," Aline points out, "although it helped somewhat that we had seen these children before in church with their earlier houseparents."

It was no problem after all, because everyone grew naturally closer, thanks to the familiarity bred by sharing a home in a Jesus-centered environment inspired by the ongoing development of a ministry complex focused on the love of God's kids. The house children, for example, see Emerson, twenty-five, laboring daily on the construction of *Lar Colméia* facilities. He's a carpenter whose skills have helped erect some of the homes and other structures. Meanwhile, Aline is the older sister whom the younger ones seek out for guidance, affection, and entertainment. All but one of the nine CHAIN of Love children are younger than Aline. "I babysit some of them, and we're often all together in the living room watching TV or a video that I have rented for their amusement. Sometimes I'll order a pizza, and they sure love that."

Meanwhile, brother Emerson, returning from work, will grab and playfully swing one laughing kid after another above his head. "They love it, and they're yelling for more as he's joking. Emerson has also taught them how to read the clock so that they can tell him the time."

Aline's popularity with the children is particularly striking in ten-year-old Tairã Machado Rodrigues. Tairã came into the ministry's care from Novo Hamburgo's halfway house seven years ago with a younger sister, Bruna, and baby brother, Pablo, who are in a different house on campus. Each is from a different father, their mother a young prostitute who has abandoned four children altogether. All three arrived with chicken pox, lice, and an under-skin growth of small worms. What they didn't have was love, supported by caring discipline.

Love and personal responsibility had already been well impressed upon Tairã by the other house children and the previous houseparents by 2001, when Aline's family came into their lives. For example, Tairã already knew he couldn't express his artistry just anywhere—that was learned within days after his arrival when his house brothers and sisters, not the houseparents, acted as a rule-enforcement squad. Shoving a pail of soapy water and a brush into his hands, they policed Tairã as he scrubbed away markings scrawled onto a ceramic floor.

Now Tairã's creative bent is flowering in a positive fashion—thanks to Aline's encouragement and love. "He hugs and kisses me on the cheek just about every day and calls me 'Sis.' Often, he'll come home from school and tape little colored card drawings onto the fridge. He signs them, 'I love you Mom, Dad, Sis.'" That's the beautiful one-on-one rapport between a family's individual members that develops when you coach and guide a kid along, as Aline does with Tairã and all the other house children, helping them with their homework, for example. "All nine children passed with good grades last year," Aline notes proudly. "And all but one are improving. And, you know, I learn too in helping them. They have taught me how to be patient, while I have learned what techniques work best in teaching." The children, she says, excitedly endorse her plan of entering college to study fashion design.

"I love it here," Aline re-emphasizes. "I thank God that He persuaded my parents to come here. They have set an outstanding example not only to myself and Emerson, but to all the house children." Aline's praise is indeed on the mark, but, then, all the housemothers and housefathers are special. They are a remarkable congregation of earthly saints serving for the love of God's kids, and their fascinating stories follow in the next three chapters.

10

MOTHERHOOD AT ITS FINEST

They're a gang of iron ladies, and yet they're the most enthusiastic of cheerleaders for the love of God's kids—these ten incredible housemothers so lovingly nurturing their flocks at the CHAIN of Love. Imagine what is required to cook for, mend for and clothe, comfort, encourage, educate, entertain, discipline, advise, give individual attention to and morally guide ten to a dozen children taken into care and legal guardianship from backgrounds as savage as those already described—unspeakably gruesome abuse, rape, homelessness, destitution, and deprivation so desperate that little ones scavenge garbage dumps for food scraps to survive. Shoulder that responsibility for children ranging from infancy to eighteen, integrating them with two or more of your own. Think of them—all in potential and often actual conflict as they clamor for your attention, for a piece of you. Meeting that challenge must require something akin to the strength of Samson, the patience of Job, the stamina of the world's top triathletes, the courage of Daniel, the faith of the apostle John, the protective nature of the Great Shepherd, and the love of Jesus.

It's a good thing they have unfailing and unwavering support and backup from their helpmate husbands, the housefathers. But the housemoms surely are the major frontline troops in a team effort of volunteers, staff, and professionals that has enabled Pastor Ken and Jerilyn Bayer over the last twelve years to develop their CHAIN of Love ministry into what could be a global role model of what can be accomplished by any worship assembly daring and committed enough to rescue downtrodden children anywhere in the world.

The children call these iron ladies "Mom," but to you, dear reader, we introduce them alphabetically as Alzira, Áurea, Cida, Deny, Eli, Eva, Marlene, Marli, Nair, and Romilda. As emphasized at the outset of this book, their loving work and play with their flocks encapsulate motherhood at its finest. God, the Master Mover, engineered the circumstances and timing perfectly to recruit them for the CHAIN of Love team.

On Mother's Day of May 9, 2004, dozens of gleeful children onstage at Good News Baptist Church sang their hearts out, smilingly expressing their abiding love in song after song to this superstar team of moms, who were seated in the congregation and dabbing handkerchiefs to their eyes to wipe away a tear or two. One song highlighted how greatly God's blessings have showered upon their moms. Moments later, tears ran even more freely down a face aglow with delight as housemother Eva Rosa dos Santos, her shoulder embraced by husband and housefather Eloi, heard one of her house children, Karine Luciana Lesing, then sixteen, recite a poem dedicated to her specifically and to all the housemothers. Karine was radiantly smiling as she stood behind the lectern onstage and fixed her eyes on Eva. Those heartfelt words of love came out slowly, distinctly, and expressively. Such has been the life-changing impact on Karine, who just a day earlier had marked the sixth anniversary of her arrival at the CHAIN of Love, so damaged that she didn't even know her real name. Hers has been a long process of healing from the effects of having been repeatedly raped since the age of five by first one stepfather (and his "buddies") and then a second. God, thankfully, brought the Bayers into her life. They took her in from a girls' shelter. Had Karine remained there much longer, she could well have been entrapped by the older girls into a life of prostitution and drugs. It's understandable that it took years before Karine could accept any adult male with trust. At *Lar Colméia* in 2004, this author observed a gracious young lady smiling, whistling, and singing as she carried out paid duties cleaning the campus technical-vocational center.

At that same Mother's Day service, the children performed a biblical theatrical presentation sharing gospel accounts of motherhood. Then Pastor Ken honored all of the CHAIN housemoms in a stirring sermon, describing them as extraordinary servants of Jesus, much like those two generations of mothers who prepared Timothy for evangelizing with Saint Paul. Ken noted that Paul had looked upon Timothy as his spiritual son and teammate in spreading Christ's gospel and starting Christian congregations. In making the analogy, Ken pointed out that Paul's second letter to Timothy recalled how his "spiritual son" had been influenced by the deep faith of his grandmother, Lois, and mother, Eunice. It was very coincidental and apropos that I had started that day by reading a devotion in *Our Daily Bread* ("Indispensable" by Herb Vander Lugt) that delivered the identical message. Lois and Eunice were indispensable to developing the faith of Timothy, and mothers like them are today indispensable at the CHAIN of Love and throughout the world for spiritually nurturing God's kids.

A quote from Abraham Lincoln underlined that devotion: "No man is poor who has had a godly mother." The children at the CHAIN of Love, once so poor in material goods, heart, and spirit, are now being enriched because of the godly nature of their housemoms. The gratitude children feel for such enrichment was especially dramatized in how the flock of then fifty-two-year-old Maria Marlene Nunes da Silva demonstrated it on Mother's Day 2002, ten months after Marlene and husband Ademar became houseparents to nine children on the *Lar Colméia* campus. Somehow, those children tricked her to remain outside for two hours while they and the couple's daughter Aline (whose story you read in chapter nine) decorated the home's interior with balloons and streamers. Marlene was stunned by the blast of color as that excited squad of children marched her back inside. Then they commanded her to sit on her special chair at the living room table, blindfolded her, and then brought in a pot of tea and a lopsided cream-filled cake. As the blindfold was removed, the gang burst into singing "Happy Mother's Day!" and presented a tearful Marlene with a heart-shaped note expressing their collective love. Covering the fridge door were each of their artful notes of love. That jubilant demonstration merely represents a microcosm of the cascade of affection showered by the children upon all the housemothers each Mother's Day at the CHAIN of Love. Varying vignettes of Mother's Day affection will be outlined as we meet with the housemoms one by one in subsequent pages.

For now, though, let's just consider encouragement. Beyond the unconditional love and faith ladled out by these shepherdesses for their flocks of God's kids, encouragement is probably the most positive medicine they dispense to their boys and girls. That's clear from how their lives have been so brightly transformed. It's given through a kind word, a hug, a kiss, a tender pat on the shoulder, a ready ear, an approving smile, a star or two pasted on a schoolwork paper that reflects continuing improvement, a warm little handshake, or a palm softly caressing a tiny cheek—treasured little things. And God only knows how much these children, many former street urchins, hungered for and needed recognition. They arrived into the arms of these moms (and housefathers) devoid of any self-esteem. Any inkling of confidence had been shattered by backgrounds encompassing, as you have already read, every imaginable family and social ill. The housemothers elevate the children's spirits along with their shoulders, just like Jesus did for people of all ages during His earthly walk and like He does today. And words are their equipment, the most powerful tool among them spelled e-n-c-o-u-r-a-g-e-m-e-n-t. Note *courage* in that word and *en,* meaning "with." That's what these shepherdess moms do: they fill and inspire each kid in their flocks with faith, hope, and courage.

All of that has been instilled, for example, by fifty-year-old housemother Marli Mello into fifteen-year-old Graciele de Lima Jardim. The interview comments from Graciele were gathered just before observing a weekly meeting of housemothers in the technical-vocational center on the *Lar Colméia* campus. Here was a girl whose self-respect had been rock-bottom when she arrived at Marli's off-campus home in July 2003, three weeks shy of her twelfth birthday. For almost two years, home and life for Graciele was in a children's shelter in her distant hometown of Giruá. Her mother, a prostitute, had visited her only once during that entire period, neglecting even to turn up to wish Graciele happy birthday when she turned eleven. No wonder Graciele's heart hardened and her outward demeanor became so hard-bitten. Understandable, since her mom merely shrugged off Graciele's sexual abuse by her stepfather, a drug trafficker who not only severely beat Graciele's mother regularly into begging and screaming panic but also forced her into prostitution. The mother also had been compelled to work late into the evenings in a detergent factory. That forced Graciele, while the stepdad was out merchandising his garbage, to care for two younger sisters, one of whom had frequent epileptic seizures.

After two years of festering negativity in the children's shelter, Graciele's behavior and outward profile duplicated that of her mother—a sensual swagger to her movements, arms crooked with hands on her hips, suggestive, foul language—the stereotypical image of a calloused hooker. That was the Graciele who arrived at Marli's doorstep after an eleven-hour bus trip from the shelter. To her, Jesus and encouragement were totally unknown. Marli more than filled the gap, pumping sunshine into Graciele's heart by first introducing Jesus and then discussing Him with her daily. Graciele's Bible and Sunday school classes at Good News Baptist Church reinforced those teachings from her worshipful mom.

Today's Graciele is Marli's right-hand gal at home, helping with cooking, baking, setting the table, preparing meals, and taking care of the baby. She is a blossoming young lady of faith and maturity. "I accepted Jesus into my heart, and I asked Mom to arrange for baptizing. I know Jesus died for me." In March 2004, a happy Graciele was dunked by Pastor Ken. It shows you what good, solid encouragement produces.

The insights Marli applied in Graciele's situation, as well as any variations necessary for other children in her flock, were likely inspired by the brainstorming at the weekly meetings of the housemothers. Minutes after we interviewed Graciele, teammate Sara and I watched Marli and four other housemothers exchange ideas that all agreed would be useful to their houseparent roles. Guiding them, as at all such meetings, were the CHAIN's private tutor, speech therapist, and psychologist. Part of the discussion that morning revolved around their "calling" to be house-moms, and each one said it grew out of a vision God had placed in her heart. The word *saint* was posed. No, they're not "saints" strictly defined, but the housemoms agreed that they could only be that in the earthly sense that God has separated them from the rest of the world's mothers for the special responsibilities now carried. Psychologist Mariene then distributed a batch of magazines and newspapers around the table, asking the moms to cut out images from the publications and piece them together into a montage conveying how they would portray themselves, and their commitment to children, to the outside world. Every creation highlighted love and encouragement. Other discussion focused on varying methods of discipline—the choice of which, all noted, would depend upon the specific needs of the child and his or her personality. "We learn from and pray for each other," one mom pointed out. "We sort out what works and what doesn't work." United in a common calling, the housemoms have a camaraderie spiritually nourished by the mini-service they share together on Thursday evenings in the campus gymnasium. Each week a different mom leads the service.

Back to Marlene, the shepherdess whose CHAIN of Love flock so elaborately honored her on Mother's Day 2002. In her *Lar Colméia* home, the living room table's centerpiece is an open Bible, there permanently for the children to peruse anytime. "I want to instill biblical curiosity in the children so they can learn on their own. My mother did the same for us seven children, and each of us would often read."

Marlene's initial leg on her route to the CHAIN began as a ten-year-old when her family moved to Novo Hamburgo, where she ultimately married Ademar, co-pastor of a church. When they left that church, God, the Master Mover, stepped in with several people who would guide their walk to the Bayers. First, Sadi Seewald, a family friend of the couple's son, Emerson, invited his buddy to Good News Baptist Church to hear him play acoustic guitar. The music and worship hit a heavenly note with Emerson, who soon was playing acoustic guitar there as well. Marlene and Ademar followed for weekly prayer meetings and a Bible study group. For about three-and-a-half years thereafter, Marlene and Ademar contributed to an evangelistic ministry focused on marital counseling.

In the meantime, God was laying the groundwork for further involvement as houseparents. The Bayers convinced Marlene and Ademar to take one boy who had run away from a *Lar Colméia* home into their own off-campus home.

He was a friend of their son, Emerson. Then came another boy from Novo Hamburgo's children's shelter, accepted by Marlene and Ademar after Clovis Scheffel, Pastor Ken's administrative assistant, emphasized that the boy would otherwise be sent to a large boys' institution that could only damage his future. This boy had been beaten brutally by his mother and had ricocheted from relative to relative.

As Marlene and Ademar became more active in Good News Baptist Church, the Bayers and the CHAIN of Love board were increasingly impressed by how well the couple had raised their own children, plus the fact that Marlene had looked after the children in one house while the houseparents were away some weekends. When that same house couple announced plans to leave *Lar Colméia* in July 2001, Pastor Ken approached Marlene and Ademar, asking them to move onto the campus and become full-time houseparents to nine more children. "For the next month, we prayed about this offer," Marlene said. "When I saw all those children needing attention, I kept thinking, 'if I don't care for them, who will?' And our own children were urging, 'Yes, go ahead!' And so we did." Here Marlene paused during the interview to wipe tears from one eye, then the other.

Her most cherished domestic task is preparing meals for the children and Ademar. Seeing her love, Marlene says, the children in turn believe "Jesus is everything in their lives." As she points out, she occasionally sits with each to emphasize the importance of Jesus in their lives.

The children also have Marlene's example of evangelizing. For instance, now attending Good News Baptist after being visited regularly by Marlene is a couple once immersed in spiritism. "They had kept inviting me back to explain Christianity, which I did. All the time I had been praying for them, then I saw the two turning up at church. They have attended regularly for the past six months."

Two scrolls on the living room mantel remind the children of Christ's presence there. One, beside a wedding-anniversary photo of Marlene and Ademar, declares from the 23rd psalm, "The Lord is My Shepherd. I shall not want." The other, received in a Christmas gift exchange with another housemom, is from John 4:14, in which Jesus declares that whoever drinks of His water shall never thirst. Walking outside later, I spot a sign on the rear windshield of a car: "Feeling Down? Jesus Wants to Show His Salvation." How could all these children not thrive with the Lord's presence tugging at their hearts everywhere?

God's Hand moves exquisitely in move after move to marshal such mothers into His CHAIN of Love. Consider, for example, the amazing sequence that ushered Marli Mello into the ministry. The story of how Marli helped to transform the life of Graciele da Lima Jardim was told earlier in this chapter. The aforementioned Deny, now a housemother herself, has been what Marli describes as her "spiritual mother" for more than thirty-five years now. They are each other's closest friend. Deny's family moved into the home next to Marli's when Deny was twenty-one and Marli fourteen. They bonded immediately. And, for years after each married, they traded turns looking after each other's children whenever the other was obliged to be elsewhere.

In 1989, four years before the CHAIN's founding, Marli was introduced to the Bayers during a child's birthday party at Deny's home. As Deny joked that day to the Bayers, "Marli sends everybody to the church but doesn't go herself." True enough, but Marli had stopped attending only because a favorite pastor at her church had departed.

Besides, husband Cezar, a non-churchgoer, was often on the road on weekends as inventory-control manager for an auto-parts company. Deny and the church pastor would drop by Marli's home regularly and expound on Jesus and His plan of salvation. At that stage, Christ was known only vaguely. But, with the seed firmly planted and ripening, connecting with the Bayers inspired Marli to accept Jesus into her heart, and in October 1989 Ken baptized her.

The Gazette of Campo Bom featured Deny Albuquerque Cezar in its Mother's Day Special in 2004.

God, the Master Mover, had yet another human "chess piece" as part of the team that would nudge Marli into the CHAIN of Love. That was Marli's mother-in-law, Grandma (Vó) Nida—Eronilda, the widow and housemom of chapters five and eight. Grandma Nida, as you recall, left behind an inspiring legacy of motherhood when a heart attack compelled her at age sixty-three to leave the *Lar Colméia* complex after several years. Besides raising her own granddaughter, Grandma

Nida had been the sole houseparent to four adolescent girls brought into care from sexually abusive situations, including Adriane, now twenty-five. You know Adriane from chapter eight as the young woman married in 2002 by Pastor Ken. To recap, Adriane had been rescued as a thirteen-year-old from such consistent sexual abuse that her reproductive organs had atrophied beyond almost the remotest chance for childbirth, yet she gave birth to Ana Raquel on October 6, 2004.

During Grandma Nida's years at *Lar Colméia,* Marli and Cezar stepped in to comfort and uplift her during a terribly grievous year of mourning and healing. Nida's thirty-four-year-old daughter, Sílvia, had died of a sudden heart attack while cradled in Nida's arms. Devastated emotionally, Nida now had inherited two more girls to mother and grandmother—Sílvia's two daughters, seven and fourteen. Along came Marli, vowing to restore her mother-in-law and see her through pain requiring strong medication. Marli and Cezar moved in with Grandma Nida for a year and did the bulk of work as houseparents during that period. "It was during this year that I began to feel God was calling me for this special way of serving," Marli says, reflecting. "Actually, I had felt the first twinge more than a year earlier while participating in a women's prayer group led by Jerilyn. Then I was approached by Ken as a potential housemother." Meanwhile, husband Cezar had been ensnared in an old trap—drinking heavily. "Both Ken and I began praying, asking God to reveal His wishes and guide us." Two months later, Cezar quit drinking and resumed attending Good News Baptist Church. Soon afterward, the Mellos' private home six blocks from the *Lar Colméia* complex was brimming with ten CHAIN of Love children and the Mellos' own four children.

With such a varied flock interacting, it's not surprising that teaching is the career goal of four girls in their care, thanks not only to Marli but also to the Mellos' two daughters, twenty-seven-year-old Daniela and twenty-three-year-old Tatiana, both education majors in university.

As our interview with Marli deepened, teammate Sara and I were touched by the intensity of the bond uniting Marli and "spiritual mother" Deny. My sponsored boy, Alexandre da Silva Fonseca, bounded into Deny's living room and planted kisses on each of Marli's cheeks, triggering a smile so luminous that it could have blown away the gray and rain outside. It was just a small everyday incident exemplifying the ties of affection binding the CHAIN of Love house families. By way of example, many years before Marli's husband, Cezar, had became a Christian, Deny and Marli had been regularly praying for each other. There had come a point when Marli was about to surrender hope of Cezar ever giving his heart over to Jesus. But Deny urged Marli to be patient, to keep praying, to never give up, that their two voices would always be united in friendship, empathy, and prayer. And the double dynamite of their prayers were ultimately answered.

Only minutes after Alexandre's cheerful intrusion, a rain-dampened Pastor Ken walked in smiling broadly, both arms struggling under the weight of many gaily-decorated packages. They were presents from sponsors to the children, and Deny's house was the current drop station. Ken certainly has a perceptive eye for only the wisest of housemoms as gifts to the children being mothered in the CHAIN of Love.

Marli is a sterling example. More than four years now as a housemom, she has been living out her childhood dream of becoming a psychologist. She loves the one-on-one dynamics of child-and-mom situations, recalling how she and her brothers and sisters would play-act as mom, dad, and children confronting specific situations.

> "We're experiencing that as housemothers, and what's helping all of us is the knowledge we're bringing from our sessions with Mariene, Fabiana, and Isabel [psychologist, speech therapist, and private tutor, respectively]. The children come crying, begging, and pleading to you with their problems, and you, in turn, always give each your undivided time and attention. They sit on your lap, and you empathize as they talk freely. Then you counsel them as kindly and soundly as you can."

Marli certainly had to employ some very careful psychology while nurturing Flávio da Silva Menezes, now fifteen, with unconditional love. The brutality this child suffered before coming into Marli's care in August 2002, two months after Marli had become a full-time housemom, is incomprehensible. Scars covering Flávio's face attest to the times his drunken stepfather tried to knife him to death before his stepmother restrained the brute. He also forced him to stand rigidly at attention while being used as a punching bag and for the occasional knife swipe. Most days, fear-paralyzed Flávio would roam his small town's streets, returning to the family hovel only after the stepdad was drunkenly asleep. One night, the stepmom set the shack on fire in an attempt to kill everyone. Somehow Flávio, failing to awaken the drunk, marshaled three younger siblings, and together they dragged him to safety outside before the shack crumbled. For all his brutality, hero Flávio and crew spared his life and then left him behind, snoring.

For the next ten days, before social workers found them, they hid near a sewage canal. They had survived on food obtained from begging in daytime and fruit stolen from orchard trees at night.

Following a month in the town's children's shelter, Flávio was brought to Marli and Cezar's home, still fearful of any adult, especially two new adults with a brood of children in a totally different home environment. It made Flávio think that once again he would be targeted for beating. So he tried to run, but he was caught by Marli after only a few steps. She quietly soothed him, asking whether he would prefer the streets to a safe, secure, and caring home. Marli's approach was convincing, and those first days of transition were eased as CHAIN volunteers included him in fun games and crafts during a Vacation Bible School sponsored by a visiting church group. However, only days after Flávio started attending a nearby school, trouble erupted. Having suffered so many beatings and violence, Flávio had become aggressive himself—he choked another boy, who ran home to his mother. In turn, the mother complained to school officials, and Flávio was ordered to the principal's office. That principal belittled him as an outcast, which angered Marli when Flávio reported his treatment. She wanted to march to the school and scold the principal for his child-damaging behavior, but she telephoned Jerilyn first for advice. Jerilyn recommended that they both pray overnight and then visit the principal together the next morning to calmly outline the situation from which Flávio had been rescued. The principal apologized, and he and Marli are now friends united in helping Flávio achieve his God-given potential.

Surrounded with love, Flávio progressively became more open, smiling easily and readily engaging with others.

Just a year after arrival, he was baptized by Pastor Ken. Flávio's amazing growth over a two-year period evoked a striking written comment from a university psychology student who had traced his progress since arrival. Love, she wrote in her university-degree thesis, made the difference in a broken boy's life. Yes, what a difference a mother like Marli makes.

Marli's "spiritual mother" Deny truly has to be a God-ordained fount of love from which children are nourished. From her interview comments and the road map of her entire life journey, it is clear that God had to be custom-tailoring fifty-seven-year-old Deny Albuquerque Cezar specifically for servanthood as a housemom with the CHAIN of Love. The Cezars, married for thirty-two years, have been with the Bayers' ministry since May 2000, and as Deny declares, "Without Jesus, we would have already fled." The Cezars stepped into the breach at the *Lar Colméia* complex when asked to succeed a house couple suddenly forced by the ministerial reassignment of Pastor Carlos Valentin, the housefather, to transfer elsewhere. This author's teammate-translator, Sara, is the wife of twenty-nine-year-old Fábio, eldest of the five children of Deny and Tadeu.

Three little words ending that headline in the Mother's Day Special of *The Gazette* of Campo Bom on May 7, 2004, aptly distill why Deny's years as a housemom have been so enriching and why each new day with her flock is treasured. "Mother Educates, Cares for, Loves and Is Still Touched When Child Says 'I love you.'" Accompanying that featured article is a photo that visibly expresses the entire family's love of Deny and vice versa. The housemom has all eleven house children gathered snugly around, smiling lovingly at their beaming queen. For a mom, does it get any better?

But for Deny and Tadeu, reaching this point was an often winding, rocky, and shaky road that indeed imperiled their marriage. As the youngest of six children who grew up on a tobacco farm, Deny was financially helped by her hard-working parents and managed to obtain an education that qualified her to teach in rural areas of Rio Grande do Sul. But with the shoe-making industry booming in the 1970s, the family moved to Novo Hamburgo to cash in on factory jobs. In the big city, Deny became a clerk in a grocery store, where she met young Tadeu, the assistant manager. Marriage quickly followed. But Deny admits arguments became routine from the start. Spiritist worship in Tadeu's family ignited the tension. Tadeu's family convinced him to attend spiritist sessions for job security. Deny, newly pregnant and raised strictly as a Catholic, had serious reservations yet went along anyway to ensure family peace. However, once Fábio was born, she bought a Bible and a book of Bible stories, intending to raise him as God's child. The following years ushered in a stream of difficulties, including daughter Monica's sickly and premature birth—problems which spiritist acquaintances claimed would have been overcome had the Cezars carried out their mystical practices faithfully.

By God's design, undoubtedly, Tadeu's mechanic had been praying for more than a year for the Cezars, who, in the meantime, had been attending one church after another seeking God and His answers for them as a couple. One night the mechanic's prayers were finally answered when the Cezars dropped by his home. Tadeu was there to pay for some work, but in progress was a party celebrating the engagement of the mechanic's daughter. Guitar playing and hymn singing by members of the mechanic's church and finally a trip later that evening to the mechanic's church laid the groundwork. There Tadeu and Deny heard the pastor leading everyone on a journey through the Bible. Following that night, the Cezars began reading the Scriptures together every day.

Tadeu, having read about various faiths, still continued searching for what he labeled the "real church." Then Tadeu's brother suggested they look in on a "small congregation served by Pastor Bayer," Deny says. Upon visiting Good News Baptist, Tadeu was soon advised that instead of looking for a "real church," he ought to look for Jesus. "We saw a difference in this little church," Deny recalls. "The people expressed their love openly, often carrying our children, even when they were crabby and sick. The fellowship was total and genuine."

For Tadeu, the experience was life changing. He bought Christian records, literature, and books, devouring Jesus' teachings every day. He seized the opportunity to convert his spiritist relatives when Brazilian evangelist Fanini scheduled a crusade in Porto Alegre. All rode to the crusade as part of a special busload organized by Tadeu. As a result, every one of Tadeu's kin became a Christian.

The Cezars, with five children, were one of the first families involved in the Bayers' church ministry. As Deny admits, she had always wanted to adopt children whose lives had undergone heart-tearing upheaval, and she had been really questioning whether that chance would ever come. "But then I was on the church board when the Bayers began researching the possibilities of starting the CHAIN of Love. They said they believed this was the way God wanted the church to care for needy children. That got me so excited—this is exactly for me, I told myself." Still, however, Deny's primary obligation remained—mothering several of her five children still far short of adulthood. So for the next six years Deny filled in whenever other houseparents were away. She was a "swing-shift" housemother, sometimes filling a gap for up to a month. All the while she prayed, "God, if you can use me as a helper, I'll be happy doing that." Then came the Valentins' abrupt departure.

"Talk about unknown territory," Deny smiles, musing over that first day in the upper story of House 5 at *Lar Colméia.*

> "Our welcoming party was a home full of upset, out-of-schedule, and crying children. Nonstop crying by the three little ones, and the baby would not come to me. The other two I couldn't tell apart. And everyone had runny noses and coughs, since it was winter. Worse, none were exactly openly accepting. But who could blame them? They feared I would be just another person they would lose—losing people had been the story of their lives. The job was not only big for me, but the children suffered as well while all of us adjusted to each other. I prayed God would give me enough love, wisdom, and mercy to overcome these difficulties and to determine how to treat these children until they could settle down."

Fortunately, eldest daughter Monica shared in teaching the children, while the Cezars' three sons assisted Tadeu with the many extra household tasks involved in caring for a large family.

Coping with and handling stress is an everyday challenge, Deny points out. It could be tiring, but prayer and calling on Jesus make that manageable. For example, as she notes,

"All the children have varied schedules, both days and evenings, so it's somewhat trying to track who is supposed to be where, when, and on what day. Besides, volunteers are in charge of many activities, and they, too, don't always follow their schedules, perhaps for good reason sometimes. But that doesn't stop the children from asking why they can't have the same privilege."

In caring for her children, Deny says she habitually reminds herself that all came from dreadfully unstructured situations and each is different. Whenever Deny feels tension pressing too heavily and fears she might overreact, she goes into the bedroom to pray it away and call upon Jesus for advice. "I'm still learning to catch myself, and then I feel so much more calm and peaceful after prayer."

Tremendously helpful to all the housemothers, she adds, are their weekly meetings. These are primarily Bible study meetings, but, as Deny says, they expand into discussions on mothering.

"We actually find we're all wrestling with the same problems, and we learn from each other. That results from telling how certain situations were handled successfully. Or we might pose make-believe situations and brainstorm on how they should be approached. I guess the most important thing all of us have learned is not to focus on little problems. Instead, we say what's most important is all our children are now finally living with a mother and a father. Throughout the week, as well, we and our husbands pray as teams for each of the other house couples."

Complementing those meetings are the Thursday

evening Bible study sessions for all women of Good News Baptist Church. Organized by the church women's group, a crowd of about seventy gather in the *Lar Colméia* campus gym to sing and pray.

Deny emphasizes that it's reassuring every day to know that she and every other housemother have such an extensive network of support underpinning their service for the love of God's kids. "After all, every day is sure to bring difficulties in dealing with emotions and feelings, not only with children but adults, too. You're juggling so many balls at once. And not everything works out the way you want." Chuckling, she says, "Sometimes I will forget to put salt in the children's meals or mistakenly flavor their food with the wrong seasoning."

As for that *Gazette* article celebrating Deny's motherhood, Deny's own words answering the *Gazette* writer's questions, translated by teammate Sara, illuminate the finest qualities of motherhood. As a whole, Deny's words add up to a primer on how to mother for the love of God's kids. In a paragraph on mother-child relationship, Deny emphasizes that she is also "a good friend" to her children, even if she is occasionally inconsistent in her attitude. That approach, she says, worked in raising her own five children. It was purposeful.

"If you always react the same to certain behavior, the children will be able to predict you perfectly. Certainly, there are moments they deserve to be punished, but I may decide not to notice what wrong they committed. But if, for example, I spot the same wrong the next day, I will certainly bring it to their attention and correct them appropriately. I don't think children should know parents completely, because it's that lack of knowledge that helps us educate them. That cultivates and sustains a certain respect while keeping parents and children as best friends. It maintains harmony in the home. And the children know you're acting in their best interests because you love them."

Deny notes that all ten children brought into her care have "difficult personalities" but that she has taught each one just how much stubbornness she will tolerate. "I am very loving and talk with them a lot, but I find that discipline and punishment are essential whenever they disobey. Both are absolutely vital to their education." Lack of discipline and limits causes families to unravel and "become unstructured," Deny points out. "A certain point must exist where a mother says, 'Enough!' and 'That is as far as you will go!' And then she must keep her word. Really, I believe this will actually help them live each moment of their lives to the utmost." On the other hand, Deny always apologizes quickly whenever she realizes she has been unfair.

"It doesn't matter if I've been unfair with the youngest or the oldest. I'll say, 'I made a mistake. I'm sorry. I'm human, and I do make mistakes.' These types of attitudes have forged a bond of trust between us, and they know that if they have made a mistake, they can speak truthfully. Certainly, the hardest challenge in raising children is teaching them to speak truthfully, and in that respect, I'm very strict. I will have them talk every time they deserve to be grounded, insisting that they speak truthfully. If they do, I won't ground them, and I will explain that they weren't grounded precisely because they told the truth. I make it clear, however, that the same mistake should not be repeated. That's how I encourage them to be honest, because, by telling the truth, they will certainly suffer less in life."[21]

In a telling comment, Deny declares that, like her own five children,

"These ten are gifts from God, too. Like any mother, I never expect anything in return, and so I'm surprised about the many times my children say he or she loves me and feels sorry for not having said 'I love you' every time he or she wished to say it. That really touches my heart, because I'm a mother who teaches, cares for, and loves her children. That's my commitment to society. Yet it's wonderful to have my children confide with me about their doubts and to see how responsible they have become, how much they have learned, and how they all love me."[22]

In a final paragraph summarizing her basic advice to each kid, Deny says:

"Every chance I get, I tell them to live today, to retain a pleasant remembrance of the past, and if possible not to harbor resentments, sorrows, bitterness, or melancholy for the past. Tomorrow, I add, it will all be different. After all, 'His compassions are new every morning.' I'm happy to be the mother of such a large and close family—a family whose strong foundation rests on an understanding love, a love that helps, that overcomes, that forgives, and that encourages."[23]

It's a boundless love such as that of then forty-seven-year-old Cida Marinho Costa that drives a housemother to dramatically turn back a child in danger of wandering astray. For the child, it's a lesson cherished forever. Remember Paulo Ricardo do Amaral de Assis, the courageous little boy of not even five years old scrounging through garbage dumps and ensuring the survival of his younger sister and baby brother? Well, even little heroes can succumb to temptation. A local grocer once approached Cida after she and husband Renato had become houseparents. The merchant accused Paulo of theft, but nothing could be proven because no items were found to be in his possession. However, several months later Cida dreamed of a child in a supermarket pilfering from a shelf and upon awakening told herself to inspect Paulo's backpack when he returned from school at noon. "Leave your backpack here," Cida told him.

"But, why?" he asked her, pacing nervously to and fro.

"Sit down to eat, and we'll talk later," said Cida, who was preparing lunch for her flock. Paulo, then eleven, suddenly not so hungry, gulped hurriedly and was about to grab the pack and head for his room, unaware that Cida had already opened it and found two cans of condensed milk and one of coconut milk. But Cida blocked Paulo's path and ordered him to eat more—and slowly. When he finished, she confronted him with the backpack and the stolen items. Here now was possibly a life-saving moment in young Paulo's life—Cida's exposure of a soul-destroying habit undoubtedly born out of and ingrained by the desperation of a scavenging little kid who had been the survival source for younger sister Vanessa, baby brother Sidinei, and himself. Strong words of correction followed from a mother to a remorseful and apologetic lamb who had veered off track and betrayed his mom's trust. Then they took a trip together to the supermarket where Paulo would often stop while walking home from school. He denounced himself as a thief and handed over the stolen cans to the market owner, who smilingly forgave him. Glum Paulo, tears trickling across his face, admitted he had learned a hard lesson and vowed never to steal again.

By Paulo's correction alone, Cida demonstrated that Pastor Ken and administrative assistant Clovis Scheffel had selected the right woman to approach about the possibility of becoming a housemother. They had been praying for God to identify a potential housemom, and both came up with Cida's name. And the sequence of events that had Cida and Renato join the team confirm that, once again, God's Guiding Hand was steering the recruitment process. "I admit I was very reluctant," Cida says, recalling the offer by Ken and Clovis in May 2003.

"They emphasized that it would be a long-term commitment but that we could leave whenever we became tired. I just felt, though, that so many other families at Good News Baptist were far more qualified. Besides, we had been members for only two years, and other families knew much more about the CHAIN of Love children from church activities. That's what I told Pastor Ken and Clovis, but they urged me to think it over for a week and pray. I'll tell you, I argued and struggled with God without hearing how He felt. But I know He wanted me here. That was revealed at the end of the week. I was working in the kitchen in early morning and listening to a Christian radio station when the show host asked, 'Have you read your Bible today?' and I answered loudly, 'No!' And wouldn't you know it, the show host replied, 'It's still not too late.' So I sat down at this very table in our previous home in Porto Alegre and prayed, then said, 'God, today I'm going to make up my mind, but You have got to show me in Your own words if I should go.' Then I randomly opened the Bible to an Old Testament passage in which God warns against disobedience by His children and, in effect, says, 'If you obey Me, I will bless you and your family and will increase the number of your days on earth.' I knew immediately God wanted us to come here, and I started crying. That night, I told Renato and our three children how I had decided."

"Incidentally, I must add," Cida says, her right palm caressing the leather-bound Bible, "that God's Word is always here on the table so that the children can use it while eating breakfast."

The Costa family had only been in their new home in Porto Alegre for a few years when the CHAIN of Love offer beckoned. They had moved from another state to Porto Alegre so that Renato would be closer to his work as a telecommunications engineer with the phone company headquartered in that city. Renato had been with the firm twenty-five years. In their new city, Renato and Cida attended a Baptist church whose youth worship team soon included son Rodrigo, now twenty-five, and daughter Renata, now nineteen. That in turn led to the first connection with Good News Baptist Church and the Bayers in Campo Bom. As members of a youth worship team, the

Costa children were part of a celebration one weekend of various teams like theirs from across the state. There they met Clovis and the younger folk of Good News Baptist under his direction. Their rapport was instant. Rodrigo and Renata liked the Good News Baptist children so much (and vice versa) that, for the next two years, the Costas drove an hour each Sunday from Porto Alegre for services at Good News Baptist. And the Costa children sang there with the youth worship team.

Cida, who grew up as the second eldest of six children in a nominally Catholic family, always wanted to mother a large family. But physical problems intervened after two children, and she complied with her doctor's advice to undergo a hysterectomy.

> "Many years had passed, and I had almost forgotten about that wish for a large family, but then we ended up attending a church where many women began telling me about their adopted children. I told Renato and the children about adoption perhaps being the answer to my dream of long ago, and they thought that would be just fine. So, I bought all kinds of baby things, diapers, a crib, and a bassinet. Then I said, 'Now the baby can be born.'"

A few days later, a friend called Cida, informing her of a new-born requiring adoption. The infant was a twin girl, just three days old and 4.4 pounds, whose twin brother had already died. Their mother, a promiscuous wanderer, had abandoned them at the hospital and surrendered them to adoption, just as she had with an earlier set of twins in another city. In fact, the infant girl's brother had died shortly after birth precisely because Mom had futilely tried to abort them.

The infant girl's lips remained immobile when Cida first put a bottle to her mouth. Eleven years later, I observe adopted daughter Rafaela—whose life was touch-and-go when she was born on June 15, 1993—studiously doing her homework with other house children at the large living room table. It's definitely a happy lot, with a vibrant, healthy, and smiling Rafaela and the others kibitzing heartily. While Rafaela has failed some grades, she is now progressing, thanks to help from Cida and the CHAIN's psychologist and private tutor.

Jesus definitely lives in the Costa household, just as the sign over the kitchen pantry states: *"Jesus Vive."* He lives in the hearts of children like nine-year-old Guilherme Mello, thanks to the love showered upon him by housemom Cida. Here was an absolutely cold fish with a demeanor so icy that his face was a frozen scowl during the Costas' first days as houseparents in 2003.

> "I told him, 'I love you, even if you don't care for me. But that's okay, I understand. And I like you, too.' Three months later, though, Guilherme began to change, and that was after he had been hospitalized for about fifteen days. It was a condition that stemmed from his infancy, we're told. Anyway, he had a respiratory condition—water in his lungs—and a fever. But then Guilherme saw how all of us care and love him so much. Today, he's a changed boy, much livelier."

Considering Guilherme's background, a cold demeanor would have been inevitable, as it indeed was initially. He had been abandoned first by his mother at six months, then by his father, who went to Social Services, reporting to staff there that he had begun working and would return later in the day to pick up Guilherme. Well, Dad never did return, and for two years Guilherme remained in the state's care, until the CHAIN brought him into legal guardianship in August 2002, placing him with the Costas' predecessors.

Like Guilherme, Taís Oliveira, now seventeen, continues thriving in the warmth of the Costas' love. You met her earlier as that wordless, lice-ridden girl rescued from the garbage dump along with older sister Ana Paula in January 1996 by Jerilyn Bayer and social workers. Taís is that child viciously skewered with barbecue spears and repeatedly raped by cowardly relatives and strangers who knew their silent victim couldn't expose them. But in May 2004, this author observed her sitting next to Cida, aglow in smiles as her mom combed her hair ever so gently with long strokes of love. Meanwhile, other links of love are being forged within the CHAIN family—the Costas' son, Rodrigo, a university engineering student, is the steady boyfriend of Clovis Scheffel's eldest daughter. Word was that they planned to marry, but no date had been set as this was written.

These housemoms have varied personalities, but the one quality they all demonstrate strikingly is the depth of their love—love of their children, their mates, their Jesus. Forty-six-year-old Eva Rosa dos Santos broke into tears a half-dozen times during our two-hour interview. Eva and husband Eloi had been houseparents for only seven months when teammate Sara and I talked with her in May 2004. Her first tears trickled down her smiling cheek with our first question, asking why the couple joined the CHAIN of Love.

"I didn't know it then, but the desire must have started faintly about eight years ago when I heard

Jerilyn Bayer speak at a women's retreat about the ministry's care of children. It was a gathering of women's groups from throughout the state. Jerilyn's message is a blur now, but I do remember her talking about a six- or eight-year-old girl who was making great progress. Then later I met Marli at an open house in our neighborhood school. She wasn't a housemother then, but she had overheard me talking to another woman about Jesus. So she walked over and introduced herself, then invited me to a women's group meeting. That's where I was introduced to Jerilyn."

As Eva and Marli grew closer in friendship, Eva confided to her about Eloi's drinking problem. Empathizing, Marli told how her approach had helped husband Cezar overcome alcoholism. Marli prayed and prayed, and eventually husband Cezar quit and resumed being a churchgoer. That started Eva thinking, so she approached her church pastor.

"The pastor said God folds His arms across His chest when His children are rebellious, in short, He remains patient and loving. So, the lesson was: I could choose how to react. I had to practice daily what God taught through His church ministers. Instead of all the hassles, arguments, cursing, anger, and contempt that erupted whenever Eloi arrived home drunk and dirty, I would greet him nicely, even if he kicked off his shoes onto the floor. I would even sit on his lap, in spite of his foul smell. And I also filled the tub and bathed him. Then I would stay up to clean and wax the floor after he

went to bed. And the next day Eloi would see everything sparkling clean. His drinking was a habit he
had learned early. His father and all his brothers are
drinkers. Of course, I prayed harder and listened to
a lot of Christian music on radio."

There were tears from Eva again when we asked her
when Eloi quit drinking.

"Despite my patience, he continued drinking a lot,
so that made me determined to leave. One day I left
home and went looking for place to rent. Honestly,
I had even forgotten exactly what had gotten me
angry, and I hadn't cleaned up at home either. I also
stopped at church and told our pastor I planned to
leave and had been out hunting for a rental home. I
told him I didn't know what else I could do. But his
reply was 'You're being tested.'"

On a morning soon afterward, Eva heard a pastor quoting
Scripture during a radio program. The message was God's
invitation to those who are weary and heavy-laden to seek
rest in Him (Matthew 11:28).

Tears trickling for a third time, Eva recalled,

"That was a wake-up call. 'Quit moping,' I told
myself. It seemed like I had been jolted from a nightmare. I cleaned the house and told Eloi that I was
going to church that evening. And was I ever
shocked when he said, 'I'll go with you.' We didn't
exchange a word during the drive or when we
arrived. So I was a bit angry at the beginning of the
service. Then the pastor announced that those
wishing to be baptized should fill out forms for bap-

tism classes. As the service ended, Eloi asked me to get those forms. Again, I was shocked. More than that, he eagerly participated in the classes and was baptized three weeks later. And it has been twelve years now that Eloi stopped drinking."

Her own walk with Jesus began in 1985 when their son, Tiago, now twenty-two, was about two years old. "I was the first in our family of six children to become a Christian." For the fourth time, tears streaked Eva's face. "My aunt took me to an evangelical church and told me how churches help people. She gave me the address of a church in Novo Hamburgo of which she was a member." Eva's first experience there was with the church's women's group, where one member was discussing prophecy and emphasized that faith restores those who are ill.

"Her message spoke directly to my problem. So I started going to church occasionally and began hearing more about Jesus. I went home happy and smiling. I had accepted Jesus as the fount of life, committed myself to Him, and eventually was baptized."

Several years later, Eva began helping friend Marli occasionally after Marli became a housemother. On some days, she filled in for a few hours if Marli had errands or appointments scheduled. Eva loved caring for the children, and the experience started her thinking about adoption and also wondering whether she could qualify as a housemom. "I figured, it can't hurt to ask, so I telephoned Jerilyn. She advised me to pray. And that very same evening, Pastor Ken phoned to arrange an interview with Eloi and myself." On March 26, 2003, the couple was interviewed by Ken,

Clovis, and Mariene, the CHAIN's psychologist. Mariene phoned the next day, thanking them for the interview and advising that, while there was no house assignment available as yet, to keep praying and that they could be called upon in future. Meanwhile, Eva continued helping housemom Marli whenever Marli filled in on weekends at *Lar Colméia* for Grandma Nida in the care of five CHAIN of Love girls. Grandma Nida's heart condition would soon compel her to retire.

Several months later, in September, Eva was walking at the top of the hill just outside the *Lar Colméia* campus and heading for Grandma Nida's house when Ken drove up beside her and offered to drive her there. During that two-minute ride, Eva was delightfully surprised by Ken's question: "Do you still want to be a housemother?"

"'Oh, yes!' I replied. Then Pastor Ken said the ministry was pleased by how well I had come to know the girls. He also said the CHAIN of Love board wanted a couple, since boys would begin being placed in the home after Grandma Nida moved next month." Then came Thursday morning, October 23, 2003. Reliving the scene creates a fifth set of tears.

"It was a bittersweet but loving farewell between the girls and Grandma Nida, and all of us were hugging and spilling tears in saying goodbye and wishing her well. The pain crossing both Grandma Nida's and the girls' faces revealed so much about the love they shared. Those pained looks also showed how grateful the girls felt toward a mother who had guided them in getting over the awful hurts of their early childhood years. Now, with Eloi and I, we will be with them for as long God wants us here. We are so very happy and at peace being here. And,

Eloi, he's so good with the children and particularly the three boys. The boys glue themselves to him from the moment he gets home from work. Eloi is on temporary disability from a shoe factory but is selling goods from a street stand downtown until he fully recovers and returns to the plant."

What's most important in being an effective house-mother? Unhesitatingly, Eva declares, "Having a disposition to serve the children 100 percent. And courage, too."

Then there is a sixth and final rush of tears as Eva pauses to unreel the scene on November 21, 2003, when the dos Santos and their flock of girls welcomed the first two boys into the household—brothers Giovani and Daniel Ribaski, then ten and four. Their father had dumped the mother of his first three children to be with another woman. After then fathering Giovani, Daniel, and three other children, he abandoned all to live with his daughter from the first woman. Their mentally challenged mother was devoid of affection or any sense of responsibility for feeding and clothing the children, despite a visiting home-care worker's efforts to teach her. So it was Giovani who stepped in, cooking as best he could with whatever scraps he and Daniel could forage. Their biggest concern was filling their infant sister Gabriela's stomach, feeding her baby beans, or rice, or stale bread and washing it down with spoiled milk or Coke. Finally, a routine visit forced horrified social workers to yank them out of a hovel reeking in a mass of filth. A judge's swift decision brought a badly hiccuping ten-month-old Gabriela into the CHAIN of Love and the private home of Marli and Cezar in August 2003, while Giovani and Daniel were placed in a halfway home for the months of legal processing that preceded their arrival at *Lar Colméia*. Snuggled in Marli's arms for that November welcome was sister Gabriela, then thirteen months old. Gabriela's smiling eyes met those of her two brothers as they walked through the doorway. After four months apart from their baby sister, both boys were crying and smiling as they dashed to her, each giving her hug after hug. The entire family of children and adults was awash in tears of joy.

God's presence is evident to anyone observing the intimate bond between these children and their shepherdess moms. it seems that God's Protecting Hand rarely permits any earthly force to rip that loving cord. Several incidents in the first half of 2006 reveal that dramatically. For example, when Altamir, who cannot hear or speak, got lost at the oceanfront, he wrote his housemother Romilda's name on a piece of paper so that beach strollers could yell it out. A relieved Romilda answered and rushed to grab Altamir into her arms. Another child wandered off in the wrong direction on another beach outing but was found by police, who returned him to his *Lar Colméia* family.

With temperatures burning at 42 degrees Celsius, extreme dryness triggered a fire behind *Lar Colméia's* homes. The blaze tore into some of the community's unused land, scorching fence posts, but was soon doused and did not get near the homes. The electrical wires and transformer that feed the homes had somehow shorted, damaging some equipment. A rear fence had been conducting sixty volts of electricity. But quick repairs got everything back to normal.

When a car carrying substitute houseparents Joel and Jacqueline hit some loose gravel, flipped over, and slid into a rice-slough trench, only the tops of the wheels stuck out of the water. Everyone thanked God that Joel and

Jacqueline, shaken but somehow uninjured, managed to crawl out of the submerged car, a write-off. The couple had been returning from a short vacation. Members of the Bayers' Good News Baptist Church, they had gladly agreed to fill in temporarily as housemom Cida convalesced after spinal cord surgery. But Cida and husband Renato resumed their mission to God's kids in four months, two months earlier than Cida's originally designated six-months' leave of absence.[24]

That motherly passion and devotion are aflame in the moms' one-to-one talks with their children. Two scenarios late in 2005 stand out, one of Eva with eleven-year-old Juliano Ribas Leuck and the other of Deny with eight-year-old Andressinha da Rosa Flesch and her eleven-year-old brother, Luciano. Eva, Juliano's new housemom, looked consolingly into his face and then softly embraced him, knowing that earlier that day he had been told by the Bayers that his grandfather recently died. Juliano erupted into tears at the tragic news, sobbing as he asked the Bayers who would visit him now, since a visit with his grandfather had been scheduled for several days later. Julian cried in anguish that his grandpa had been his only loving relative, and he moaned that he had no one left in the world. Here was a lost child who had just been shepherded into the CHAIN's care after social workers decided *Lar Colméia* would be Juliano's only safe and caring refuge, since his ailing grandpa was about to die. That grandfather's home had been Juliano's shelter almost since infancy. His mother had abandoned him and an older brother when Julian was just two months old, and the boys' alcoholic father abandoned them as well soon after, leaving them with their grandparents. However, he would periodically drop by to beat

Juliano and slur, "It would have been better if this pest had not been born." At age seven, Juliano was left with only his grandpa after his grandmother died, while his older brother was being raised by an impoverished aunt.

As the social workers wisely emphasized four years later when approaching the CHAIN to assume legal guardianship, no one could imagine what kind of horrendous damage Juliano's father could inflict once Grandpa passed on. As Juliano's CHAIN biography says, this studious, quiet boy felt at home the first day he came into Eva and Eloi's home. And on that night of grief for Juliano, there was Eva, explaining to Juliano and the other children how the CHAIN's homes represent the opportunity to learn what it is like to love and be loved and how to live in a family. Juliano, though, was struggling with the idea of forgiveness to his father. So, Juliano asked Eva why no homes existed to teach the same things he would learn. Eva replied that his alcoholic father didn't need a home but, rather, Jesus, and he could find Jesus at anytime. Eva then led the children in prayer for their parents. "It was such a special time," she said.

As for forgiveness, housemom Deny provided insight and an object lesson into both that Jesus-like quality and compassion when she escorted Andressinha and Luciano in November 2005 on their first visit to their biological mother since being rescued into the CHAIN's guardianship on September 16, 1999, when Andressinha was just two and a half and Luciano was five. Andressinha had always envisioned her mom as very pretty, but the woman she saw that sorrowful day with Deny and Luciano was a ghoulish soul totally disfigured and dying of AIDS, much like the skeletal image of the two children's father, who had died earlier of AIDS. In fact, much of Andressinha and Luciano's family has been decimated by this ugly killer. Their mother had a long history of abandoning her children, and one of her and their father's legacies was transmission of AIDS to the older children, including a sibling slightly older than Luciano who likely will have joined their mom in death by the time these lines are read.

Mercifully, Andressinha and Luciano's mother had already voluntarily gone into a government program before their births. Under that program, the fetuses that were Luciano and then Andressinha were treated in the womb so that each entered this world AIDS-free. Still, Luciano was born with club feet, his right foot much more deformed than the left one. Yet he managed to get around, and recent surgery has enabled happy little Luciano to run and play just about like any other kid at *Lar Colméia*. He loves to skateboard, and an art class being taught on campus has caught his fancy. As for Andressinha, she's a self-confident, dirt-laden tomboy with an artistic flair. Her Mother's Day poem and drawing were published in the local newspaper in 2006, and she has learned to play the keyboard by ear and is determined to play the bongos. That November day in 2005, their faces were downcast as they visited their dying mom, a comforting and supportive Deny at their side. As Deny reports, their mother told them she herself had been abandoned as a child and had been abused. "But she also shared of her new-found faith in Christ and the hope of being with Him eternally. The children were elated to know that she belongs to the family of God now, too." Luciano was so excited by the meeting that he asked to enroll in the next baptismal class.

When the Bayers' daughter, Jessica, was nervously about to run the Power Point equipment for the first time, little Andressinha approached her. She had perceived Jessica's butterflies, so she insisted on praying for her. With both of her tiny palms placed atop Jessica's bowed head, Andressinha prayed aloud, thanking God for Jessica's willingness to serve and asking the Lord to eliminate Jessica's nervousness. "Amen," Andressinha ended, immediately asking Jessica if she felt better. Poof! The butterflies had fled![25]

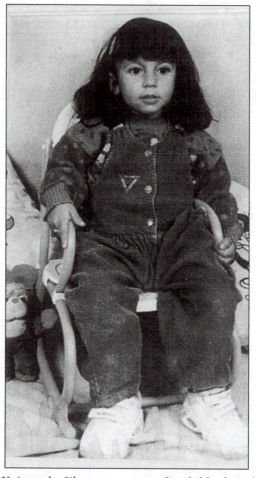

Angelica Kaiane da Silva was an angelic child of God who had
"lived life to the fullest."

11

AN ANGELIC CHILD, HEAVENLY MOTHERS, AND THE POWER OF LOVE

Little Kaiane da Silva was almost six years old when she died painfully in Romilda's arms. Despite all the physical shortcomings with which Kaiane entered this world, housemother Romilda de Vargas Lencina da Silva says this child of God "lived life to the fullest—always so enthusiastic, bubbling over, and flashing smiles." The legacy of their daughter-mother bond lives on in Romilda's heart, and the vision of it remains with everyone privileged to have witnessed that love in action.

Here was a little one who had undergone thirteen surgeries and would have undergone a fourteenth if extreme viral diarrhea had not ruptured the flesh of the previous operation, poisoning her, and ultimately passing her from Romilda's caring arms into those of our loving Lord. This was a child whose last words in life, despite the sickening agony, were only, "Mommy, it hurts." Picture it—not what

Kaiane came into life with, but what she so courageously endured while always being an effervescent bundle of joy to Romilda and all those whose lives she graced. Kaiane was born without an anus or urinary tract, and with only one wall for her uterus and bladder. Immediate post-birth corrective surgeries included a colostomy, an operation on the colon that opens the abdominal wall enough to provide an artificial one. Minus a kidney, she required a separate bag for urine. This was the birthright of a biological mother who had been injecting cocaine while pregnant. Both her mother and father were hard-core druggies, but fortunately her mom wasn't injecting during the three pregnancies that produced Kaiane's three older brothers.

The amazing irony is that her suffering, her angelic example, and her death were precisely what jolted her father, Sérgio Luis da Sillva, into such a remarkable turnaround that he is today long past hopeless drug addiction, one of the CHAIN of Love's housefathers of distinction. The pain of sharing and caring for Kaiane during her ordeal also brought Sérgio and Romilda together into a partnership that today is a solid marriage. Their wedding was performed by Pastor Ken nine months after Kaiane's funeral. God's abundantly amazing grace was obvious in Sérgio's miraculous turnaround. That inspiring story will unfold throughout the next chapter.

For the first two-and-a-half years of Kaiane's life, Sérgio was continuously with her. He quit his shoe factory job to undertake his ever-present and prayerful watch at Kaiane's side in hospital. Hospital staff taught Sérgio the techniques for her care. While his blood tested as satisfactory and was used for transfusions for Kaiane, her mother's blood test turned up HIV positive. That was her last visit to hospital;

shortly thereafter, she and a male companion were found dead of a drug overdose. Meanwhile, unable to support sons Levi, Saulo, and Isaac and desperately needing nursing help for Kaiane, Sérgio made some timely decisions. At Sérgio's insistent urging, Pastor Ken placed the three boys into CHAIN of Love homes and agreed to find assistance in nursing Kaiane. That choice was Romilda, with Sérgio thoroughly instructing her in Kaiane's total daily routine.

Kaiane's monumental impact on the lives of Romilda, Pa Sérgio, and all of her house brothers and sisters speaks out from a framed eight-by-eleven-inch photo adorning a living-room wall of their CHAIN of Love home on the *Lar Colméia* campus. Radiating from that picture is the widely smiling presence with which Kaiane blessed their lives in the home for almost three years, from the minute she arrived at Romilda's doorstep with Pastor Ken on October 30, 1997, until she drifted into eternity on September 11, 2000. Romilda's most cherished image of her is touching.

> "She did this so spontaneously, wherever and whenever she felt affectionate: she would grab both my arms out of the blue and kiss the entire length of them up and down—whether we were riding a bus, walking outside, or shopping in a store. And every time she did it, she said, 'Mom, I love you.'"

For Romilda, looking after little Kaiane was unbelievably demanding, but she notes, "This beautiful child merited all I could give." The toddler's diaper had to be changed up to fifteen times a day to prevent possible infection. The Bayers drove Kaiane and Romilda to the community hospital every couple of days for checkups and evaluations. Of course, the entire CHAIN and church families were rallying to her side with countless prayers and vigils during the hospitalization periods for those thirteen surgeries over thirty-four-and-a-half months. Jerilyn and two members of Good News Baptist Church donated blood when Kaiane was in surgery for construction of an anus. The surgery succeeded, but Romilda had to carefully prepare Kaiane externally for urination and bowel movements. That required meticulous cleaning and the use of antibiotic solutions. There was not the slightest whimper of complaint, however, from the ever-smiling Kaiane. Observing her sunny attitude, Pastor Ken marveled time and again, "Kaiane has springs in her feet."

"The Lord provided for her needs in many ways, but one response particularly touched me, " Romilda points out. "A Porto Alegre newspaper appealed for diapers for Kaiane, and a diaper manufacturer adopted Kaiane's need as a special project. Delivered in a massive bag with the company's prayer and blessing was a supply of 500 disposable diapers."

In the meantime, Romilda was increasingly impressed by Sérgio's frequent visits to Kaiane in hospital, the love he showered upon her, and the appreciative words she always received for looking after Kaiane.

Finally, the surgeons felt confident that they could undertake the extremely delicate and complicated operation of connecting Kaiane's urinary tract. Mom Romilda was at her daughter's side as they prepared her. All necessary tests were completed in August 2000, and surgery was scheduled for September. Then a virus struck. Kaiane's abdominal pains and diarrhea began on a Sunday afternoon, preventing Romilda and her from attending Sunday evening services at Good News Baptist. That evening the Bayers led the congregation in praying for her. Jerilyn telephoning

Romilda afterward and learned that the diarrhea had intensified and become more frequent. "On Monday morning, she was barely alive," Jerilyn recalls, recounting the desperation sobbed into the telephone by Romilda. The Bayers left daughter Julissa with a neighbor and drove speedily to Romilda's for the mad rush with Kaiane to hospital at 3:30 A.M. Rushed into emergency, Kaiane apparently was already gone.

Sighing, Romilda relives the emotional pain. "I had gone into a back room to pray and begged God for help, but not long afterward the doctors and nurses came out to the reception area, and I could tell by their grim faces that Kaiane had died. It was so very hard on all of us at the CHAIN of Love, but those doctors and nurses also were terribly grieved because all of them had become so attached to Kaiane. After all, she had been in the last leg of her surgeries, and success appeared to be looming, but the recovery effort failed. They fell apart emotionally in tears, too, paying their respects at Kaiane's funeral." The Lord took Kaiane on September 11, 2000, exactly one year before the 9/11 suicide hijackings and terrorist attack on New York's World Trade Center rang up a death toll of nearly 3,000.

"Probably the hardest time I have ever had was at Kaiane's funeral," Jerilyn says. "And the hardest moments were when I tried to sing a solo of 'Celebrate Jesus,' as our worship team had requested. That had been Kaiane's favorite hymn, and my rendition was the congregation's tribute to her life and the legacy of love she had bestowed upon us. In and out of church, that little angel sang it everywhere. Tears flowed freely, and my voice cracked, but I somehow struggled through the words." Reminders of Kaiane's inspirational life hang today over stagefront railings in Good News Baptist Church—two gold-lettered "Celebrate Jesus" banners on a dark-blue background. And on the *Lar Colméia* campus, the playground bears her name.

"For sure, I confess I was very disappointed with God," Jerilyn continues,

"but in my heart I knew it was better for Kaiane now because she was about to start school. Going to God when she did was probably even a blessing from God. Her father, for one thing, came back to the Lord, and that was the one positive impact from everyone's loss. Sérgio absolutely fell apart at the service, denouncing himself and crying that life wasn't worth living now because he had lost his wife and his children. So, I told him, 'What you need is a new life, Sérgio, and the One Who gives it is here today.' Then we all prayed together with a group of men, and Sérgio vowed to accept Christ from that moment on."

Retracing those moments himself, Sérgio says,

"I determined to seek the Lord with all my heart and not go back into drugs. And the acceptance and support of so many people there was overwhelming. One fellow even pulled me aside and promised, 'Whenever you are tempted by drugs, give me a call, and I'll find you wherever you are and take you home and feed you.' That started me going back to church, where I again saw and became reconciled with my sons. That was so comforting, and I also got to see Romilda."

Houseparents Romilda and Sérgio Luis da Silva with most of their lively house flock.

It seems that Romilda's journey toward becoming housemom to the CHAIN's neediest children was being charted by God several decades ago. Her father died when she was six, but her sole-support mom did an admirable job raising Romilda and the other children. They faithfully attended the local Baptist church, and all grew up believing in the Lord. However, as a teenager she drifted from worship after marrying a non-churchgoer, a drift that worsened five years later when he was killed in a mining accident, leaving Romilda a widow with two small sons to raise. Financially strapped and lacking emotional support, she moved to Campo Bom to be near her mother and family. Romilda erroneously thought her own security and that of her two sons would be assured simply by living with a man—any man. Fortunately, her disillusioned drift ended in 1993 when she rediscovered her faith and resumed attending church. Romilda's man, however, said "no thanks" to the Lord, and that ended their relationship. But the first steps of Romilda's return to Jesus apparently were taken seven years before Kaiane and the CHAIN of Love entered her life in 1997.

It happened this way: for seven years, Romilda helped to raise the child of her neighbor's sister, a prostitute. During the day, while the neighbor worked, Romilda fed and looked after the child, named Carol, meanwhile praying daily for the rescue of Carol's errant mother. The little girl's mom, who had always provided financial support, eventually gave up prostitution, got a regular job, and at Romilda's urging underwent professional counseling. Finally, that mother even began attending church occasionally. As Romilda declares, "It's God Who uses us, and it's only because of God that Sérgio and I are able to do what we're now doing."

Romilda reflects again upon Kaiane's contribution to her life.

> "Well, I always loved children, but when Pastor Ken asked me to take Kaiane, I only wondered if I were capable enough. Then, when I saw Kaiane, I instantly fell in love with her and just knew God would give me all the grace, love, and strength necessary to meet my little angel's needs."

Romilda admits she was so traumatized by Kaiane's death that for some time she felt she could never again love any child with such intensity. But then two other little angels already in her flock rallied to her side. Handicapped physically, this pair must have sensed the gaping hole in the heart of their shepherdess mom. Therefore they have never let up overwhelming her with love. You, dear reader, know them from their chapter nine stories as the two inseparable and sometimes mischievous pals Altamir Matias and Linda Débora de Lima. Altamir, who cannot hear or speak, is now ten, and his sidekick Linda, neurologically afflicted, who steals everyone's heart with her toothless grin and spontaneity, is twelve years old. Romilda learned sign language soon after Altamir's arrival. He had been with Romilda seven months and Linda exactly a year when Kaiane died in 2000. Romilda's heart is happily alive because Altamir and Linda always add a zesty topping to all the love radiating from the other house children.

Altamir's adventurous curiosity once prodded him to somehow open the emergency door of the school bus and wander out into a busy maze of vehicles. He nonchalantly hand-signaled cars to a halt and kept meandering until the flustered bus driver dragged him back aboard. Tadeu, Deny's husband, who drives many *Lar Colméia* children to and from school daily, was the victim in a second such incident. Although the door on Tadeu's old van couldn't be opened from inside, perceptive Altamir found that by rolling down the door window, he could reach the outside handle and thereby exit. That misadventure sent Altamir into snarled traffic. Soon afterward, Tadeu bought a 2004 vehicle incapable of being locked or unlocked by anyone but the driver.

As for Linda, Romilda now feels this ever-bubbly angel of the toothless grin is taking a special place, like Kaiane's, in her heart. When placed in Romilda's care at five and a half, Linda's drooling was continuous and her motor skills almost nonexistent. She would put her shoes on backwards on opposite feet, and she would slip into a dress backwards. Drooling was her way of communicating. That has long stopped, and

Linda now uses gestures to say her piece. Obviously, the work of the CHAIN's professionals with both Linda and Altamir has been a godsend of support to housemom Romilda's nurturing. On Mother's Day 2004, this author admired a creation by Linda that expressed her love for Romilda. It was a heart-shaped paper flower colored in blue-and-black crayon and adorned with her drawing of a green tree. It also had her own artful script handwriting. Linda had made it at school. Holding Linda's creation and smiling proudly, Romilda pointed to the Portuguese words: *"Mamãe Romilda, reserve amanhá, dia 15/05/04 (Sábado) para grandes emoções. Beijos, Linda."* Translated: "Mom Romilda. Reserve the morning of the fifteenth, a Saturday, for big emotions. Kisses, Linda." That was Linda's gracious invitation to a special celebration for mothers at school. The gift of a child's love—can't get much better!

As Abraham Lincoln said, "No man is poor who has a godly mother." Maria Alzira Cavalcante Tavares is a mom and housemom whose godly influence is evident. Alzira and husband José's nineteen-year-old daughter, Raquel, is determined to become a missionary, and their eighteen-year-old son, Josias, is focused on becoming a Baptist minister. When Alzira herself was in the second year of her twenty-three-year marriage, she was enthusiastically urged, "Sister, you should be a missionary!" Those encouraging words came from renowned missionary Richard Rabenhorst, whom Alzira and José had heard as featured speaker during a church-growth clinic.

Alzira and José have been houseparents for eight years with the CHAIN of Love. Besides Alzira and housefather José, the CHAIN's ebullient bus driver, the flock of house brothers and sisters are blessed by the godly influence of their houseparents' two children. As Alzira says, beaming,

> "Oh the wonders of God's way! God has placed a fire
> in Raquel's heart. She has wanted to be a missionary
> since she was twelve. Raquel always speaks openly
> about Jesus to her friends and encourages these high
> school children to look to Jesus for inspiration and
> follow Him. Religion is her favorite course. It's also
> so great knowing the lessons we've taught Raquel
> and Josias about Jesus are being passed on by them to
> all the other children in our home!"

Judging by the sequence of events that brought Alzira
and José to the Bayers' ministry, it's plain the Lord was navigating their movements. Raised as the second youngest of
seven children in a nominally Catholic family in Natal, the
capital of Brazil's Rio Grande do Norte province, Alzira is
grateful that her upbringing was traditional, wholesome,
and strict. No one smoked, drank, or partied. A school girlfriend once tried to coax her into conversion to what Alzira
describes as a "legalistic" church, but she refused, believing
herself to be as morally upright and honest as anyone of any
faith. At fourteen, she moved to Porto Alegre, where she
lived with an uncle and was introduced to his Independent
Baptist Church. There Alzira attended Sunday school for
three months.

> "A woman in that church was just wonderful,
> explaining Christ and clarifying misconceptions,
> and Jesus really invaded my life. Regretfully, how-
> ever, I stopped attending church after moving into
> my sister's house. I didn't go for three years, simply
> because I had no one to go with."

For those three years, she cleaned various houses as a live-in maid during the week and resided with her sister on weekends. Those three years of stalled faith also saw Jesus slip from her heart and mind. Alzira was, in effect, a slumbering prodigal daughter. But then, at seventeen, she met José in a discotheque. After a night of dancing and a movie, Alzira opened her heart to José.

Late in their year-long courtship, a conversation signaled the start of a life-changing relationship for each of them and was a fitting prelude to their marriage soon afterward in October 1982. Alzira said, "I remember the happiness I felt in my uncle's church, and I still want that happiness. I know that joy was coming from Jesus, so I never want to leave the church again."

Jose's replied, "If you want that happiness, and you want to serve Jesus, I will too." A few nights later they went to Cristal Baptist Church in Porto Alegre and stepped forward in response to the minister's invitation. They both accepted Jesus as their Savior.

Then came missionary Rabenhorst's perceptive comment in 1984 about Alzira being ideally suited for missionary life. That remark followed an evangelistic church-growth clinic that stressed that God has a purpose for each life. Alzira politely thanked Rabenhorst for his confidence in her, noting, however, that she lacked sufficient education, was ineligible for seminary, and wasn't keen on learning a different language. "But I'm going to raise children to be missionaries."

As it turns out, Rabenhorst did prod her in a missionary direction. Her missionary zeal has been richly rewarded, first with her family. Thanks to Alzira's kind evangelizing, everyone in the nine-member family except her father and an older sister are baptized Christians. Her mother, who is illiterate, committed to Jesus after listening for months to Alzira's Bible readings. Now her mom never misses a Sunday attending church and, regardless of distance, will go only to those churches where God's Word is read as an integral part of the regular service.

Alzira also made a courageous one-woman mission to evangelize in a brothel. For three hours she clung to a neighbor's back as they rode on a motorcycle from Porto Alegre north to Alzira's hometown of Natal. She was fixed on introducing Jesus to her father's mistress and bringing His message of salvation into her residence—a house of prostitution. Before leaving on that tiring ride, Alzira prayed, asking the Holy Spirit to compose and instill in her a specific message for delivery to her dad's mistress. Almost instantly, there an answer. It was the story from John 4 of the Samaritan woman Jesus met at the well and told of the Living Water (Himself)—the woman so overwhelmed when Jesus identified her as having had not one but five husbands during her sordid past; the woman who led other Samaritans to accept Christ as their Savior. Armed with that message, Alzira would be a female Daniel venturing into a lion's den of iniquity with the Bible as her sword and shield.

A woman answered the brothel door, then scurried away, embarrassed, when Alzira, a Bible in hand, asked for the house mistress. That mistress strode out boldly from a rear room, accompanied by a young daughter fathered by Alzira's dad. They exchanged pleasantries, and Alzira was amiably frank about her intentions. That impressed and ultimately endeared her to the mistress. And what a contrast the outcome would be to the minute of arrival! The ladies of the house were stunned, then abuzz with questions. What was a customer's daughter doing there? Was she going to wreak havoc rebuking everyone and pick fights?

Alzira offered personal interpretations of the salvation message, connecting it to real-life stories of others who had been saved.

> "Five women in the drawing room listened in rapt attention. They were spellbound. I used the Samaritan woman at the well to convey to my father's mistress that God loved her and wanted to be with her always, but in a different way of life. I felt at peace reading, and the words contributed were not mine but those given by the Holy Spirit. I presented the entire plan of salvation lovingly and compassionately, and, really, that even surprised me. Later, I was told the mistress had intended to punch me when she first came out."

Alzira is convinced that Jesus captured the heart of that lady of the night. Inside her Bible later, placed when Alzira had set it aside, was a wad of Portuguese currency. It was that day's ill-gotten proceeds by a house of ill-repute, money surrendered to the Lord.

A few years later, on December 29, 1986, still another dramatic experience underscored the Lord's intervention and preparation of Alzira for His special mission. On that Sunday morning, Alzira, six-and-a-half months into her first pregnancy, had gone alone to Cristal Baptist Church for the service and was the first of about 100 to arrive. Soon afterward, José arrived but was unable to locate her. He frantically asked the caretaker, "Where's Alzira?" Told she had been rushed to the hospital unconscious, he dashed off to the hospital while the entire church congregation prayed for his pregnant wife.

The joyful climax to this crisis proves again the power of prayer and reinforces the saying that the strongest army marches on its knees. In hospital, Alzira lay unconscious for thirteen hours in the stranglehold of eclampsia—the medical term for a condition involving high blood pressure and convulsions that trigger a coma, especially during pregnancy. Eclampsia, claimed by some to be a hereditary condition, had taken the life of her cousin's mother.

"The doctors were amazed when I regained consciousness. Then, they offered medication to abort the fetus, but I refused, so the doctors performed a Cesarean section. Raquel came into the world at just three pounds, four ounces. The pediatrician said it was a miracle, and I say Raquel's survival was a miracle answering a prayer."

God's healing hand brought forth an aspiring missionary. As Alzira says, "I see God's hand in her life to this day." Shortly after Raquel's birth, the doctors told Alzira's mother that her daughter had been strong and courageous. Alzira's mom agreed and added, "Jesus invaded her being."

That faith-testing ordeal convinced José and Alzira that she should be a stay-at-home mother. That would ensure their children's best interests, since they not only would thrive on their mom's love and constant presence but would become thoroughly educated in Christianity. After Josias was born two years later, Alzira, without compromising her maternal duties, taught Sunday school for several years and served as president of a ladies' group.

In 1999, Alzira and José were hosting and leading weekly Bible studies in their Porto Alegre home. The study series was entitled "Knowing the Mind of Christ." During one session, their pastor reported having just returned from a pastors' retreat. There, he said, he had heard Pastor Ken Bayer describe the CHAIN of Love and the ministry's need for another couple as houseparents for a newly constructed home at *Lar Colméia*. The pastor then led the study group in prayer for the Bayers' ministry and success in finding "a couple who loves children and senses a missionary call." Later that night, Alzira hesitantly asked José whether they might qualify for such servanthood. Her hesitancy was based on José's devotion to their own two children. She rather doubted that he would willingly agree to have them team up and divide their time with ten or more children. But José's reply was surprising. He praised Alzira for an entire lifetime of excellent care-giving to children, both their own and those of other people. As José said, "You have done a good job raising ours, and I know you can raise more."

For further confirmation, Alzira questioned various church members. Their unanimous reply was basically "Of course, go ahead; it's God's will."

And their own children? "That would be fun." The entire Tavares family pledged to devote themselves to this ministry of love for God's kids. Alzira and José quickly won Pastor Ken's approval following an interview and then the board's okay after a meeting. Soon they were in House 3 at *Lar Colméia* as a part of a ministry team going to bat for the love of God's kids.

The family's link into the CHAIN of Love coincided with that of Ana Paula Langer da Silva, who was brought to *Lar Colméia* as a twelve-year-old in April 1999 with four younger brothers and sisters, all of whom were entrusted to Alzira and José's care. That young lady's 360-degree change over seven years is a glorious testimonial to the chemistry of love flowing between the nurturers and the nurtured in this unique ministry. Worshipers everywhere, consider Ana Paula's progress as signaling what your particular congregation can accomplish, salvaging one or more children anywhere on this planet, merely by tailoring the Bayers' prototype to your own congregation's unique plan.

Social workers had found Ana Paula and her four younger siblings wallowing in a hovel repugnant with wall-to-wall human dung and garbage. As one social worker gasped, "Not even a rat would live here." The five children had been abandoned by a father so delusional that he walked city streets as a homeless vagabond throughout the day, identifying himself as a pastor and preaching gibberish to himself, the trees, and the lampposts. To build his "church," he would steal bricks nightly from construction sites. No less deranged was Ana Paula's mother, who was institutionalized. Although she had been released occasionally to be with the children, her condition is now so severe that even short leaves from hospital are impossible. During one stay with the children, she barged into a neighbor's house and, wielding a knife, threatened to kill everyone there unless they handed over food for herself and the children. Police hauled her off in a straitjacket.

Written reports by social workers described the parents as extremely authoritarian and repressive. Ana Paula arrived at the Tavares CHAIN of Love home extremely withdrawn and barely capable of uttering an intelligible word. She had been sexually abused regularly by cousins from age five on. Often she would timidly sit alone in a corner, head bowed. Other times she would hide when her name was called. And her hands would shoot up, defensively covering her face, whenever anyone tried photographing her. For some time, she recoiled and cried hysterically if Alzira tried to cut her long hair—just as she had in the halfway house when a barber did succeed in cutting it short. Only long hair and certain clothes were moral under her father's faith. She would often scowl or frown or make ghastly faces when provoked.

It's no wonder that millions of children like Ana Paula fall through the cracks in Brazil. Sociologists designate five social institutions as constituting any nation—family, economy, education, politics, and religion. In Brazil, none of these appear to be of any positive support to each of the others. The economy, for example: as Pastor Ken noted in chapter seven, 3 percent of the population of 176 to 180 million controls 70 percent of the wealth. The middle class of 17 percent controls 20 percent of it, and the bottom 80 percent scrambles desperately for the skimpy 10 percent of leftovers. The creaky health-care system is supported entirely by taxing all financial transactions. How much life can there be in a system unable to rely on any injection from that poverty-stricken 80 percent who are lucky if able to scrape up food for the day, never mind make a bank deposit or withdrawal! And the justice and social services systems are a mess, as Jerilyn Bayer emphasized in chapter six. The overloaded courts are so stymied by underfunding that decisions on the futures of even the neediest children remain interminably on hold, leaving a small portion of them lingering in government-run halfway houses that are pathetic by any societal standard. Meanwhile, the millions of others not in the state's care wander the streets, homeless and starving and, in some cases, as noted in chapter two, becoming so bothersome a "blight" that "death squads" are hired to kill the "infestation." As these numbers and realities show, very blessed indeed are those few who land in the loving care of the CHAIN of Love. This underscores the enormous opportunity in Brazil alone for worship assemblies to rescue deprived children.

From its inception more than twelve years ago, the CHAIN has been looked upon as an escape valve by the hard-pressed, cash-starved social services and justice systems. The inherently sick condition of those systems themselves produces bad decisions. As Pastor Ken emphasizes, "Our homes will not become an easy dumping ground." The CHAIN's requirement, he points out, is that government social workers exhaust all available options beforehand. "We want to make it impossible for them to extract a kid from here after placement. There are just too many broken homes because of broken families. And, with our children, we want to break that pattern from continuing on generation to generation."

That cycle-breaking certainly is very likely to materialize in Ana Paula's generation. Had nothing happened, would Ana Paula and her four younger brothers and sisters have been entered anonymously into statistical data as street-kid deaths? God only knows. Thank God for what love has accomplished in nourishing Ana Paula's soul over ten years in the *Lar Colméia* family of Alzira and José. That once withdrawn mouse now easily trusts people, is very outgoing, and talks amiably and charmingly. Having regained lost ground in school, when we interviewed her in 2004 she was enthusiastically looking forward to attending university, although she had not yet decided on a study major.

Not one of the ten CHAIN of Love families lacks some dramatic, life-transforming story akin to that of Ana Paula Langer da Silva. In fact, all of the children's stories in every house are dramatic to some degree. And a large part of the dynamics generating their life changes is motherly love, passionately driven by servanthood to Jesus.

Housemom Nair da Silva Pires exemplifies this superbly with nine children and her own eleven-year-old son, Mateus, in their off-campus home in Novo Hamburgo. God engineered the connections and events that brought forty-nine-year-old Nair and her fifty-year-old husband, Enaldir, into His CHAIN of Love community of families in April 2002. First, a neighbor, Rute Piangers, hosted Nair and Enaldir for supper one evening. As they socialized, Rute presented Christ's plan of salvation. Until then, Rute had never openly discussed her faith with her neighbors. But Nair didn't accept any of Rute's invitations to attend church together.

A year later, on Good Friday in 1996, Nair and Enaldir had just alighted from a bus downtown and were about to transfer to another for home when an impulse struck Nair. Bitten by curiosity, she urged a reluctant but accepting Enaldir to drop in on Rute's church, which happened to be nearby. There they heard the choir sing "At the Cross." Nair was touched, and her heart was doubly overwhelmed by the pastor's sermon. Sure, this was the dark Friday marking Christ's crucifixion, the pastor said, but he urged that it not be considered wholly a sad day. He continued on for most of his message celebrating the resurrected Jesus, ending it with an appeal: come to the front if you wish to accept Jesus. Nair did just that. Then, walking out the church following the service, she and Enaldir spotted former neighbor Rute standing at the door and smiling. Rute threw her arms around Nair in a gigantic hug and said, "I've been praying for you for the past year and a half."

For the next two years, Rute, Nair, and Enaldir attended church together, with Rute's husband driving them home after the services. But then Nair and Enaldir moved across the city, and because of the great distance and lacking a vehicle, they fell out of the churchgoing habit. But, thank the Lord, that was only temporary. God had another servant waiting in the wings to bring the pair closer to their ultimate linkup with the CHAIN of Love. That was Nair's cousin Marli—the same Marli Mello whose own recruitment as a housemother into the Bayers' ministry was detailed in chapter ten. One day, Marli mentioned that Rute was now attending the same church she attended. Nair thought that perhaps she could connect there with the same Jesus she knew when attending Rute's former church. On that first Sunday that Nair and Enaldir attended services at Marli's church, they not only renewed their friendship with Rute but were introduced to Canadians Ken and Jerilyn Bayer, who were the minister's guests that day.

During the year that Marli and Cezar were residing with and carrying out many of the houseparent duties for the ailing Grandma Nida in her *Lar Colméia* home, Nair would occasionally pitch in assisting them. Meanwhile, Marli and Nair began attending Grandma Nida's church, Good News Baptist. The Divine Hand was again in action as the Bayers' ministry saturated their souls. Jerilyn, for example, persuaded Nair, Marli, and another church lady to participate in a women's retreat, where all three committed to pray and fast for their unsaved husbands. On each Friday for two full years each wife knelt in prayer for a half-hour and fasted until noon, then maintained a praying spirit throughout the day, the regimen focused wholly on their husbands. As a result, all three husbands were baptized in January 1999.

An interesting prelude to that conversion is a personal close-up in 1998 of a couple lingering for a moment in a pew at Good News Baptist as the service ended. Enaldir and Nair were sharing an intimate conversation. A reluctant and luke-warm churchgoer for the past few years, Enaldir, in that spiritual awakening, confessed that his faith had actually been growing slowly. And that Sunday, Pastor Ken's sermon had touched him particularly. Nair recalls Enaldir's words: "I'm sorry you went alone to church for so long. I have lost so many years not going with you. Now, I understand the love you have for Jesus, and why you would want to work for the CHAIN of Love." Pastor Ken's message that Sunday prodded church "benchwarmers" to get off their butts and onto the field of action for Jesus. "That's it—no more bench-warming for me," Enaldir decided. After all, for several years he had already been observing how passionately Nair had been teaching children during the children's church ser-vices while also helping housemothers at *Lar Colméia*.

Over the next few years, the Bayers and CHAIN of Love board members became increasingly convinced that such a faithful couple could be terrific houseparents. Thus one day in late 2001, Pastor Ken urged them to temporarily care for a thirteen-year-old girl who had been causing trouble with the children and houseparents in a *Lar Colméia* home where she had been placed with her younger sister. Aline (Ane) Katiúscia Viana and sister Patricia had been with CHAIN of Love since February 1997. Ane's stay would be only for a fifteen-day cooling-off period, Ken explained.

As it turned out, a municipal judge subsequently decided she could be placed permanently with Nair and Enaldir in their off-campus home. As you may recall, Ane and Patricia are the sisters from chapter nine who had been repeatedly bru-talized by their mother with the closest weapon at hand—a garden hose, a belt buckle, anything—and even forced them to stand or kneel on sharp rocks or open pop caps for an hour. After just five months of Ane's linkup with Nair and Enaldir, Ken and the CHAIN board were so pleased with how everything worked out that Ken telephoned Nair and urged her and Enaldir to accept eight more children from *Lar Colméia*. A crisis had developed out of an unforeseen emergency involving one of the ministry's house couples. It was 11:30 A.M. and, when Nair accepted, Ken said the eight would be there by 3 P.M. This, indeed, was a pivotal day in the lives of both Nair and Ane. When told, Ane cried that she didn't want to share her mom and dad with eight other children. But Nair, with her innate maternal sensitivity, convinced Ane this challenge would bond them even more closely. "You will help me, and the Lord will teach us both how to care for these young children," she told Ane, then fourteen. "Before long, they will be like brothers and sisters to you."

Preceding that fateful call from Ken, a heartwarming scene had transpired. As Nair was standing at the kitchen stove preparing their lunch, Ane came up from behind and hugged her, saying, "I didn't like you at first, and I didn't like praying and reading the Bible, but now I sure like you, and I like doing that, too." What a change from that first day five months earlier when the rebellious teen entered the Pires home! She would scowl whenever Nair or Enaldir attempted reading the Bible to her, sometimes leaving the room when the couple began to pray and shuffling back and pouting only after Enaldir ordered her back. And she would frown and jerk away anytime Nair or Enaldir tried comforting her with a touch. Such behavior prompted weekly counseling sessions with the CHAIN's psychologist, Mariene Tammerik, which continue even today. Today, this totally transformed eighteen-year-old is a friend and guiding light to her nine younger house brothers and sisters.

Having learned forgiveness, Ane now visits with her birth mother occasionally. But when asked by Social Services in 2004 if she wished to return to her, she replied, "No, I have found a real home." Her voice rings with loving affection when she calls Nair "Aunt." Those house brothers and sisters of hers, incidentally, motivated Ane in her career choice—she aims to be an elementary school teacher. This is the girl whose abusive upbringing triggered two grade-one failures before coming into CHAIN of Love. She was, however, a bright child. After an ophthalmologist discovered that she had only 10 percent sight in one eye, she wore a patch over the good eye for months to induce strengthening of the bad one. Not only has Ane's vision improved substantially but so too has her vision of the future and her image of herself. Infinitely wondrous are the tools of unconditional love, acceptance, and the caring warmth of a godly family!

Nair became tearful while answering our question, How important is Jesus to you? She answered it slowly, first pointing out that her oldest son, Márcio, was almost twenty when son Mateus was born on June 2, 1995. Nair says she began worrying when Mateus began standing at eight months and always cried as he stood. He could only stand, painfully, on his toes, not his feet.

> "My pediatrician told me to wait until Mateus was a year old, and if the problem persisted, to then consult an orthopedic surgeon. But nothing changed, and one-year-old Mateus always cried as he walked on the front part of his feet. The surgeon ordered physiotherapy and rejected surgery, saying that even if performed, Mateus would still continue walking

only on his toes. Everything looked hopeless. But one day I went to a neighbor, with Mateus in my arms. He consoled me and asked, 'Do you believe your son can be healed?' I nodded sadly. That's when he laid his hand on Mateus' shoulder, and the two of us prayed. Then, back in our home, I had the most wonderful, peaceful sensation placing Mateus back into his playpen. For the next several months, the physiotherapist worked my baby's foot muscles. Finally, it happened. Mateus was one year and three months old. The physiotherapist saw it first, telephoned the surgeon with the news, and then called me into his office. He placed some toys onto the floor, and Mateus walked flatly on his feet to pick them up. I was so overcome with crying and gratitude. I dropped to my knees and thanked the therapist, and I thanked Jesus for the miracle. It was all so exciting. Jesus healed my son, and when Jesus heals, He heals completely. That miraculous moment is engraved in my heart forever."

Since then, of course, Nair has been flooded with the affection of nine more children. "I love them as my own," she smiles. Can more miracles be anticipated? Why not? As you have already read, the *Lar Colméia* campus has proven to be remarkably fertile for miracle making. As this was written, housemom Nair, housedad Enaldir, and their flock were looking ahead to the day when they would move from town into the seventh home, nearing completion, on that blessed campus.

Eli Cavalcante and her husband, Raimundo de Jesus, have been with the Bayers' ministry since late 1995, just a year after its launch, and their backgrounds almost shout that the Lord tailor-made this couple for the love of God's kids at *Lar Colméia*. Eli thanks God for having had a happy childhood in a middle-class family of thirteen, eight girls and five boys. "I love kids, and since I grew up being around a lot of children, it's just so natural wanting a big gang of them around me. Like the eleven in our home now, and that's besides our own three children." Eli and Raimundo are of like mind in shepherding children, and one incident reveals that clearly. When a missionary showed him a pamphlet describing needy African children, Raimundo wanted to go there, but other commitments then made that impossible. Like Eli, Raimundo is from a large northern Brazilian family. He's the eldest of seven—five brothers and two sisters.

Actually, one of Raimundo's sisters was the link in bringing the couple into Christianity about eight years after they married. The couple's spiritual pilgrimage began when the sister invited them to church. Their curiosity stirred, they began looking into different faiths, eventually deciding to attend a Baptist church in the northern Brazilian state of Maranhão. It was about then, too, that Eli and Raimundo adopted Monica, now seventeen but then twenty-six days old. They were already raising two sons, nine-year-old Márcio, now twenty-six, and five-year-old Marcelo, now twenty-three. Since Eli could no longer bear children, adoption was their answer to prayers for a daughter. That infant could not have been placed into much more caring hands, considering her condition. As Eli recalls,

"The mother had agreed to give up the child, but we were supposed to get Monica when she was four days old, not twenty-six days. When we got her, she was so dehydrated she couldn't urinate. Monica was the fifth child the mother had given up, and we were told the mother had not been feeding her. Poor child, that's why she was in such horrid condition—her body emptied of liquid."

Six months later, Eli and Raimundo moved south with their three children to Novo Hamburgo, with six-month-old Monica healthfully restored and bubbly with smiles.

Soon afterward, Raimundo bought land behind their home, constructed a metal-shop building there, and began taking sheet-metal orders. His earnings supported the family. Meanwhile, he enrolled as an evening seminary student in a nearby city. However the load proved a bit much, and Raimundo dropped out two years short of ordination. That calling, as Raimundo told Sara and me, had arisen fifteen years earlier in a dream. "It was a vision: the face of God shining and His Body dressed in golden-lined clothes of many colors. God was pointing sideways to a crowd of people looking up and screaming for help. I interpreted His pointing as summoning me to minister." Two of his four younger brothers are already pastors and the other two were then in seminary, and his two sisters became Christians still earlier. In fact, all seven of the de Jesus children accepted Christianity in their twenties. What an incredible outcome, considering that their parents practiced no faith! Raimundo's mother accepted Jesus nine years ago and is now one of her church's most active members, thanks to Raimundo's gentle teaching and persistent praying. His father, opposed initially to religious talk, is now attending church as well and is gradually growing in faith while accompanying his wife. Raimundo and Eli are currently ministering as houseparents to eleven children, not counting, of course, all those previous children who are now adults leading independent adult lives but continue visiting their "mom" and "dad" frequently.

The Lord's Hand was guiding the recruitment of Eli and Raimundo into the Bayers' mission for the love of God's kids. His intermediary was the pastor of the Novo Hamburgo Baptist church that they were members of.

"This was our friend and pastor, Stan, an American missionary," Eli smiles, recalling the fateful events. "I don't know why Stan would recommend us to Ken as possible houseparents, and I never did ask him. I figure maybe it was because of how we had been raising our adopted daughter, Monica. Anyway, I had been praying to God for years to give us something special to do. And, when Ken approached us, caring for a houseful of children sounded perfect."

The CHAIN of Love was then in its first year of existence, with just one home up on the *Lar Colméia* campus. For Eli and Raimundo, their first taste as houseparents occurred when they filled in for a couple away on vacation for several days. They survived looking after eight children, with no major catastrophe, and found the children liking them and vice versa.

"Meanwhile, we kept praying to hear from Ken again. And Ken responded. One couple had left the ministry, so we started taking children into our own home in Novo Hamburgo while a second home on campus was being finished. We moved into House 2 at Lar Colméia less than a year later, in 1996, with our family of fourteen children."

One of those children was André da Silva, now twenty-two. There could not have been a much more sullen and rebellious ten-year-old than this now positive and optimistic young man when he came into the care of the ministry's first couple in September 1995 and then transferred in December of that year into Eli and Raimundo's off-campus home.

His temper in those early days was explosive, particularly in spitting out violent expletives. This was a kid ripe for becoming a street criminal until Social Services brought him into the Bayers' ministry. He had totally ignored an elderly grandfather too old to really look after him. Instead of going to school, he hung out in the streets. His hard-nosed demeanor was hardly surprising. To this day, his father's identity is unknown, but rumors describe the dad as a nameless vagabond wandering from town to town. André's mother cared for him for a few years but was brutally murdered in his presence when he was a toddler. How could André possibly emerge with anything but a negative self-image? This was a kid without a single mooring. In fact, at heart André was a totally withdrawn child. No way would he accept Eli as his "mom"—initially. But Eli and Raimundo were the earthly embodiments of Christly patience. No words were said until he cooled off following an angry outburst. Then, often together, they would explain the wrong he had committed and how it contrasted with God's expectations of proper behavior.

It took several years, but André really began listening and accepting their wise counsel. Unquestionably, he was a full-scale rebuilding job. His rescue and ultimate transformation are wholly thanks to Jesus and His CHAIN of Love servants. Along the way, André also learned auto mechanics in a trades course, while attending high school at nights. A biographical sketch from the CHAIN of Love in May 2004 spoke volumes in addressing potential sponsors: "He feels loved and accepted, and is a very happy boy. He enjoys church and learning about God's love." A letter five months later noted that André and twenty-year-old house brother Leandro, his closest buddy, had moved off campus and with two other older boys were renting an apartment owned by a widow from Good News Baptist Church. The two pals, as adults officially released from the CHAIN's legal guardianship, were a little nervous making the change, but they are living in what the ministry terms "a semi-sheltered environment" while journeying toward full independence. André aspires to become a professional soccer player—the loftiest of goals in a nation, so entranced with a sport that produced the immortal Pelé, the game's greatest player ever.

Having observed André perform skillfully with about fifteen other brothers from the various campus houses during a Saturday afternoon soccer class in the *Lar Colméia* gymnasium, I wouldn't bet against him being tapped some day to represent his nation. André's deft hands and feet are artistry in motion. But these children are all skilled, thanks to thirty-five-year-old coach-instructor Antônio Carlos Rodrigues do Nascimento, a volunteer whose full-time job is teaching soccer and physical education in a local school. Coach Antônio was recruited into service by César P. Nunes, coordinator of volunteers at *Lar Colméia*'s technical-vocational center and a nephew of Raimundo. It is intriguing indeed how the Lord connects and positions people to fulfill His goals on Earth—it was Uncle Raimundo who recommended his nephew to Pastor Ken! You will read about this dynamic young man and the program he leads in chapter thirteen. Raimundo's house is directly across from the *Lar*

Colméia gym, and adjacent to that building is the large campus playground. That proved handy for André during those nine years growing up under the watchful and intensely interested eye of Raimundo, who was often out there on the field kicking the soccer ball around with André and a gang of house children. In addition to his fatherly love in action, Raimundo is a role model as a successful business owner. He expanded the shop he constructed behind their former home in Novo Hamburgo into a sheet-metal finishing company employing fourteen workers.

One weekend afternoon in the living room of his home, Raimundo was surrounded by a pack of fifteen excited children, all cheering, laughing, groaning, and simultaneously participating in an ongoing commentary as they viewed the huge television screen. Flashing from it were videotaped simulations of Brazil's most momentous games over many years in world competition, inspiring images of teamwork triumphant. That living room was bursting with energy and happiness, a parallel to the enormous voltage of happiness in the gym and playground across the road, in the other houses, and in the technical-vocational center, where the children learn trades and life skills. The housefathers and housemothers of CHAIN of Love function as a victorious team for the love of God's kids, all of it because of passionate teamwork for Jesus. You see it in the joy and thrills spilling over in the gym and onto the playground. You see it in the swarm of smiling and yelling children scrambling wildly to climb aboard the bus Sunday mornings for Bible classes and services at Good News Baptist Church. You see and hear it in everyone—adults and children—during worship services, especially in hymns sung exultantly.

While the housemothers are, because of their full-time household duties, the primary generators of such happy results, the housefathers contribute much as well to that success. Indeed, the CHAIN of Love family is blessed with dads who shelter like the great oak tree the children love climbing, stand tall across the years like the nearby mountain, and are as deep as the ocean waters and as wide as the cloudless skies above. To their sons and daughters, they're rocks of strength and reassurance. Fifty-year-old Enaldir Pires is always joking with them and telling stories and is raring to play soccer with the boys anytime. Forty-three-year-old José Carlos Mota Tavares, a self-employed microbus driver and delivery service courier, goes the extra mile for all of the CHAIN's children as the jolly bus driver whose humor and commentary buoy their spirits on Sunday morning rides to church. Forty-eight-year-old Cezar Mello's beaming smile and outstretched arms lovingly invite the children into his embrace when he returns home daily from his job as inventory-control manager with an auto-parts company. Fifty-year-old Renato Oliveira Costa, a mechanical engineer and telecommunications engineer with a Porto Alegre telephone company, is a friendly encourager and educator who goes from one kid to another with solid help while they're doing homework—and he's great if anyone's stuck on a math problem. Fifty-one-year-old Eloi dos Santos' weekend barbecuing always attracts a circle of hungry children, and he seems always to have three or more of them glued to him at belt-line height or tagging along with him as he cooks up a feast of stories. Fifty-one-year-old Ademar Correa da Silva is a metal worker and former co-pastor of a church, and his biblical lesson guidance and spiritual advice consistently has his children asking questions and hungering for more.

Fifty-nine-year-old Tadeu Cezar is a retiree who's nearly clocking as much mileage now driving children to and from school and appointments as he did during a thirty-year career as a sales rep. Tadeu loves kidding with them, and he's a master at easing their anxieties, especially for something as scary as dental work. Plus, with roughly ninety children housed on and off campus, Tadeu is as busy as any regional cab driver. The extensive network of contacts he fashioned over his long career is a major asset to the Bayers. For example, he helped Jerilyn recruit many of the doctors and dentists who have committed to the ministry on a reduced fee-for-service schedule. In another instance, one of his contacts helped Tadeu find a Christian glass-lens manufacturer in New Hampshire whose plant is now producing spectacles of greater quality and much less expensively than the CHAIN's former source did.

Then, there's fifty-one-year-old Lauri Guilherme Bastian. Not only is Lauri a manly role model to his own two teenage sons and the six boys in his off-campus home, but he's also an elder in Good News Baptist Church and the lead instructor of the shoe, handbag, and leather making enterprise at *Lar Colméia*. Moreover, it was his leadership that launched that expanding enterprise and stamps it as an outstanding winner. You will come to know this man of inspired Christian devotion and entrepreneurial vision more intimately in chapter thirteen.

Finally, there's forty-seven-year-old Sérgio Luis da Silva, Kaiane's dad. Read on and marvel in the next chapter about this incredible gent, a former hard-core drug user and pusher saved and uplifted by Amazing Grace.

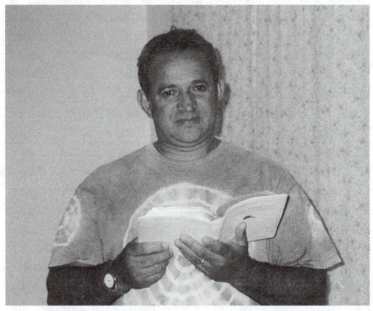

Sérgio Luis da Silva: from a wicked wretch to a heavenly house father thanks to Amazing Grace.

12

TOUCHED BY AN ANGEL, TRANSFORMED BY AMAZING GRACE

Wicked and wretched—a perfect summation of most of forty-seven-year-old Sérgio Luis da Silva's life. Sérgio's pitiful lifestyle for almost three decades was getting zapped daily on drugs and frequently drinking himself into oblivion. The father of angelic Kaiane had been a wreck before her suffering and death jolted him into a life-changing transformation. Today, as a housefather with the CHAIN of Love, he is a Christlike role model to the ministry's children.

As Sérgio recalls, drugs had enslaved him for twenty-eight years. He started at about age eleven, building up to an average monthly usage of one-half kilogram of marijuana and cocaine for most of that living hell. He was also a prodigal son degrading himself as wastefully as that infamous carouser of Jesus' parable—although the father to whom Sérgio returned was not his own dad but the heavenly Father of all of us. In fact, Sérgio's own boyhood descent into wretchedness was influenced by observing the behavior of a father he detested, a drunk who regularly visited prostitutes and whose alcoholism often had him fired from short-term menial jobs while Sérgio's mother struggled to hold the impoverished family together with her earnings as a maid. Sérgio was the middle child of nine children lucky to have the bare necessities, never mind toys and games—these they devised themselves.

Left pretty much on his own, Sérgio quickly developed entrepreneurial street-savvy, thanks to his innate amiability and clever talk. As Sérgio told teammate Sara and me, he has always regarded himself as somewhat of an impresario earning his own way. Soon after starting school, for example, he was buying school supplies with earnings made by crafting and selling moccasins. At nine, Sérgio's curiosity was aroused when he overheard school mates bragging about their "highs" from marijuana and other drugs. So he told his mother he would like to try pot. That triggered a slap across his face and a stern warning to lay off such garbage. By grade five, eleven-year-old Sérgio had dropped out of day school in Campo Bom and started working full-time in a shoe factory (child labor was not yet illegal in Brazil). Meanwhile, he attended school at night.

Hoping to buy a bicycle, Sérgio faithfully gave his earnings to his father to save. But he soon learned that his father had been wasting that money on prostitutes, so Sérgio declared that he wouldn't receive another penny. Father would not be denied, however, ordering Sérgio to begin handing over one-third of his pay for room and board. That Sérgio did, turning over most of his remaining earnings to his struggling mother.

Still, temptation lingered—he kept wondering about that "high" so vaunted years earlier by his school friends. His slide into the abyss of the drug culture began with legal drugs taken at home. Sérgio swallowed twenty-three pills bought at a pharmacy and became dazed. He was rushed to hospital by his parents, where doctors told them pumping Sérgio's stomach would be useless since the drugs had already been absorbed into his blood. That had Sérgio flying "high" for four days. Just a week later he smoked his first joint, and thereafter it was an accelerating drive into drug hell. That first marijuana "experiment," he says, was prompted by a radio commercial promoting pot usage, and, those first drags were, ironically, on soil now occupied by Pastor Ken's Good News Baptist Church. Part of the site was then occupied by a storefront club, with the rear used by prostitutes for transacting "business."

In those early days, Sérgio managed to hide drugs from his mother, a naive soul who just wouldn't believe neighbors who accused her darling son of being on drugs. Even the scent on his clothes couldn't convince her. He would partake only on weekends when his gang stole cars and frolicked on joy rides. Sure enough, though, dope seized the driver's seat of his life and became more expensive. For Sérgio that first night, it was solely pot, but, eventually it became pot and sex and sundry other drugs in an area of perdition. Praise the Lord for having torn down that Satanic nest and planting a divine ministry on that earth, a place of salvation where Sérgio prayerfully kneels every Sunday in gratitude for having been rescued by Amazing Grace. But during those early hell-raising days, Sérgio's pot-induced cockiness and disobedience soon got him expelled from night school along with two other pot-smoking sixth-grade buddies who constantly riled teachers by laughing and mouthing off. The last straw came when a power outage forced students outside, and an instructor observed twelve-year-old Sérgio hugging a girl a mite too exuberantly amid a cloud of marijuana smoke.

Within weeks of expulsion, Sérgio had graduated to higher levels of drug and alcohol experimentation in hopes of inducing a more powerful "jag." He filed off shreds of his fingernails and deposited them into liquor and beer along with the ashes from smoked cigarettes, then drank the concoctions. He mixed street sand with marijuana. Smoking that trash, Sérgio says, made him feel as if some contortionist was pushing in his back while grinding his knees down upon his head. That crushing pressure had him limping like a dog on both arms and legs. Thus, working in a shoe factory ultimately gave way to what Sérgio deemed a higher occupation—trafficking in drugs. Entrepreneurial Sérgio always sold enough to cover his debt and resupply himself. "I got children hooked by giving the drugs away free; then I began charging them when they became desperate." Sérgio admits having overdosed on cocaine so many times that he has lost count of the number.

> "I would pass out and awaken days later not knowing how long I had been unconscious. My eyes would open, and immediately I would be gasping for breath. It was so terrifying—fearing I was suffocating to death. I would hold on to and even chew the bedposts for dear life."

His degrading existence was a revolving door of swinging into and out of detox centers. How many times is unknown even to Sérgio, but the two longest stays were forty and thirty days. That thirty-day internment was in an isolation unit, where his digestive system could tolerate only fruit and watching television was all that his energy level could endure.

At seventeen, Sérgio was arrested for stealing cars. His mother was crushed when he was jailed for a few months. After being released, Sérgio continued living at home, but on weekends he would set out aimlessly to laze on the beach and partake of "the good life." That so-called "good life" ultimately lured him away from his mother's Campo Bom home to a coastal community, where he achieved his mark as a high-roller selling drugs. Outwardly, he was a sartorial dandy, always attired in fancy, crisply-pressed clothes.

Sérgio's sales enterprise died at age twenty when his drug lords got busted, cutting off both his merchandise and his own supply. But savvy Sérgio would not be denied. Hallucinogenic mushrooms filled the void. Like an animal he roamed the fields on an empty stomach, gorging himself on the fungi and collecting enough for another meal back in his room. "Wow, was I ever crazy! Often I would be hallucinating for more than twenty hours. Mixing it with marijuana became potentially deadly, and within three months I again began turning myself into detox centers." Later, his supply of pot was disrupted when police intercepted shipments by barricading border crossings. Again, clever Sérgio found a substitute—a wild flower that grew in ditches. Never mind that nature's contribution was stronger than LSD and a known killer. Sérgio's addiction was his god.

Ultimately, Sérgio says, he drifted into becoming a hippie in the 1970s, wandering the country for about two years in hippie-style clothes and taking temporary jobs, earning just enough to keep afloat in alcohol and drugs. "I figure I could have died many times, remembering how often all of us would drink until we dropped." But his mother's death brought him back to Campo Bom. While that move soon sunk Sérgio even more deeply into the drug culture, in the end it would, by Amazing Grace, bring him into the Lord's arms.

He was back at his trade in a leather shop, and there fellow worker and drug user Márcia came into his life. Her parents had disowned her. Sérgio claims she had been even nuttier than he was. This was the woman who would give birth to Kaiane—the fourth child of her union with Sérgio, the angelic darling whose story of heroic life and death unfolded in chapter eleven. Those early courtship days, as Sérgio recalls, were an accelerating whirlwind of drugs and sex. Marcia soon became pregnant, and Sérgio married her reluctantly, even as he sensed that wedlock could prove disastrous for both. They married a month before the birth of Levi, first of three sons before Kaiane. In the months before Levi's birth, Sérgio taught Márcia how to craft leather goods, which they sold readily in their travels. Things ran rather smoothly until their marriage, but thereafter it became hellish. On their first New Year's Eve as a couple, a drunken Márcia insisted on leaving her sister's house for still another party. But Sérgio refused, feeling enough booze was available there for both to get hammered. When Márcia refused to back down, Sérgio slapped her, and that exploded into a major war of words. "That night reflected our whole rotten marriage." Nursing Levi took a back seat to Márcia's alcoholic thirst. Inexplicably, however, as Sérgio recalls, both Márcia and himself lapsed into an untypical flash of parental responsibility and decided to swear off drugs for the sake of eighteen-month-old Levi. That aberration failed at the first offer of marijuana from Márcia's sister and brother-in-law. And the marital warfare escalated along with increased drug usage.

Sérgio and Márcia separated several times, and when Levi reached age five, Sérgio convinced a judge of Márcia's parental incompetence and gained legal custody of Levi. Subsequently, Márcia repeatedly went into and out of detox. Just as repeatedly she would knock on Sérgio's door, asking him to house her for awhile. It was during these interludes that she became pregnant with their second and third sons, Saulo and Isaac, and finally Kaiane. Cocaine and alcohol, however, continued demonizing them, whether together or apart. The courts ultimately declared both to be incompetent parents and had civic authorities place the children with relatives, an arrangement that also failed. Even today, Sérgio cannot recall precisely the sequence of events from those drug-fogged days that eventually brought the four children into the loving embrace of the CHAIN of Love.

Whatever the chronology in those wasted years, it was an unfolding horror story. As Sérgio says, buying drugs consumed all but perhaps a week's portion of his yearly earnings. He lied to his sister consistently, persuading her to look after their children while Márcia and he left to binge on dope. That same sister today continues to disbelieve that the new Sérgio is, in fact, a genuinely committed Christian.

Several wake-up calls brought Sérgio to Jesus, he notes. He points out that his three sons have biblical names, names that he came upon as a fifteen year old in a religious booklet that initially exposed him to the gospel. The first wake-up call occurred after a fellow worker, actually a former drug pal, became a Christian and persistently invited Sérgio to attend weekly prayer meetings at his home. Finally Sérgio relented and went, but only because he wanted to please his friend and to test God's response to a prayer for Levi, then five. Although toilet trained, Levi was still dirtying his pants. "I said, 'Lord, if you will cure my boy, I will be yours.'" A few weeks later, Levi was fully toilet trained. So Sérgio started attending the meetings every week. Sérgio always took Levi along, but gossipy neighbors assumed Sérgio was simply going to another brothel. "They ridiculed me, refusing to believe any good in me. Finally, I surrendered and went back to drugs."

At some point in this scrambled timeline, God dispatched another wake-up call, Sérgio adds. "I was really shaken when a fellow worker disgustedly slammed a tool down on a counter and, glaring, told me, 'God has shown me you are going to lose your boys, your house, and your wife.'" Shortly after Kaiane's birth, Márcia left Sérgio and their sons. Meanwhile, Kaiane, struggling against so many physical deformities—particularly the absence of an anus or urinary tract—needed blood transfusions from her mom and dad, but tests had shown Márcia to be HIV positive. She had contracted AIDS while shooting up drugs and sharing a syringe with a transvestite. In the divorce settlement shortly thereafter, the judge stipulated that Sérgio and Márcia divide the house down the middle and live in the separate halves.

To his credit, Sérgio took his workmate's tongue-lashing to heart. He strove hard to look after the boys, struggled valiantly to get off drugs, and spent increasingly longer periods at the hospital at infant Kaiane's bedside. A local newspaper, at the same time, exposed the rat-infested conditions in the shared home. And while Sérgio was maintaining his vigil with Kaiane, Márcia was taking the three sons along and educating them in the seamy world of sexual "entertainment" and providing condoms to Levi, the eldest. Márcia had quit visiting Kaiane in hospital after learning of her own AIDS. That negligence resulted in a twenty-day period during which courageous Kaiane fought on alone without visitors since father Sérgio was working to keep the family intact. Then Márcia and her male friend were found dead of drug overdoses. Understandably, her unloved sons shed no tears. Sérgio, meanwhile, was so busy at work and tending at all hours to hospitalized Kaiane that the boys drifted into the street-drug culture. Fortunately, their way-wardness was cut short by placement in a drug rehab center, and recovery was complete.

In the meantime, Sérgio's heart was undergoing a terrible beating as he helplessly observed infant Kaiane enduring her agony. So he quit his job and virtually lived in Kaiane's hospital room for the next two-and-a-half years, sleeping under her bed with a keen ear perked for any whimper for help. Hospital staff trained him, and the government subsidized him as a parental caregiver. Occasionally, Kaiane would be released to go home with her dad, but the stench and filth in Sérgio's neglected home would quickly force her return to hospital. The infection risk to her fragile system was just too great.

Throughout this emotionally draining ordeal, Sérgio began seriously questioning his own worthiness as a father and a human being. Was God confronting Sérgio and prodding him out of his wretched past? What but the Divine Hand of God would prompt him to weigh his parental liabilities and call upon Pastor Ken for help? Sérgio urged Ken to take the three boys into the CHAIN of Love because of his full-time commitment to Kaiane's care. Ken hesitated and suggested some other options, because he felt Sérgio was not the type of father to surrender his children. "I can tell you really love them deeply."

Yes, Sérgio agreed, and it was wholly because of his intense love for them that he wanted the three nurtured in loving Christian homes. "I don't want them leading the kind of life I have had." And his next desperate remark was the clincher. "If you won't take them, I'm going to put a revolver to my head and end it all." All three boys are thriving today because Ken, himself an outstanding father, listened compassionately to another father's aching heart and brought three brothers into the Bayers' CHAIN of Love on October 30, 1997.

It was on that same day of October 30 that Kaiane legally came into the care of the CHAIN's ministry. Sérgio had devoted almost two-and-a-half years to caring for Kaiane, who was born on December 12, 1994. With so many corrective surgeries looming for his little girl (thirteen before she died on September 11, 2000), it was obvious Kaiane would require care far beyond Sérgio's capability. Someone would have to be with her around the clock, and that's when the ministry's Romilda stepped in to demonstrate motherhood at its finest. As Sérgio recalls, "She vowed to commit herself entirely to my daughter, both in and out of hospital." In turn, Romilda says,

> "Sérgio gave her completely into my care and carefully trained me in every step of Kaiane's daily routine. And whenever she was in hospital, Sérgio would visit often. He deeply loved his little daughter, and he sure didn't look or behave like an addict. And he always thanked and praised me for the care I was providing."

For Sérgio, one moment illuminates the loving bond he saw deepening between Kaiane and Romilda. "When Romilda came to take Kaiane home from a halfway house following one surgery, Kaiane's face lit up in a big smile as she grabbed Romilda's hand and said, 'Let's go, Mom.' That was so very, very touching. It warmed my heart." The Lord undoubtedly was drawing them together more closely in respect, friendship, and affection as they tended to Kaiane's needs. Over time, Romilda became Sérgio's crutch and his anchor, whose prayers helped redirect the lost sheep that he was into the arms of The Great Shepherd, Jesus.

While Romilda began looming ever larger as a tower of strength in Sérgio's eyes, so also was another womanly tower of strength rallying to his side. That was Jerilyn Bayer. While Sérgio felt God was remolding his life, he, nonetheless, was tormented mentally, questioning his fitness as a father.

"I told myself, I have these beautiful children and yet I'm not raising any of them. What kind of father am I? And I can't even keep a job. I was plagued with questions, and I brought all of them to Jerilyn. Everything she said was so encouraging. Jerilyn told me I could do nothing alone. 'Give yourself completely over to God,' she said, and He would do everything to uplift and empower me so that I would not fall again. Then she emphasized, 'Sérgio, what you have done for your sons is best, because they're happy, they're learning about Jesus, and they're going to school.' Would they ever forgive me, though, I wondered. Jerilyn's answer was so very comforting. She said, 'Yes, Sérgio, they will forgive and respect you so long as you demonstrate that, although you have failed, you are now determined to do what's right.'"

Just as Jerilyn had said, God was there, empowering Sérgio over the next few years to fight his drug demons and establish loving ties with his sons. Then Kaiane died, when extreme viral diarrhea ruptured the flesh from her thirteenth operation, releasing the fatal poison that claimed her. As detailed in chapter eleven, Sérgio was beside himself with grief at her funeral, not only denouncing himself as a father but uttering suicidal words in regret for having led what he called a worthless life. Jerilyn prodded him to begin a new life right then with the Lord. She and a group of men surrounded him, and they all prayed.

> "It was at that moment that I accepted Christ and vowed to kick drugs. Everybody in church on that mournful day was so kind and so supportive. Sorrowful as it was, however, that day was the major turning point in my life. I have been going to church ever since, and I am now reunited in love with my sons."

Sérgio said, "I knew I loved Romilda from the moment I heard and observed her first express her love and dedication to Kaiane." Following Kaiane's death, the two found comfort in and strengthened each other as they grieved. They also discovered that they shared common interests and viewpoints. They started dating about three months after Kaiane's death. In church, they sang hymns enthusiastically and worshipped God with Sérgio's sons and other children from housemother Romilda's *Lar Colméia* home.

"Eventually I proposed marriage, but Romilda said she would accept only if I obtained Pastor Ken's permission. I was scared going to him. But Pastor Ken said he had been impressed by my lifestyle changes over the past eight months. As he said, I had been straight most of that period, and, whenever I did lapse, I always returned for God's forgiveness. Nevertheless, Pastor Ken cautioned against rushing into marriage. He described Romilda as 'pure gold,' and he didn't want her hurt. So he urged that we both take our time while we strive to know each other more intimately. 'Get to know your strengths and weaknesses, and, yes, then get married. You have both my permission and blessing.' We courted for six months, and then Pastor Ken married us."

There Sérgio and Romilda stood on June 8, 2001, smiling radiantly and exchanging vows with God's blessing in Good News Baptist Church. Observing Sérgio and Romilda worshipping in Good News Baptist Church one Sunday in May 2004, it struck me that Sérgio's high-spirited and reverent singing is galaxies removed from the guy once ensnared on that very site in the dregs of degradation and the chains of devilish addiction. There he was, smiling and belting out the Portuguese words with Romilda and about a half-dozen children from their household flock. *"Eu entrego tudo a Ti, eu entrego tudo a Ti"* ("I surrender all to You, I surrender all to You").

Reviewing his lost decades during our interview, Sérgio declared: "I really didn't have a life before. So, never again will drugs be my lord. For one thing, mixing cocaine with alcohol produces an awfully lethal weapon, a fast killer, which, thank God, didn't kill me. But pot is a slow killer. It's also a bad trip because it dulls your senses. And I certainly don't want it as a shield against anything. The only escape from troubles is knowing Jesus. He is the only salvation. With drugs, the trips are up and down continuously. But with Jesus it's a steady-going journey that's eternal. I'm so happy here now, helping Romilda, knowing also that whenever God calls, I will be ready." Sérgio's son Levi, now almost twenty-one, left upon reaching legal adulthood in 2003 and is happily succeeding in the work world. His two younger brothers, Isaac, almost sixteen, and seventeen-year-old Saulo, are also flourishing, thanks to the love being showered upon them in the *Lar Colméia* complex, where they are with houseparents just two homes away from each other.

Sérgio's story proves that no one, however wretched, is beyond the power of God's redemption once he or she genuinely renounces sin and seeks forgiveness. Other prodigal sons saved dramatically include John Newton and Charles Colson. Once a rude, lecherous, profane, and slave-trading sailor, Newton credits the Lord for saving his wretched life when he cried out to Jesus from his storm-battered ship in 1748.[26] He became an Anglican cleric and gratefully wrote what is probably the world's best-known hymn, "Amazing Grace." Colson, a notoriously manipulative strategist in the 1970s Nixon Watergate scandal in the United States, is the born-again Christian who founded the Prison Fellowship ministry while imprisoned for his role in Watergate. Today. thousands of volunteers serve in that ministry, bringing the hope of Jesus to prisoners throughout America and overseas.[27]

Similarly, the famous Dutch painter Rembrandt is actually reflecting himself as prodigal and profligate in his monumental painting *The Return of the Prodigal Son*. In corre-

spondence to his son, Titus, Rembrandt blamed ostenta-
tious recklessness for his bankruptcy and credited Titus for
the business management that enabled him to continue contributing his incredible artistry to the world. Surely, the
Divine Presence was gracefully at work in the family. In his
letters, Rembrandt confides that he composed *The Return
of the Prodigal Son* (1669) as a poetic, loving message of
hopeful destiny to anyone's life journey.[28]

Observe the closed eyes of the father in *The Return of
the Prodigal Son* and you see the promise with which Sérgio
now lives. Those closed eyes are a metaphor suggesting that
human love, in emulating Divine Love, will be blind to the
past and infinitely forgiving and merciful to a repentant lost
sheep. Observe the bent father gathering in his beloved son
with age-stiffened hands and believe that Sérgio and all of
us can find rest and meaning in divine redemption. Listen to
the opening verses of Newton's "Amazing Grace," and you
hear what Sérgio feels today:

"Amazing Grace! How sweet the sound
That saved a wretch like me!
I once was lost, but now am found;
Was blind, but now, I see.
'Twas grace that taught my heart to fear,
And grace my fears relieved;
How precious did that grace appear
The hour I first believed."

Through all of Sérgio's trials and misery, God was
regenerating and molding him to become the super housefather now guiding children in the upper story of House 6
at the CHAIN of Love. I was touched seeing how joyfully

the children gravitated to him the instant he reached the top of the stairway after a day's work in a Novo Hamburgo shoe factory. In fact, the children's faces lit up the moment they heard his motorbike roar through the *Lar Colméia* gateway. I was privileged to see that precious scene reenacted nightly when I was the family's supper guest throughout twenty-five days there. What a treat it all was to share in Romilda's generous suppers, lively play and camaraderie with the children, and a close-up on a worshipful family deeply in love with Jesus.

Commit, trust, surrender—those three words are ablaze in Sérgio's heart because of their profound significance to a soul brought into Amazing Grace. That's why he delights in and identifies so meaningfully with Psalm 37, in which David urges, "Commit your way to the Lord, Trust also in Him" (Psalm 37:5, NKJV). When I asked to photograph him, Sérgio immediately picked up a Bible from the living room table and turned to the page containing that psalm, which was flagged with a bookmark bearing an artist's conception of Christ's image. There in front of the living room wall, beaming happily for the camera with the open Bible in his hands, stood a man saved by Amazing Grace. How appropriate that from the wall behind him Kaiane's smiling face radiated from a framed photo so that it appeared an angel was settling onto Sérgio's shoulder.

13

SOLDIERING ON SELFLESSLY IN SERVICE TO GOD'S CHILDREN

Only God knows how many millions of homeless and orphaned children the Indonesian earthquake of May 2006, coupled with the Southeast Asian tsunamis of December 2004, have added to global total of such young souls adrift, hopeless and despairing. Ponder the grim reality of an estimated eight million to twelve million alone in Brazil—the nation acknowledged as having the world's highest number. As horrific as the devastation is in the dozen tsunami-ripped countries and the Indonesian quake, these tragedies present an enormous challenge and opportunity for Christians and those of all other faiths everywhere on Earth to unite on this global disgrace of homelessness and emulate what the Bayers' CHAIN of Love ministry is accomplishing in Brazil.

The tsunamis and the earthquake have dramatically driven the global homelessness nightmare into the world spotlight. But imagine the impact if each worship assembly across the earth stepped out one by one and established in a nation other than its own a CHAIN-like ministry doing what the Bayers' team has been doing in Brazil's southern-most state of Rio Grande do Sul. What the Bayers initiated through their Good News Baptist Church in Campo Bom for the rescue of homeless children is a speck so infinitesimal that it would be almost invisible in the ocean of the millions of homeless children globally. The ninety children currently being showered with nurturing love there are priceless in God's eyes. But if all the world's congregations were to unleash an earthquake of ecumenical Good Samaritanism for homeless children as thunderous as the two aforementioned disasters, is it just possible that this worldwide problem could be swept away or at least hammered down to negligibility? Worshippers, please think about it. And, while doing so, consider how God may be speaking to you in such biblical passages as the two in CHAIN of Love ministry leaflets published by the International Missions division of the North American Baptist Conference. From Lamentations 2:11: "My eyes fail from weeping, I am tormented within...because children and infants faint in the streets of the city." From Psalm 82:3-4: "Defend the cause of the weak and the fatherless; maintain the rights of the poor and oppressed. Rescue the weak and the needy; deliver them from the hand of the wicked."

The dedicated workers in the CHAIN of Love ministry know that a life of significance, far more than one of so-called worldly success and materialistic accumulation of goods, is eternally blessed and honorable in the Divine scheme of things. But, before detailing their fascinating personal stories, let's set the stage by observing that lives of significance, as this writer understands the concept, are interlinked across humanity as motherhood to fatherhood to sisterhood to brotherhood—lives intended by our Creator to touch other lives positively, to reach out beyond ourselves.

In this connection, hear the voices, as I did, of two pastors whose messages echoed and reinforced each other strikingly on our crucial duty of touching other lives positively. The first one came from Pastor Ken Bayer in Brazil in May 2004 and the second from Senior Pastor Tim Schroeder in my home church—Trinity Baptist, in Kelowna, British Columbia—five months later in Canada.

Pastor Tim's sermon was entitled, "From Success to Significance." He emphasized that even a so-called "successful" person by shallow earthly standards could well reach a stage in life feeling dreadfully empty and hanging on the question, "Is that all there is?"

Is that all there is? There is such utter emptiness, even after having achieved by stupendous wealth and conspicuous consumption a mountainous pile of shiny goods and worldly toys. No, that is not all there is. A life of significance transcending any so-called temporal "success" is one of sacrifice, sharing, and giving, as Pastors Ken and Tim both emphasized. A life of significance, in short, is one centered on others.

Pastor Ken drove that message home by noting the tragic fate of a prominent Brazilian politician's son. That young man leaped to his death from the roof of a building—a suicide. Yet he supposedly had it "all": piles of money, power, fame. But his self-centered life was poverty-stricken in purpose and plans, and apparently he lived without an Anchor and Foundation (God).

Pastors Ken and Tim could have contrasted lives of self-indulgence and self-aggrandizement against those of such humble, selfless, and acclaimed international heroes and heroines as Mohandas Gandhi, Dr. Martin Luther King Jr., Mother Teresa, Terry Fox, and Clara Barton. What outstanding lives of significance! Gandhi was the Hindu "brown saint" and "soul force" whose active, non-violent resistance spearheaded India to independence from the British crown. Dr. King was the southern Baptist preacher whose hero was Gandhi and whose 1960s civil rights movement transformed American society, indeed a heroic crusader, whom I was privileged to interview in 1961 as a reporter for the now-defunct *Columbus Citizen-Journal*. His vow moved this hard-nosed journalist deeply—declaring that he would do "whatever it takes," including repeated imprisonment (and implying death), to achieve full equality and opportunity for black Americans. Mother Teresa, of course, was that sweet Catholic nun who tended so lovingly to the poor and starving on Calcutta's streets. She founded the Missionaries of Charity religious order, which now provides food for the needy and operates hospitals, schools, orphanages, youth centers, and shelters for lepers and dying poor in fifty Indian cities, with branches in thirty other countries. Terry Fox was the Canadian lad whose own cancer fatally undercut a valiant attempt in 1980 to run across Canada on one leg to raise funds for cancer research. His inspirational legacy has since raised more than $360 million (Canadian) for his cause in the twenty-six annual Marathon-of-Hope events—events respectfully honoring Terry's famous quote: "I want to set an example that will never be forgotten." Clara Barton, International Red Cross volunteer and founder of the American Red Cross, was that valiant nurse of the

American Civil War endearingly revered as "the angel of the battlefield," a caregiver who went to extraordinary lengths tending to the sick and wounded under hellish conditions.

Those renowned heroes and heroines shared that same life of significant selflessness as the unknown and unpublicized heroes and heroines at the CHAIN of Love. Like Gandhi, Dr. King, Mother Teresa, Terry Fox, and Clara Barton, the lives of the CHAIN's staff are reflections of the admonition in Philippians 2:3: "Do nothing from selfishness or empty conceit, but with humility of mind regard one another as more important than yourselves" (NASB). So, also, has this honor roll of the dead and living honored the call in Hebrews 10:24: "Let us consider how we may spur one another on toward love and good deeds."

Look into the eyes of a child, it's said, and you see God— a light that beams in the eyes of the children at the CHAIN of Love, thanks to the likes of Clovis Scheffel, Lauri Ghilherme Bastian, César P. Nunes, Sara Esther Luna Cezar, Sally Antholzner, and Calvino and Katie Taylor. Observing forty-nine-year-old Clovis makes it obvious why those children are so vibrant. He's the ever-bouncing worship-team leader at Good News Baptist Church and administrative assistant to Pastor Ken for more than seven years at the CHAIN of Love. Multiply many times over this enthusiasm, exploding out of the other adults in the ministry, and one realizes how promising the future now glows for these children once mired in abject deprivation, many of whom distrusted adults because of having been abandoned and despicably abused.

"Must be my tennis shoes!" Clovis laughed, when I asked how he triggers the springs in his feet—the dynamism so engaging and inspiring to the church congregation during Sunday services as a smiling and waving Clovis exhorts them along in belting out the hymns. The children in the pews love it, jumping and shouting out the words joyously. Of course, today's dynamic 143-pound Clovis is a much slimmer version of the 308-pound guy described in chapter four whose lively bulk during a rehearsal back in 1988 sent him crashing through the rickety floorboards at the earlier site of Good News Baptist Church. While that was a resounding start to his relationship with the Bayers, Pastor Ken realizes Clovis had earlier been a guardian angel of sorts. Had it not been for Clovis and wife Anita, Ken might not even have had that church to minister in. The couple had transferred there from Novo Hamburgo's Central Baptist Church, mother church of Good News Baptist, and were actually keeping the little church alive for the six months before Ken and Jerilyn would arrive for their new Brazilian posting after a year-long furlough on home assignment in North America. As Clovis says, Good News Baptist had just one or two members when he temporarily took the helm with Anita and two other members from Central Baptist. Slowly, membership grew into the double digits, and the church was at least still breathing when the Bayers took charge.

With the Bayers' arrival and such a crashing start personally, Clovis realized the time was now ripe and urgent for downsizing—not for the church, but for himself, physically. Otherwise, a grave could claim his body. Due to business pressures, Clovis had gradually descended into severe depression and, as a result, had been overeating to ease the stress. Five and a half years earlier, he had been told the commercial and residential real estate company of which he was a partner would ultimately close because it lacked the resources to sustain itself financially. Meanwhile, wife Anita began working more hours as a teacher to supplement the family income. "I believe that crash through the floorboards, hilarious as it was, was a wake-up call from God," Clovis says.

"My joints were swollen, and at the rate I was going, I knew I wasn't going to live very long unless I changed some things. At first I stopped eating, sometimes going for two days without touching food. There was a lot of pressure, and Anita was working long hours. But, always, she was so strong, so supportive, and so optimistic. And Ken and the church members were always encouraging, too. What I learned early during this worrisome ordeal is that the worst problem for a person like myself is not financial but lacking something meaningful to do and living without purpose. First I changed my dietary regimen. No more poor foods, I lectured myself. So I began eating more fruits and vegetables and less fatty meat, while eliminating other fat-loaded foods. Pop and pizza were junked. I ate more white meat and fish. Bananas were eaten regularly for potassium. My stomach cramps eventually stopped, and my energy level shot up. Every day for three years, I went to the gym to lift weights and do aerobics."

The real estate firm did close in 1998, but by then Clovis had forged a new, more hopeful perspective on life. Pastor Ken, valuing his intensity, discipline, accounting skills, and proven leadership and administrative abilities in church affairs, hired him as administrative assistant for the CHAIN of Love.

The "real estate" for which Clovis has been toiling the past seven years—the CHAIN of Love homes and related facilities—will bring infinitely more lucrative investment returns in the spiritual market. Salvaging children's lives outweighs all the realty-market deals ever transacted. Still, the material gains promise to be handsome as well. Thanks to what's being taught in the technical-vocational training center completed several years ago on the *Lar Colméia* campus, the children are supplementing their basic formal education by learning trades, skills, and crafts that should reward them well in the work world. Clovis was integral to the administrative input that brought the center to reality, just as he is now to its ongoing operation. Since he was born in Novo Hamburgo and has spent his entire life in the area, he knows the so-called lay of the land and how the natives think and feel. He grew up in a nominally Catholic home but embraced the Lord after he joined teenage friends in a small group that called itself "Jerusalem." His best buddy convinced him to accept Jesus. He and his wife, fifty-two-year-old Anita, are devout Baptists and have been married twenty-four years. Their two daughters are university students—Ticiana, twenty-four, in nursing, and Tatiana, twenty-two, in law.

While he believes the CHAIN of Love is temporarily at its limits now, Clovis is faithfully confident that God "will continue showing us when and how to grow." As he says,

> "If God puts a plan into someone's heart, and the person follows that plan, God will be faithful and bring that plan to reality. In that sense, nothing is impossible. On the other hand, if we think we can help God by somehow becoming self-sufficient, then things don't work out. Never should we at the CHAIN of Love allow ourselves to point proudly at 'what we have done.' It's the Holy Spirit who implants the visions in people's minds. Our greatest

joy will come when we see that the children here now have grown into good adult citizens and servants of God."

Like Clovis, fifty-two-year-old Lauri shines with life-of-significance selflessness. He's both a housefather and the volunteer instructor in shoe and leather making in *Lar Colméia*'s technical-vocational center. Every morning, he drives there from his off-campus home to guide children in crafting shoes, belts, and other leather goods. Shoe and leather making is the region's major industry, so Lauri's instruction is equipping dozens of children with a highly-marketable skill that will enable them to support themselves and their families as adults. As mentioned earlier, Lauri also is one of the two elders at Good News Baptist Church, where he teaches baptismal candidates and Sunday school.

The shoe- and leather-making class started in March 2004, and already big plans are percolating. Lauri envisions the operation expanding into a plant wholesaling its products to regional shoe and leather stores, with all earnings pumped back into the CHAIN of Love. A thriving domestic enterprise would offset any great need to ship the goods to other nations, thereby avoiding the expense of high export taxes. Tax money saved would remain for the CHAIN's benefit. Also, visiting groups of volunteers would be urged to buy as many leather "souvenirs" and gifts as possible. Lauri is sharing his thoughts with Pastor Ken and volunteer coordinator Nunes.

My sleeping quarters during a twenty-five-day stay there were in the technical-vocational center's second-floor men's dormitory. From all the excited chatter and machinery sounds echoing up from the class in the center's basement, there's no doubt Lauri's instructional leadership is a resounding success. Every morning offered a cheerful treat looking down from the stairwell railing on a gang of children, including my own sponsored boy, Alexandre, beaming with smiles and learning enthusiastically from Lauri and a few assistants. Lauri and his crew were developing a nifty skateboard-style sneaker of synthetic material and nylon that could be fitted to a jogger. The brand logo adopted for the five skate-shoe models is a honeycomb spelling out the Portuguese acronym for CHAIN of Love. The children are already adept in making sandals, which sold briskly during the Brazilian summer.

Two classes, one in the morning and the other in the afternoon, are a profile of cooperative teamwork turning out shoes and belts. Some punch out patterns, others sew, and the rest assemble the belts and footwear—almost like an assembly line. The belts, in a variety of colors, are both durable and fashionable. By the fall of 2004—several months after I had left—the children were producing more than 300 belts weekly, or from sixty to seventy a day, and then had about 1,000 available for sale. Several were so keen that they were each turning out ten belts a day. As sales rise, more needed tools and machines will be bought, enabling even more creative output. A couple hundred belts are being sold in Canada by church-group volunteers who had been at *Lar Colméia* in late 2004, helping in the late-construction stages of a seventh campus house.

In Lauri, the ministry and the children are blessed with an ideal instructor for shoe and leather craftsmanship. A seventh-generation Brazilian of German ancestry, he has thirty-plus years' experience in the trade. Lauri worked in other states previously and at one stage was the foreman in a factory employing 370 workers. Moreover, one of the worshipful ways in which Lauri visualizes Jesus is as the Great Entrepreneur and Teacher, an image befitting the analogy that teaching a person to fish equips that person to be self-supporting, thanks to the skill acquired. That's why he posed the idea of a shoemaking class to Pastor Ken and volunteered to lead it. Now the dividends are pouring in. Word reached this author in June 2006 that a business contact has been firmed up in central Brazil for sale of the belts, a deal under which the boys in Lauri's class receive a commission for each belt produced.[29]

Looking back over the years, he says, "Long before I knew of the CHAIN of Love, I somehow knew God was feeding my heart with the desire to teach children, street children especially. This whole idea grew out of God's heart, not mine. His message was that if a person knows how to make shoes, the Lord could use him to help others." As Lauri explains, "I grew up in a rural area of this state and was raised by good parents. I was the oldest of four children, and my brother and two sisters grew up as nominal Christians in the Lutheran Church. However, my father was an alcoholic." At eighteen, Lauri moved to the central section of Teutônia, a small city in the same state, got his first job in a shoemaking plant, and completed his high-school education by attending night school.

"During the five years I lived there, I saw no street children, nor any of the degradation they suffer. But soon after I moved to Novo Hamburgo as a twenty-three-year old, I saw all these poor areas with so many children begging for money to eat. They looked so sad, pitiful, and humiliated. Everything was so new and shocking to me. I saw a lot of prostitutes roaming these poor areas. They were the mothers of so many of these children. These women would have up to a half-dozen children and would simply abandon them to eke out a living selling their bodies. Guess the mothers were desperate; I don't know. Anyway, there was no birth control, and some children would wind up being looked after by grandparents—if they were lucky. Seeing these street children made me think it seemed unchristian that they were going without help."

Those initial street-kid images lingered in Lauri's subconscious after he married. He and his wife, fifty-year-old Áurea, have been married twenty-five years and have a twenty-one-year-old daughter, Lillian, and a seventeen-year-old son, William. From Lillian's mouth seventeen years ago came some innocent but stabbing words that were among the most fortunate Lauri has ever heard. Lauri had acquired a taste for booze almost akin to his father's. He was half-asleep on the sofa when then four-year-old Lillian yelled to her mother, "Guess we're not going out. Daddy's been drinking again, and he's drunk." He had promised to take the family out that evening.

"Her words pierced my heart, and I would never drive drunk, anyway. In those days, I drank everything, including moonshine. What Lillian said that day made me determined to stop drinking. And in a week I was off liquor. I know the biggest reason I didn't have to seek help—as I learned later—was because Áurea and my mother-in-law had been praying for me for years. Áurea has been a Christian from the age of twelve. And their power of prayer was dynamite for me."

The prayerful rescue also spurred Lauri into gratefully accompanying his family to church more regularly. Six years later, he was baptized on the day before his fortieth birthday.

For many years, the Bastians had lived in another state, but Lauri's leather-selling travels would frequently take him to Rio Grande do Sul and Novo Hamburgo. For Áurea's convenience, Lauri shopped for a second car so she could drive to church activities and services if he happened to be away a few days. And, as the Divine Manipulator would have it, the glove compartment of one of the used cars he checked in Novo Hamburgo contained a notice featuring the services and ministry of Good News Baptist Church. It just happened to drop onto the seat when Lauri opened the compartment door. He filed that information mentally, and when the Bastians moved to Novo Hamburgo in late 1997, Good News Baptist became their home church.

As Good News Baptist and the CHAIN of Love grew, so also did the Bastians' service to Jesus. Áurea, for example, leads the church's evangelism and visiting ministry. And six years ago, they accepted Pastor Ken's invitation to become houseparents. Besides their daughter and son, they are "Dad" and "Mom" to four teenage boys in the CHAIN's guardianship plus two adopted boys of eight and two. "God has been teaching us all along that we are capable of helping His children."

Like the earlier glove-compartment "discovery" by Lauri, it seems that God's hand was moving a few years ago when Pastor Ken asked Lauri to scout around for potential real estate on which to construct the new church in Novo Hamburgo. "Ken had asked me to look for land near the old church," Lauri recalls. His research turned up a property ideal for the expanding congregation's needs, a building of 32,280 square feet. The structure housed a brothel, and Lauri delighted in the prospect of good uprooting evil. So did the board of Good News Baptist, and thus an area of perdition was demolished for construction of an area of salvation. And wonder of wonders, among those attending the inaugural service on May 1, 2004, were the leading madam and three owners of that destroyed brothel!

The Lord's strategy of bringing gifted players into action for the love of God's children was demonstrated again in the life of César P. Nunes, or just Nunes, as he prefers. He's the twenty-eight-year-old coordinator of about twenty volunteer instructors whose dedicated teaching is equipping the children with skills, trades, and learning that has their confidence soaring while preparing them for earning their way as adults. The classes are in the technical-vocational center at *Lar Colméia,* where the constant buzz of activity is in itself a tribute to the youthful leadership of Nunes, a computer whiz whose expertise is bringing the CHAIN's children into today's electronically wired global village. As I saw, day after day, the children sit smilingly enthralled for hours while pecking away at the keyboards of the half-dozen computers in the center's computer room. Nunes came to Pastor Ken's attention via a recommendation from housefather Raimundo.

Raimundo is one of Nunes's six uncles—the brother of Nunes's mother, Clara. You know Raimundo from chapter eleven. He's the entrepreneurial owner of a sheet-metal-finishing factory. So shrewd Pastor Ken, knowing Raimundo's business-contact network likely would turn up just the right person, asked Raimundo who would be best qualified. He listed these qualifications: a person who could recruit and handle volunteers to teach a variety of subjects; one who is amiable, decisive, and fluent in both Portuguese and

English; and, especially, a person who is brilliant in and passionate about computer technology. Raimundo immediately replied that Nunes would be perfect. And when Pastor Ken telephoned Nunes with the offer on January 23, 2003, Nunes accepted immediately. "I was so surprised and excited—I would be paid doing what I love to do!" Actually, Pastor Ken knew somewhat of Nunes's communication skills from three years earlier, when Nunes translated for some visiting North American groups there to team with Portuguese workers in house construction at *Lar Colméia* and teaching the children various skills as well.

Two months after his phone call from Ken, Nunes launched the program with sixteen instructors for a smorgasbord of courses in the center, whose construction had been completed less than a year earlier, in 2002. He had spent those first two months assembling his "faculty." Nunes visited several churches as a guest, explaining the CHAIN of Love project and its mission by projecting photos of the children and activities onto an overhead screen. His call for volunteers wishing to be interviewed ushered in a flood of inquiries. As the first computer instructor, Nunes taught with a half-dozen computers donated by North American individuals and organizations. Six months later, they were replaced by six up-to-date models selected by Nunes, which he had negotiated bargains for after thoroughly canvassing the market. Of course, donated money financed their purchase.

Currently, there are about twenty instructors. Besides the highly-popular computer and shoe-making courses, subjects include car mechanics, dance, guitar, sewing, baking, cooking, singing, English, woodworking, welding, soccer, and arts and crafts. Arts and crafts is a category that includes such subjects as embroidery, cross-stitch, quilting, drawing, and painting. The regular instructors are Brazilian, but the program benefits as well from additional teaching by North American volunteers, there with church groups working on *Lar Colméia* construction or some other mission such as the Jesus-film showings by Campus Crusade for Christ.

Coach Antonio Carlos Rodrigues do Nascimento with some of the many enthusiastic students on his Saturday team.

In just about every class, children chatter excitedly and beam with enthusiasm. *Lar Colméia*'s gym on Saturday afternoons, naturally, is the most explosive, when a couple dozen boys gather for a soccer-playing feast with Antônio Carlos Rodrigues do Nascimento, the coach-instructor. Like baseball in the United States and hockey in Canada, soccer is Brazil's national sport and pastime. And smiling Antônio, a high-school soccer coach and physical education teacher, makes everything fun. The entire gang laughs through drills, games, and even calisthenics. Judging by the ball-shifting footwork and shot-kicking power and finesse, there could have been several superstars in the making. I was impressed by the amazing saves in goal by Edinei Calderini (then thirteen). Edinei and brother Deniclei, two years older, had been prime candidates for street-kid misery until rescued by the CHAIN of Love in 1999. Now they're two gregarious, fun-loving brothers wearing baseball caps and soccer jerseys that came to them as gifts from North American sponsors. In fact, at *Lar Colméia* there just might be more soccer balls in play and jerseys worn per square yard than anywhere on Earth.

Kids are taught the Word of God in dance class as they step out and sing the Portuguese lyrics of *I Seek You, Lord.*

In the dance class, the little ones were gleeful balls of foot-bouncing and arm-waving energy, moving in unison to the left, then to the right, and vice versa. Giggles erupted whenever someone goofed with a misstep. It was lyrical worship in motion as the small fry sang "I seek You, Lord" in Portuguese with then twenty-three-year-old instructor Gisele Silva conducting. Assisting her that happy day in May of 2004 was Vanessa Strelaw, then fifteen, who came into the CHAIN's care as a four-year-old abandoned by her prostitute mother. Now Vanessa, experiencing love within a family, is singing and dancing happily.

The baking class was still another hot spot of interest. Delicious aromas wafted out of the center's kitchen. There Katiúscia Suellen dos Santos was the guiding hand with the kitchen tools, fetching bread and sweets out of the oven to the approving nods of several of her "sisters" in the CHAIN of Love. That scene was possible thanks mainly to Nunes. He had convinced the CHAIN's board to finance the six-month course that certified her as a professional baking teacher. Katiúscia, who turned twenty-one in 2006, is today a proud and ambitious young lady of bright promise, a universe removed from the May day in 1996 when she arrived at *Lar Colméia* to join a younger sister and two younger brothers already in the CHAIN's guardianship for two months. These were children of nine, five, four, and two who had been fending for themselves for more than six months in an abandoned hovel. Their drug-trafficking mom was imprisoned, and their drug-addicted aunt left the children at the abandoned shack.

Nunes, through his program leadership, is contributing to the transformation of lives. That's obvious in the computer room as Nunes, standing at the blackboard with chalk in hand, unravels the complexity of computers with such clarity that the keyboard-keen children smile and nod knowingly as the bulbs turn on in their brains. He substitutes as needed for volunteer instructors in three computer classes and the English class, and his office is always open to the children whenever they need help. Observing then fifteen-year-old Deneclei Calderini in a computer class with instructor Janderleia Batista, I marveled at how determinedly the CHAIN of Love strives to develop their children into versatile, well-rounded individuals bursting with confidence. Deneclei, Edinei's older brother, is passionately focused on becoming either a professional soccer player or an English instructor. As I had seen in the gym, his soccer talents and those of Edinei are formidable. The computer class will push Deneclei toward achieving either or even both of his goals. As related back in chapter nine, these Calderini brothers, so upbeat in talk and manner, were ripe for street-kid destitution until the CHAIN's timely rescue.

By his own example, Nunes inspires the children, and their respectful affection is vocalized whenever they call him "Uncle"—as most do. He's ambitious, devout, energetic, visionary, and thirsty for knowledge. Although born into a Catholic family, Nunes came into the Baptist faith as a boy, following the lead of his mother and six uncles. On Sundays during the worshipful singing in Good News Baptist Church, the children see him playing the piano. Nunes learned that instrument at the age of fourteen after mastering the flute at eleven and the guitar at thirteen. He has played in the church band since 2000 and has attended Good News Baptist since the age of nine.

Nunes became a computer whiz by taking courses at night in the community, on top of his university course load. He graduated with a bachelor of science degree in biomedicine research from Novo Hamburgo's Feevale University in 2005. He's keenly interested in cancer research and plans to work toward a Ph.D. in preventive medicine so that he can serve God's people as a missionary doctor. Nunes is self-taught in English—his learning sources were books, movies, videos, and an English-language Bible. The Bible came into his possession several years ago as a gift from Dr. Herman Effa, the retired Canadian clergyman and missionary who is Jerilyn Bayer's father. "Someday, I will be able to speak several other languages as well—French and German, for sure," Nunes adds. When interviewed, Nunes was engaged and spoke of plans to marry sometime in 2005.

In the strongest sense, Nunes truly coordinates. It's often challenging—especially when course volunteers change, sometimes requiring a rescheduling of class hours. He always keeps housemothers updated so that they can carry out their own time planning accordingly for themselves, the children affected, and their house families. "We have a good working relationship because we're all focused on doing what's best for the children. Whatever happens, though, we all know God is in command, and He has always provided for us."

God is always providing, as Nunes declares, and He has been especially generous in sending volunteers from the United States and Canada to inject skills, talents, and expertise into this Brazil-based CHAIN for the love of His children! They heard God's call through some persuasive voices—Ken and Jerilyn Bayer directly during their North American visits to sponsoring churches over the past thirteen years, and indirectly through those many teams who have returned from construction and other projects at *Lar Colméia* with touching tales, not only about the miracles being forged there but also about how the experience has permanently colored and even transformed their own lives. Imagine the impact by merely considering the numbers of voices participating. Pastor Ken and Jerilyn have addressed an average of 100 church congregations during each of several support-raising journeys in North America. Without the selfless labor of those volunteers the CHAIN of Love would not shine today as a global role model. Take Bob Brown, who went to Campo Bom in 1998 and helped the Bayers set up a computer system that simplified the many administrative intricacies of bringing children into the CHAIN's guardianship and monitoring their progress. Brown was then accounting and computer-operations manager at the international office of the North American Baptist Conference in Oakbrook Terrace, Illinois. What he accomplished during his three weeks as a volunteer enabled the Bayers, staff members, and professionals to not only efficiently manage their administrative load but eventually to electronically transmit the ministry's story to a global audience. Again, God only knows how many sponsors came aboard or actually set out on a working mission to *Lar Colméia* because of Brown's contribution. Nunes, who has organized a second worldwide Web site, is building on this man's invaluable groundwork.

Brown wrote that year in *NAB today*, the bimonthly newsletter of the North American Baptist Conference, "I didn't expect Brazil to change me." It was his first missions trip. Until that journey, Brown's office duties had always prevented him from fulfilling a long-nourished desire to participate in some worthy overseas project. He signed up immediately when he heard about the CHAIN, pleased that the mission's time frame worked perfectly into his schedule. His team worked on the initial construction of *Lar Colméia*'s third home. "I wondered whether I would have the stamina to deal with the thirty-two children on site after spending twelve hours digging and pouring concrete—my other job."

Brown emphasizes that the stories told about the CHAIN's children "were worse than any I had heard in the Chicago area, where I have worked in halfway houses." So he decided to get his own close-up of street-kid desperation and took a late-night bus ride downtown.

> "As I got off the bus after midnight, I saw three children—not older than ten—sitting on a doorstep begging for money…I had heard that some parents sent their children out begging for money all night, but now I believe the stories. As I emptied my pockets for these children, I thought, 'The children with houseparents could easily be here on the streets if not for the CHAIN of Love. I began dreaming about bringing a group of my friends, Generation Xers, back to Brazil. I could just imagine challenging them to discover what's important in life and get involved in ministry. Brazil changed me, and I believe it could change them, too!"[30]

It seems just about everyone from North America returns home from Brazil changed forever, including those youth so many of us older folk sweepingly and often unfairly label as "spoiled." The children in the CHAIN of Love teach just about anyone who goes there more about love, joy, warmth, and wonder than we can ever impart to them. Take the word of Stacy Siedlecki, of Parma Heights, Ohio. "Taught by Children" is the headline over her story in the September-October 2001 issue of *NAB today,* the bimonthly newsletter's "youth focus" issue. Stacy, then sixteen, wrote on behalf of twenty-seven teens and adults from Parma

Heights Baptist Church who helped in early construction of the technical-vocational center and other projects.

> "You name it, we did it. From carrying roof tiles to teaching vacation Bible school. There was so much to do and less than two weeks to do it in. We knew with the Lord's help and guidance, we could finish it all...sure enough, we did."

Although the Ohioans went to Campo Bom intending to teach others, Stacy admitted,

> "...the children did most of the teaching. We learned more about ourselves than anything else, and probably more than we would have liked. We saw how selfish we can be, and how we take so much for granted. I learned to take time to see the beauty and wonders this world contains. I learned we need to notice one another and the potential each person holds. All the compassion we feel needs to be directed into the hearts and souls of others. This trip helped me do just that."[31]

Stacy described it as "the most fantastic experience of my life." Stacy and the others repaired and replaced doors, windows, hinges, and locks; scrubbed homes and bathrooms; weeded the garden and greenhouse; sifted manure and separated worms to make humus for planting; washed more than 200 chairs in Good News Baptist Church; moved heavy loads of brick over rough terrain; spliced hundreds of eucalyptus logs for use as concrete-form braces; pulled thousands of nails from old boards to be used in new buildings; dug out the backfill from a sandstone-block retaining wall five feet deep and twenty-five to thirty feet long, then rebuilt the wall; hauled and poured cement flooring; stacked and organized wood; prepared team meals; sorted and organized children's clothing and school supplies; covered school notebooks with plastic, and finished six quilts for children's beds. Furthermore, the *NAB today* report points out,

> "That was just during the daylight hours! Children's rallies were held each evening, including crafts, singing, games, and puppets. Time was spent with the children on the playground, in the gym, and in their homes."[32]

Everyone shed tears as the team left for Ohio. As *NAB today* adds, team members left feeling challenged to consider careers in missions or ministry.

The lessons implanted in the hearts of visitors by God's children in the CHAIN are forever cherished and far-reaching. As Pastor Ken notes, "Many who worked here have initiated projects, missions, and ministries in their own communities. Four from one team alone became ministers."

Almost without exception, those who come to Campo Bom do so in the spirit of "Linking Lives to God's Purposes," as another headline of *NAB today* proclaimed in a 1996 issue, matched to the sub-heading "A different way to spend a vacation." Instead of opting for leisurely vacations, for example, Fred Pahl and Ewald Konrad of Edmonton, Canada, spent a mercilessly hot month in 1995 laboring side by side with Brazilian Christians in building the first house at *Lar Colméia*. Konrad's wife, Ruth, meanwhile, assisted at a Vacation Bible School for up to 200 children, made clothes for children, and helped in gardening. They were part of a mission organized by Edmonton's Central Baptist Church. Imagine laying bricks with the tropical sun burning down unrelentingly at almost 38 degrees Celcius. As Pahl told Alberta's *Peace Arch News,* "You have to drink water like a fish and use sunscreen—I've never used it in my life, but I went through an unbelievable amount of sunscreen."[33]

For many older volunteers, like Les Miller, building the CHAIN homes enabled them to contribute valuable skills they used daily before retiring. Miller, a retired line superintendent for Oliver-Mercer Electric Cooperative in North Dakota, was on the team in 2000 that finished the upper half of the fifth home where houseparents Tadeu and Deny shepherd their flock of eleven children. Miller, of Hazen, North Dakota, also got to meet the boy he and wife Cynthia sponsor. Mateus Machado Seidler, then a chunky three-year-old, soon warmed up to Miller and readily sat on his lap for a group photo with his house brothers and sister. His big dark eyes shone above a huge smile. Mateus typifies the kind of kid Miller and everyone connected with the Bayers' ministry are rallying for. Mateus and older sister Aniele came into the CHAIN's embrace in 1998. Mateus, then just nine months old, had been raised practically from day one in Novo Hamburgo's halfway house. The offspring of a broken union, the two children were given up to Social Services by their sixteen-year-old mother, a prostitute, and their drug-trafficking father of about the same age.

As for so many other teams that have labored at *Lar Colméia,* the trip by Miller and fifteen others was organized by Jerilyn Bayer's parents, Dr. Herman and Ardath Effa, of Edmonton, Canada, who keep returning to Brazil and helping everyone through their lifelong experience as Brazilian missionaries. The Effas translated for the workers—four Americans from North Dakota, including

Miller, and twelve Canadians. They also translated for another team involved in finishing that fifth home in 2000, a fourteen-member Canadian crew led by Bev Stober, of Bowsman, Manitoba. Besides Stober, there were a dozen others from Manitoba's Swan River Valley, one from Ochre River in that province, and another from Ontario. Some of those fourteen used their skills to start building the sixth home once the site was ready. Among other duties, they dug foundation holes, built forms, poured concrete, worked in gardens, and finished interiors. Only the roofs and ceilings of the CHAIN's homes are built with wood—that's standard throughout Brazil. Construction is constrained by the voracious appetites of Brazilian termites, certain to quickly digest any structure made entirely of wood. Houses at the CHAIN and elsewhere are shaped from concrete, brick, and tile. "This is one of the joys of frost in Canada—no termites," Stober joked in an interview published by the *Swan River Valley Star and Times*. With temperatures exceeding 38 degrees Celcius, Stober said, "We had watermelon breaks instead of coffee breaks."

The support of that Canadian team's mission illustrates outstanding teamwork by community churches. Four churches aided the team in planning and gathering supplies and funds. They were Temple Baptist in Swan River, First Baptist in Minitonas, Grace Baptist in Ochre Rive, and Moosehorn Church. Later, team members shared their experiences at those churches, emphasizing how life-changing the mission had been for everyone. "It has changed how we think about ourselves and other people," Stober said. "The children—they're just craving for love; they want to be held. They called us by our first names. It got kind of emotional for all of us when we left."[34]

Sure, there's plenty of work in these missions, but there's no less fun! The children and the workers love playtime. Children were roaring with laughter as water balloons and buckets of water rained down on them in November 2004. They were screaming delightfully in the refreshing wetness. Tossing the stuff from a second-story window were their laughing American and Canadian pals. Other times the children and their visiting friends are on the playing field mixing it up in soccer, using the swings and slides, or engaged in games of their own invention. There's even evidence of creative fun on the computer-room walls in the technical-vocational center. Hanging from them are the paintings of children taught for a month in 2003 by a Canadian art teacher. She accompanied a busload of these aspiring artists to the art museum in the big city of Porto Alegre, thirty-one miles south. It was their first taste of culture. Even tastier later was ice cream at McDonald's, for many a first-time outing to the golden arches. The children also respond sweetly whenever visiting ladies from North America turn up at their homes with jars of jam and other homemade goodies.

Like the Brazilian volunteer instructors working in the program coordinated by Nunes, these short-term volunteers on teaching missions from the United States and Canada are endowing these children with skills they can carry into their adult lives for profitable use in the labor market and at home. For example, in 2003, girls were taught sewing by Helga Berg, and boys are now handy in the mechanics of vehicle repair and maintenance, thanks to Caleb Peckham and Art Isaak. The three, from Trinity Baptist Church in Kelowna, Canada, did double duty in the region, first teaching at *Lar Colméia* for the CHAIN of Love and then joining a Jesus-film-project mission sponsored by Campus Crusade for

Christ. For the Jesus-film showings in various communities, Berg, Peckham, and Isaak were among nineteen Canadian teammates who harvested, on initial count, 182 people who accepted Christ and committed to Bible studies.

Peckham and Isaak taught auto mechanics at *Lar Colméia* for two months prior to the film project. During that time, Peckham demonstrated the under-the-hood and under-the-frame functions of a 1984 Volkswagen van while Isaak, fluent in Portuguese, translated Peckham's English for the students and added a few pointers himself. That van was bought by Isaak for $2,000 (Cdn) and completely overhauled by students under his and Peckham's guidance. The ministry used it extensively over the next year. What Peckham and Isaak did at *Lar Colméia* was actually an extension of their service at Trinity Baptist, where they then headed a car-care ministry of volunteers who, free of charge, regularly repair and service the vehicles of needy single parents in the community. In Brazil, the overhauled van's first journeys from *Lar Colméia* were jarring hour-and-a-half drives taking the Jesus-film teams into mountain villages. The most touching moment to Peckham and Isaak, particularly, was a tearful pastor's gratitude to one team for having ventured to such bumpy heights to deliver the Lord's message.

For Berg, the crowning tribute to her sewing instruction occurred when a smiling thirteen-year-old girl flashed a thumbs-up salute, proudly thumped her chest, and displayed the green apron she had created from remnants of fabric. "You never know what you sow into the hearts of people," Berg says. She just may have woven into the girls a love of sewing that could prove of lifetime value and enjoyment. To encourage such passion, she left behind a stack of books and a binder full of sample patterns.

Throughout the experience, Berg was astounded by the many doors God kept opening. Before departure from Canada, for example, a friend's request to an open-line radio show produced a donation of four sewing machines, which were carted to *Lar Colméia* along with dresses, blouses, T-shirts, and slacks made or donated by sisters, relatives, and friends.

In fact, it seems God has showered His blessings upon the CHAIN of Love since day one. His faithful North American servants have poured out a torrent of gifts. After a year-long home assignment, for example, Ken and Jerilyn Bayer returned to Campo Bom in June 1994 with eighteen boxes of clothing for infants through age five and commitments to build the first four homes of an envisioned ten.

Judging by the CHAIN's progress over twelve years, the giving by volunteers to this very moment has been remarkably unremitting in love, time, money, gifts, labor, skills, and professional service. Their servanthood in the first six months of 2006 is astounding, for example, yet typical. A dental team from Spruce Grove, Alberta, treated 118 patients—including all ninety children, their houseparents, and the children of those houseparents. This included 105 cleanings and 157 fillings. Cavities had been reduced by eighty-six since the team's last visit. Outside the dental rooms, meanwhile, other volunteers were painting, repainting, and repairing houses; quilting; and sorting and mending clothing. Another earlier team had made 187 jars of grape jam, finished twenty-three quilts, planted ten palm trees, did wide-scale landscaping, and built a huge retaining wall and steps with brick and mortar. A professional photographer took photos of each child and taught jewelry making and how to craft scrapbooks. Others taught tie-dyeing and painted the exterior of a new addition to the technical-vocational center.

Still another group from Iowa, comprised of fifteen teenagers led by four adults, laid a concrete floor for the volleyball court and skateboard ramp. That meant children are now off the internal road, away from cars and other smaller children at play. This contribution spares the expense of more frequent repairs to skateboards, since the polished concrete eliminates the jarring to both the boards and the children's bodies by the old cobblestone driveway. In late 2005, two teams totaling thirty-four from Minnesota and Alberta dug out the base for House 8 at *Lar Colméia,* raised the retainer wall, and laid the sidewalk. They painted, stained, replaced rotting wood, welded, and gardened, yet still played games with the children in much of their spare time. Some children even learned to play the recorder and handbells, thanks to volunteer input. Worshippers at one of Pastor Ken's Sunday night services were delighted with a handbells number learned by the children.

Incidentally, soon after the base of House 8 had been excavated, with other construction progressing, word came that a Canadian couple had volunteered to underwrite a major portion of the home's financing. God had spoken to their hearts, just as He had spoken to the hearts of others whose professional skills are enhancing the children's lives. Altamir Matias, the ten-year-old who cannot hear or speak, whose sad story of maternal abuse and neglect unfolded in chapter nine, loved displaying his new handbell-ringing skill during that aforementioned church service. In fact, one of the little girls had to grab his wrist to stop him from playing past his part. A month or so earlier Altamir had been fitted with hearing aids, and the sensational news was that he could hear. Although Altamir had trouble distinguishing origins of the various sounds, his verbal noises changed. He could only wear those devices for fifteen-minute periods, and later they were changed. The hope is that he will learn to talk within a few years.

The CHAIN's prayers, meanwhile, were going out to two girls, one being fitted for a fourth time with contacts to prevent potential blindness and another being fitted with braces in the early treatment stages to remedy a crooked jaw. Thanks to those volunteers, it seems each new week and month the CHAIN's children and adults are being equipped with some new skill. Craft teacher Sueli, for example, somehow obtained a loom and taught rug-weaving to children and houseparents.[35]

Perhaps some idea of the impact of the CHAIN of Love can be gleaned from one volunteer's grateful letter to his supporters. The writer is Carl Beck, of Leduc Fellowship Church, in Leduc, Alberta, Canada. Beck was at *Lar Colméia* in the fall of 2004 with a construction team from his church. He writes,

"Shortly after I arrived, I had a very sleepless night till I prayed to God and asked Him what He was trying to tell me. His answer to my prayer was very clear, and was as follows: I have brought you here to show you what true love is really like. This place is as close to heaven on earth as you will ever find. You will see it in the eyes and the smiles of the children here. They have been placed here to show you a new appreciation for what I have prepared for you in heaven, and whatever you are capable of doing for them here, you must do for Me, to make this a better place. I went to sleep and slept like a baby. Woke up the next morning and asked Pastor Jon what he had for me to do. He said the men's washroom needs cleaning, and would I do it. I said sure, and did it gladly. The next day I asked the same question, and he said we have some painting to do. I don't like painting, but I gladly picked up my brush and painted shutters for two days and loved it. I was able to do many other jobs, as well as helping the men on the new home to install supports for the rafters they were installing. I praise God for His leadership in my life."[36]

14

JESUS-DRIVEN MISSIONARIES STRENGTHEN GOD'S MINISTRY OF LOVE

ara, Sally, Calvino and Katie Taylor in 2005, and Rev. Chris and Ingrid Kidd in 2006—in that order of succession since 1998—have been responsible for the myriad details of accounting, bookkeeping, promotion, and communicating with everyone sponsoring children under the ministry's guardianship. Sara is Sara Esther Luna Cezar, my teammate in authorship of *For the Love of God's Kids* and the superb Portuguese-to-English translator for our exhaustive interviews of several dozen men, women, and children at the CHAIN's *Lar Colméia* site over twenty-five days in May 2004. Sally is Sally Antholzner, of Buffalo, New York, who succeeded Sara in March 2001 after a two-month training period and served until missionaries Cal and wife Katie agreed in September 2004 to fill in for her while she completed her obligatory home assignment in the United States. Sally, conversant in Portuguese like Americans Sara and

Katie, and Cal, a Brazilian, were helpful whenever this author needed vital information on children and the current operation. And, although we haven't met, I have grown to admire Cal and Katie very much, thanks to our e-mail exchanges. Like the stories of Sara and Sally, theirs also fascinates and inspires. As a package, the tales of Sara, Sally, and Cal and Katie demonstrate the divine perfection with which our Lord was mapping step by step each of their life journeys toward that gang of children stealing the hearts of everyone connected with His CHAIN of Love.

For thirty-two-year-old Sara, a Mexican-American, that journey started back in Monterey, Mexico, where she was born to missionaries Juan and Amanda Luna. An only child, she was from day one under the influence of two devoted servants of Jesus. Her father, Juan Luna, now sixty-six, had just completed seminary in the northern Mexico town of Torreon when he met Sara's mother, Amanda, now sixty-one, who had finished studies at another Bible school. Soon after marriage, her dad was ordained a Baptist minister, and the Lunas teamed in ministry at a mission church in Camargo, Mexico, a small town on the Texas border along the Rio Grande River. Sara was then two, and the Lunas ministered there for about four years.

The Lunas loved the area and their assignment, but both were beset by health problems that forced a move to the metropolitan city of Guadalajara in west-central Mexico for quick access to medical services. A cardiologist advised the move after Reverend Luna suffered a mild heart attack and Mrs. Luna was diagnosed with hyperthyroidism and diabetes. Medical services were free to pastors of all faiths at Guadalajara's Baptist hospital. While undergoing treatment, Reverend Luna served a local church as a visiting pastor, feeling that once his health had improved the family could return to tiny Camargo. An American friend living in Camargo, Branch Jones, convinced Sara's dad and mom to return anyway and minister just across the border in Rio Grande City, a Texas community of about 50,000 a mile north of the Rio Grande River.

There was the Holy Spirit, again working in people's hearts and connecting them in ways that would eventually bring Sara as a servant into the CHAIN of Love. You see, Branch Jones had come to accept Christ some time earlier in Camargo, thanks to Reverend Luna's godly influence. Like Sérgio, Jones had wasted his past life as both a user and drug trafficker. Only Jones, as Sara related his story, was much more a high-roller. Based in Rio Grande City, he had preyed on the poor and vulnerable on both sides of the border. He was well known to the authorities. "After he accepted Jesus, Mr. Jones would say he was far wealthier with nothing on this planet, and that heaven with Jesus is where the real rewards are stored."

Incredibly, Jones himself became a minister. And Sara, then about eight, personally saw how the love of Jesus can polish someone as dirt-laden as Jones had been into a model of servanthood to God and humanity. Her child's eyes saw him as a hero. His indeed was a sensational turnaround.

Jones and Sara's father would go to the homes of people Jones knew in Rio Grande City and evangelize. "It was Mr. Jones's idea. He would say to my father, 'Let's go see some friends I know, and let's tell the good news about Jesus.'" Reverend Luna, as pastor of Garcia's Ranch Church in Rio Grande City, was ministering in a region desperately in need of the message of Jesus, a downtrodden corner of Texas notorious for illegal immigration and drug running. As Sara says, "There's no industry and no jobs, and a lot of people depend upon federal assistance. Even today, drug trafficking is so bad that a dirigible flies along the corridor to scout for illegal activity."

During that decade in Rio Grande City, Sara distinguished herself as a top-flight student through every grade. Meanwhile, her parents had been strongly urging the North American Baptist Conference to open a mission field in Mexico. Dr. Herman Effa—Jerilyn Bayer's father—who was then director of international missions for the North American Baptist Conference, agreed with them. Dr. Effa saw them as perfect for opening Mexico to missionary work. During that first year in Mexico, Reverend Luna served alone in Mexico City, returning monthly for visits to Rio Grande City where Mrs. Luna had stayed behind with Sara until she completed high school. Then, Reverend and Mrs. Luna journeyed on to Mexico City to start churches, while Sara went on to Baylor University in Waco, having graduated fourth in a class of 350 from Rio Grande City High School. At Baylor, Sara started as a music major, focused on a career playing French horn with a band (she had played French horn in high school). But she switched to an English major as a sophomore after realizing she no longer enjoyed all the hard work a major in music entailed.

"One reason I changed my mind is that God spoke to me during that first summer before returning to Baylor for my second year. I was in Mexico City with my parents, who were hosting some youth teams there on missions from North America. The young people and I quickly became friends, and I translated for them at various places. I really enjoyed helping and told myself I wanted to do more of this. And that's what I did during my next summer break from Baylor."

The Lord had sown a seed in Sara's heart. In the meantime, her dad's heart problem had returned. Mexico City's pollution and high altitude had exacerbated the condition, which was further worsened because he had developed diabetes as well. In the meantime, Mrs. Luna's diabetes had disappeared. During Sara's final year at Baylor, Reverend Luna returned for a short time to McAllen, Texas, and underwent treatments to remove a blockage to his arteries. Then, just before Sara's graduation, the good pastor underwent triple-bypass heart surgery.

> "He came through incredibly well, We did a lot of praying, and God pretty much gave him back his health. Dad was always saying, 'There's more to do, I still have so much more to do.' He was always making plans, and he always had a new one. Really, I came to appreciate and love my parents as lifetime role models. Through all their ups and downs, they were passionately and continuously in love with God. At first, I didn't want to be like them, particularly when I was a teen. It seemed too hard. Dad did everything. He counseled mothers troubled about their children, dealt with the fallout of people coming out of failed marriages, and prayed for everyone, deeply feeling their wounds."

Sara admits she was "surprised" herself when she told her father she had been considering the missionary field. Sara had already been accepted for Baptist seminary studies at Sioux Falls, South Dakota, before graduation in 1997 from Baylor with a grade point average of 3.3.

"Dad was so happy when I returned home to Mexico City and told him about my missionary hopes. But he suggested things could work out even better if I experienced some short-term missions first before entering seminary. So we telephoned the Baptist international missions office in Illinois, and the director listed three choices: Japan as an English teacher, Brazil assisting with administrative duties at the CHAIN of Love, and as a youth-ministry official in Mexico City. Mom was so practical. Japan was too far, she said, and in Mexico really no experience would be needed, but Brazil, on the other hand, was similar to Mexico in many ways, and there is where I could gain needed experience. It was an excellent suggestion, but I still had no idea of what the CHAIN of Love was. All I knew of the Bayers were their names and photos on prayer cards for missionaries."

The officials at North American Baptist Conference headquarters in Illinois interviewed me and recommended I go on an exploratory trip first to *Lar Colméia* to observe the construction proceeding there and judge whether I would feel right with the ministry. So I got a visa and went to Campo Bom.

And, there, to personally train Sara for about ten days in November 1997, was another member of that remarkable Effa family. It was Jerilyn, Dr. Effa's daughter and the CHAIN's co-founder with hubby Ken. Roughly eight years after Dr. Effa had persuaded Sara's father to undertake missions in Mexico City, the daughter of the former international missions director for North American Baptists was reassuring and pep-talking Reverend Luna's shy and worrisome daughter that she would work out just fine.

"I didn't feel qualified, because I had never done anything in administration, and much of this would entail gathering information on children taken into the ministry's guardianship. But Jerilyn and Ken both said they would love to have me on the team. I spent some of the time with Jerilyn, organizing and boxing clothes for missions. She instructed me in bookkeeping and coached in the writing of letters to churches, organizations, and individuals connected with the ministry. A big part of that correspondence would be with people sponsoring a child under the ministry's care. Jerilyn and Ken were so supportive, telling me the training would be ongoing and that they would always be helpful."

So, Sara says, she arrived confidently at Campo Bom in June 1998 with no expectations. "Everyone was so receptive. Everyone welcomed me so warmly at Good News Baptist Church. That was the small one before the new one was constructed." Again, Jerilyn, who sings with the church worship team, took charge, telling team members of Sara's musical talents. Sara added a new instrument to the group, purchasing a keyboard. And, thanks to her skilled touch, the congregation's musical praise to the Lord has been all the more gloriously uplifting over the past eight years of Sundays.

Already with the worship team when Sara joined was drummer Fábio Cezar, the eldest son of Tadeu and Deny Cezar, church members who two years later would become houseparents at *Lar Colméia*. (Deny was spotlighted by the local newspaper, *The Campo Bom Gazette,* in its annual Mother's Day Feature in May 2004.)

Six months after joining the worship team, Sara accepted the leader's invitation to participate in a weekly small discussion group in the bass player's home. Fábio was in that same group, and for the next two years the daily activities of Sara and Fábio pretty much followed the same tempo. In addition to the discussion group, they participated in the same church youth groups and rehearsed one or two evenings weekly with the worship team. "What initially attracted me to Fábio was that he always wanted to do the right thing for God," Sara said with a smile.

It sounds like the Luna and Cezar parents were on the same wavelength raising Sara and Fábio. "Deny has always been involved with ladies' activities at the church," Sara notes.

"And, for years, Fábio and his two brothers and two sisters have been constantly active in church youth-group activities. Still, that's not all. Fábio was always studying and working while he attended university. He actually worked his way through university and has a bachelor of science degree in electrical engineering. He's now a shareholding owner and partner in an electrical engineering company that also develops computer software."

A bond of mutual admiration and affection gradually strengthened between Sara and Fábio. In June 2000, Sara completed her two-year mission assignment but agreed to remain in her position until Sally, who would succeed her, finished gathering her support funds and obtained a visa and other vital immigration papers. However, parting eight months later in March 2001 was not that sweetly sorrowful. Joy was beckoning. Sara and Fábio proposed marriage to each other before she left for Texas to rejoin her parents. "We didn't know what was going to happen, but I said I would be back in Campo Bom for Christmas vacation."

Back in Texas, the Lunas were again in Rio Grande City, where they had returned a year earlier and bought a house. The stress of missions in populous and polluted Mexico City had exacted a toll on the health of Sara's parents, so they opted for semiretirement. Sara soon found work at her alma mater, Rio Grande City High School, teaching both English and English as a second language in the evening division.

As agreed, she and Fábio were reunited at Christmas amid the joy of a Savior's birthday celebration. They officially proposed marriage and exchanged identical engagement bands, a Brazilian custom. Sara returned to Texas to finish the school year's teaching duties and finalize a permanent move to Brazil, and through e-mails they fixed July 27, 2002, for wedlock in Mexico City. "First, we had a small civil ceremony before a justice of the peace in Campo Bom, followed by an evening reception with guests at a local restaurant." After the civil ceremony and reception with church friends and Fábio's family, Sara and her parents traveled back to their home in Texas, where they made the necessary preparations for the religious ceremony and reception with Sara's family. "Meanwhile, Fábio and his parents remained in Brazil to prepare for their journey a week later to Mexico City, where my father married us."

Children? "I think we'll settle for two." On January 19, 2005, Ana Cezar was born, weighing 5.7 pounds and measuring 18.5 inches. As fate would have it, Pastor Ken and Jerilyn Bayer weren't in Campo Bom to share the Cezars' happiness and welcome God's lovely gift into the church and ministry family. On that very day, the Bayers were here in my home city of Kelowna, Canada, doing morning and evening slide presentations in my home church, Trinity Baptist. The

Power Point presentations highlighted milestones of progress at the CHAIN of Love and updated everyone on where the ministry is headed after ten years. Ken had been in Canada since November 23, 2004, because of the life-threatening liver cancer of his mother, Irma, in Edmonton, Alberta. Jerilyn and their three daughters joined him early in December, after staying on at Campo Bom for the CHAIN's tenth-anniversary celebration on November 26. (Descriptions of the celebration, by Jerilyn and others, will be featured in chapter sixteen.) Because of the family emergency, the return to North America by the Bayers for mission-support help and fund-raising was advanced, and they visited about fifty-five churches in five Canadian provinces, Michigan, and Illinois. Ken returned to Brazil in mid-March 2005, Jerilyn a month earlier.

Sara and Fábio were house-sitting the Bayers' home during their absence. Meanwhile, when Sara's little doll was just four days old, here in the living room of my Kelowna home I was interviewing Ken and Jerilyn for the wrap-up chapter of *For the Love of God's Kids*. I feel a strong link to that little girl. After all, her mom was my teammate in this labor of love for children. I spent almost two years of my army service in Sara's home state of Texas, most of that time as editor of the camp newspaper at Fort Sam Houston in San Antonio. As well, Ana's grandparents, Tadeu and Deny, are the houseparents to my sponsored boy, Alexandre, and his younger brother, Regis.

Likewise, I share a connection with Pastor Ken, as much of my journalistic career was with the *Winnipeg Free Press* in the Canadian city of Winnipeg, Manitoba, where Pastor Ken grew up. I acquired some insight into the plight of deprived children as the *Free Press* social services reporter. I already had some knowledge of notorious urban streets and the hurts inflicted on God's children like Alexandre and Regis before they come into the loving embrace of folks at *Lar Colméia*. That stemmed from having grown up in crime-scarred Detroit, having witnessed deadly, city-wide race riots there as a boy, and later covering police and courts for a time as a reporter for the old *Detroit Times* before its death with sale to the *Detroit News* in 1960. God is often, if not always, engineering these types of connections for His purposes.

Sally, Sara's successor, was recruited into the CHAIN by God's direct marketing through exceptional salespeople. He spoke emphatically into Sally's heart through Canadians Don and Moni Nickel, of Kitchener, Ontario. In 1996 Nickel, an ophthalmologist, and his wife were at Sally's White Haven Baptist Church in Grand Island, New York, showing slides of *Lar Colméia*, the children, and the house construction. They had been part of a team building a house the previous year, and they were proposing that the church sign on as a financial sponsor for the CHAIN.

> "Those photos were riveting, and they made a huge impact on me. Powerful images of love, especially in the faces of the children. I envisioned becoming a full-time missionary, and I knew in my heart God wanted me to go, but at that moment I thought it was way above me physically, mentally, emotionally, and spiritually. I felt some other experiences would be needed as training."

So, Sally consulted her pastor and close friends, all of whom advised work similar to that of the Nickels as a means of getting a "feel" for missions. But a call to North American Baptist Conference headquarters determined that no team opportunity was then available. Sally persisted, buoyed by supporters who urged that she patiently await "God's timing." And God's timing came in March 1998, with formation of a Conference-approved eighteen-member "Gateway" team to work at *Lar Colméia*. Half of them were from California churches, and the other half were from Sally's Buffalo-area congregation and Latta Road Baptist Church in Rochester, New York. The idea underlying the "Gateway" term used by North American Baptists is that the team experience is one that could potentially open the minds of participants and, perhaps, the "gates" to full-time ministry. The two-week construction-work mission was scheduled for late July to early August. "Tough as it was," Sally said, "I drove the one and a half hours from Buffalo to Rochester with a broken elbow to join the New York contingent for the flight to Brazil. I had broken it six weeks earlier when my bicycle overturned. A tire had blown out, and I went crashing to the pavement." So, during those two weeks at *Lar Colméia,* Sally landscaped around the site, did a lot of gardening, and washed the team's laundry. And she fell head-over-heels in love with the playful gang of children who crowded her. She returned to Buffalo prayerful and impassioned to land a two-year missionary commitment to Campo Bom.

Sally is the youngest of nine children, four sisters and four brothers, with those older brothers having the strongest sway over her. "Boy, was I a tomboy! Had great rapport mixing it up with the four of them. I was into wrestling, boxing, baseball and basketball with them. Everything." That high-octane energy, she figures, is derived from parents who were "German workaholics." Although raised by their parents in another denomination, Sally was led into a Baptist church by brother Christopher. He accepted Christ when he was eighteen, then started taking Sally to church meetings. "Chris felt he needed a stronger, personal relationship with Jesus, and that's what he found, thanks to a Pentecostal church friend who had discovered it earlier. Same thing happened to me, thanks to Chris." She started attending White Haven Road Baptist Church a year before graduating in 1991 with a degree in public accounting from the State University of New York at Buffalo. Thereafter, Sally worked as a certified public accountant at several Buffalo companies. Meanwhile, as her faith deepened, she became increasingly involved in her church's women's ministry and was serving as the congregation's youth-ministry leader in 1998 when she undertook the Gateway team mission to *Lar Colméia.*

Almost immediately after returning to Buffalo, Sally began seeking a missionary assignment to the CHAIN of Love. She offered her public accounting education and experience to fill whatever vacancy could exist in that area. However, Carol Potratz, international missions recruiter for the North American Baptist Conference, thanked her and said the position embracing accounting and promotional responsibilities was already filled (by Sara). Nonetheless, Sally's name went into the file. She was contacted for a weekend of interviews when the international missions office learned that Sara had decided not to stay beyond the end of her two-year assignment in June 2000. For Sara, family obligations had arisen in Texas, while marriage to Fábio loomed in Campo Bom. As demanding as it was, an energized Sally was very much up to the challenge of that long weekend of grilling in 1999 at North American Baptist Conference headquarters in Oakbrook Terrace, Illinois. She was queried, sometimes separately, by the psychologist and five other conference executives. "I was a little nervous about the unknown, but I guess I did all right. They asked about how I would deal with living overseas, and how I might deal with different personalities. Plus, they wanted to know everything about my personal life." The day prior to Thanksgiving, Carol Potratz telephoned to inform an elated Sally that she had been accepted. "I was supposed to leave in August 2000, but because of visa-approval problems I didn't arrive in Campo Bom until January 2001." Pastor Ken trained her for the next two months.

So, here was Sally, finally, at *Lar Colméia* on a mission whose seed had been planted five years earlier during that slide presentation in her Buffalo-area church by Canadians Don and Moni Nickel. Personally-raised mission support and recruitment of an ongoing-prayer team are mission prerequisites, and the Nickels are among her mission-support sponsors at the CHAIN of Love. From even before their first meeting, the Lord was obviously at His people-chessboard, mapping the intersecting routes of Sally and the Nickels. They have been regular e-mail friends from the beginning, and Sally has visited them in Ontario. Besides sharing in Sally's financial support, the Nickels are among the thirty team members from various churches praying for her.

As Sally recalled during our interview, the *Lar Colméia* complex had doubled in size in the two-and-a-half years since her Gateway-team mission there in 1998. Growth in the three and a half years since her second arrival in 2001 has been equally stunning, she added. Moreover, she points out, the environment contrasts markedly with much of the Brazilian urban landscape outside *Lar Colméia*.

"There aren't many parks in the cities, and many schools don't have playgrounds. But look at this place—it's a role model focused on children. There's a bocce-ball court here, a gym building, a playground, a sand-volleyball area, and the children feel safe and loved."

A passing motorist might mistakenly conclude that the campus is a closed condominium community, anything but a refuge for deprived children. They are not the "normal" ramshackle quarters for the so-called "underclass." Sally's comments reinforce those of Jerilyn Bayer, whose forceful answer to skeptics is: "Why shouldn't these children deserve first-world treatment? We try to give them the normal, dignified life of any middle-class Brazilian family."

Sally's competence and devotion at *Lar Colméia* quickly caught the notice of the international missions office. Just a year into her two-year commitment, at the end of 2001, she answered "yes" when a headquarters official invited her to become a full-time missionary. Now, as a full-time missionary, Sally had a new two-year assignment with the CHAIN of Love. During that first year, the Buffalo dynamo had forged close bonds with the entire gang of children, in no small part thanks to her pet German shepherd, *Boneca* ("Doll" in English). It doesn't hurt to have such a playful, affectionate, amusing pet around as a drawing card to charm the children.

That year was replete with touching moments with children like Mateus Machado Seidler, then a four-year-old little butterball, who jumped onto her lap, put his chunky arms around her neck, and delivered a big smooch. That occurred during Sunday school at Good News Baptist a day before Sally was to leave *Lar Colméia* for a brief vacation in Buffalo. She had driven several children to church that day and worshipped with them. In fact, as I witnessed, Sundays routinely featured a rambunctious bunch of laughing children gathering around Sally's car, each pleading for a seat on the fun-filled ride from *Lar Colméia* to the church in Novo Hamburgo. "That was a sad last day," Sally said, recalling the big buss from Mateus. "I was tearful, thinking, 'I want to be here to see him get married someday.' That solidified my desire to stay in Brazil."

What a lesson in love for the world to behold from Sally and Mateus—a kid who could well have gone a lifetime without such joyous love had he not been rescued at nine months of age from the brutality of abandonment by his mother, a teenage prostitute, and his drug-trafficking teenage father. Mateus, now a playful nine-year-old with big brown eyes, shows how "a kind word is the oil that takes friction out of life." That popular expression is reflective of Sally and many others who have empowered these children with love and encouragement. At the CHAIN of Love, kind words and deeds include Sally's to Deneclei Calderini, an eleven-year-old when Sally gave him a compact disc. On it was a hit song by Phil Collins. Months later, Deneclei knocked at Sally's door, then with a smile burst into song as she stood in the doorway. He had memorized Collins' song in English. A tear or two glistened as Sally listened to Deneclei's heartfelt rendition of "You'll Be In My Heart."

"What the children learn most here is that God loves them, and they see Him using people as instruments to demonstrate His love. I would say the most vital food and medicine being dispensed here is the human love transmitted from houseparents and everyone else. This ministry wouldn't be possible without God's Hand moving people."

Several interviews crystallized how Sally has flourished under God's Guiding Hand in Brazil. She had just obtained her permanent visa from the Brazilian government and would leave in September 2004 for her obligatory one-year furlough and home-mission assignment. "I have fallen in love with Brazil. I wouldn't want to be anywhere else." Sally has one other reason to return to this "second home." Her name is Gabriela Maciel Machado, and she is Sally's godchild. The then eighteen-month-old blonde cutie bubbled over with smiles as I photographed her being held by Sally and others in Good News Baptist Church. Gabriela was passed around from row to row into arms thrust out invitingly for the privilege of her company while she flashed smiles at everyone. Here was a delightful tyke now thriving in a community of love after being rescued from a mother so neglectful that Gabriela could have suffered permanent health damage had she been left with her much longer.

Born on October 17, 2002, Gabriela was the fifth child of a mentally unstable woman whose husband abandoned the family shortly after Gabriella's birth. Woefully inattentive, this mother seldom fed Gabriela and rarely changed her diapers, leaving her in a crib as little more than a storage item. Authorities failed in their attempts to teach her proper mothering after placing Gabriela in a home-care setting specifically for that purpose. Frustrated, they approached a judge who agreed this infant's welfare would best be served with the CHAIN of Love. So Gabriela came into the off-campus home of Cezar and Marli on August 29, 2003, horribly undernourished and about half the normal size of a baby ten months old. As Sally recalls, Gabriela appeared almost lifeless, her tiny body showing only scant ripples of movement. "She was severely dehydrated. And I fell in love with her on sight."

Meanwhile, the children were having fun kidding Sally whenever she walked around *Lar Colméia* with Gabriela snuggled in her arms. "'Sally has a baby! Sally has a baby!' was a chant I heard often. Well, they heard me say right from the start, 'This one I want,' and they knew I was serious." Gabriela's ten house brothers and sisters were also instantly overwhelmed with affection for her, consistently vying for a chance to hold her while asking what they could do to help with their baby sister. Sally said, repeating what she declared concerning Mateus, "I want to be at Gabriela's wedding." As Sally noted, should Gabriela ever be left without any legal caregivers, Sally would share responsibility for her with her other godparent, Monica. Housemother Deny's daughter, Monica is a twenty-seven-year-old schoolteacher studying at seminary to become a missionary.

Sally has become fluent in Portuguese, having attended classes for three hours weekly over two-and-a-half years, then one hour weekly since the beginning of 2004. Assisting me during a medical emergency and treatment—a bite from a stray dog that required anti-rabies inoculations—she shared information that reinforced what Ken and Jerilyn Bayer cite as Brazil's structural shortcomings. For example, the rickety health-care system is supported by income from taxing all financial transactions. There's just too little money in the health-care pot, because the millions of poor certainly aren't transacting with banks. "The tragedy of life here is that the poor have to work the system," Sally notes.

"A poor mother, for example, has to arrive at 4 A.M. to get a numbered ticket at the medical clinic,

then return several hours later so that she can be
among the first numbered in line when doctors
arrive at 8 or 9, and even then there's no guarantee
she will be seen. People die waiting for surgery."

Hourly pay at McDonald's, Sally adds, is maybe thirty
cents. "Street beggars earn more."

When these lines were written, Sally was in New York
gathering support for further missionary work and had just
spoken to me on the phone. Back in the United States since
October 2004, she was in the midst of an itinerary that had
her speaking gratefully to the twenty-five churches in various states that had financially sponsored her missionary
work over the previous four years. She was also visiting the
approximately forty individuals who did likewise. (Sadly,
an e-mail message from her more than a month later
reported she would not be returning to the CHAIN of Love.
No reason was specified, but Sally offered best wishes and
expressed gratitude to the Bayers' ministry. She also
requested prayers from all for her missionary future.)

Meanwhile, back at *Lar Colméia*, Cal and Katie Taylor
were demonstrating how perfectly the Lord selects the
replacement troops. There is no doubt that His Guiding
Hand shaped the forces that brought Cal and Katie together
and then directed them to the CHAIN of Love. Cal, twenty-
six, and Katie, twenty-five, are committed to serving His
children. Katie, an American from New Jersey, first came to
northern Brazil as a tenth-grade teenager with her parents on
a missions trip to Vianopolis, where Cal, a Brazilian, was
living in the mission boarding school. His parents are missionaries in northern Brazil. Katie completed the eleventh
and twelfth grades at the school, dating Cal only occasionally at first but more seriously as graduation approached.

Then Cal accompanied Katie and her parents back to Deptford, New Jersey, where all four attended a Bible institute for two years and graduated with associate degrees in biblical education. In June 2003, Cal and Katie married in New Jersey, then moved to Waukesha, Wisconsin, for a year. They became active in a Baptist church that was recruiting a construction team headed for *Lar Colméia* early in 2004. Who better to tap as the team's translator than Cal?

"We loved being at *Lar Colméia,* and we really fell in love with all the children," Katie said. "As we were leaving, I was crying and telling Pastor Ken that we would be back again." Back in Wisconsin, Cal and Katie became increasingly more involved as church volunteers. Then, with Sally soon to leave on home assignment, the Taylors were asked by the Bayers if they would consider returning. "After much prayer and many miracles, we arrived here in August 2004," Katie says, "and it has been so wonderful since." Meanwhile, Katie's parents were in Canada, studying to be missionaries in Brazil like Cal's mother and father.

As Sara and Sally will both attest, the duties handled by their successors were varied, stimulating, challenging, voluminous, and, above all, always fulfilling. They were in close ongoing contact with all those lovable children and the vital bridge of communication between the children and their sponsors. Under the multiple-sponsor arrangement designed by Pastor Ken and Jerilyn Bayer, that means the Taylors had been keeping about 900 or more sponsors updated on ministry activities and the lives of their boys or girls until they completed their term in May 2005 and returned home. Their secretarial duties for some months thereafter were being handled temporarily by Jerilyn Bayer's mother, Ardath Effa. Each kid in guardianship has at least ten sponsors, and some have a maximum of twelve. So that estimate of 900 is based on a fluctuating number, ranging from eighty-four to ninety-one children in care during the writing of this book. Mrs. Effa, as Cal, Katie, Sara, and Sally did previously, kept a notebook highlighting the progress and development of each child and sent personal letters to each sponsor. Other duties include translating all the letters sent to the children, processing all funds on the computer, personally presenting overseas gifts and birthday money to the children, and writing a monthly newsletter to all sponsors.

As this book was being updated in July 2006, Americans Chris and Ingrid Kidd had been at *Lar Colméia* for slightly more than three months and were studiously absorbed in Portuguese language classes while being trained in their duties by the Bayers and Ardath Effa. Mrs. Effa and the Bayers were also educating the young couple in Brazilian culture, customs, and history. Chris arrived at Campo Bom on March 23, just four days after he had been ordained as a minister. Exactly two months after his ordination came another milestone when son Anthony Philip entered the world, at just over nine pounds on May 19, as a brother to toddler Elizabeth. In his biographical sketch from the North American Baptist Conference, Chris stresses that he's determined to fully employ his technical, instructional, leadership, and relational skills in service to God's Kingdom. Ingrid emphasizes she will use her love for children and teaching for God's glory. Moreover, their marriage mission statement adds, in part:

"To allow God to use us as a dynamic team to share His love with each other, with our family, and with others, and also share all of our resources that He has blessed us with so that others will see God in us and desire Him in their lives as well."

Like their predecessors, Chris and Ingrid can be assured of and anticipate one far-reaching spin-off inherent in all the work. It generates a CHAIN reaction—and that pun is intended. Sponsors are motivated to encourage the CHAIN-supporting churches of which they are members to undertake such helpful projects as making quilts or collecting good clothing for the CHAIN's families. And word does get around. For example, in January 2004 in Kelowna, Canada, I read about Jeremy Chwastkowski, then nine, in the January-February issue of *NAB today,* the news periodical published by the North American Baptist Conference.

Jeremy was featured in the back page *NAB today* profile. As his profile's headline proclaimed, he was "Striking a Different Kind of Goal." His mother, Ruth, encouraged him to consider transforming his ninth birthday party on August 23, 2003, into a giving, instead of getting, celebration. No doubt his mom matured into that giving attitude and way of life, having it instilled by her own parents, Reverend and Mrs. William McLatchie, who pastor Hillcrest Baptist in Highland Heights, Ohio. She suggested that Jeremy might want to ask those invited to bring, instead of presents for him, donations to a good cause. She promised him that he could still enjoy pizza with his soccer teammates and other friends. He thought it was a good idea and searched for awhile, trying to find something just right—something children his own age could deeply and instantly identify with. Then a bulb switched on when "I heard about children that were suffering and living on the streets with no home." They were children his own age, many even younger. So on the party invitations Jeremy requested that each kid bring not a gift but a donation to the CHAIN of Love homes in Brazil.

Jeremy had already been saving much of his allowance, spare change out of his dad's pockets, and money awarded for doing extra household chores. Donations on his birthday brought to $216 the grand total sent to the CHAIN of Love. Totally committed, Jeremy went on to raise another $105 from his savings and earnings by early January 2004, when *NAB today* went to press, reporting that Jeremy was still "figuring out new ways to give more to church and CHAIN of Love."

Bet you those soccer-crazy children at *Lar Colméia* in the world's foremost soccer-loving country would just love booting the ball around with Jeremy, a defensive mid-fielder with his Ohio school team. Bet you, too, Jeremy would fit right in with the gang gathered on weekends in housefather Raimundo's living room for a rousing time viewing televised soccer games. Language barrier notwithstanding, they would hit it off grandly in more ways than just soccer.

As his *NAB today* profile notes, Jeremy's interests are wide-ranging. He's computer-savvy, plays trumpet, plays baseball and collects baseball cards, collects stamps and turtles. He's also on his school's soccer team's defensive frontline as a mid-fielder, out to stop opposing players from scoring. He's a "stopper." But, as *NAB today* adds, Jeremy is also a "striker" off the field. In soccer jargon, that's a forward player whose major purpose is to "make things happen, or score." Jeremy does make things happen, as his CHAIN of Love initiative reveals. This is very much in the spirit of the CHAIN of Love itself, making things happen for the love of God's children. Millions of homeless children remain out there, but Jeremy and company, one by one, have strikingly demonstrated the art of the possible in extending loving arms of rescue.[37]

15

PRO SUPERSTARS WIN BIG FOR GOD'S ADORABLE CHILDREN

Mariene Tammerik, Isabel Maria de Souza Pinto, Fabiana Bergman Ribeiro, and Kénia Witeckoski epitomize what all championship teams know: winning is a result of teamwork executed by players suitably and strategically positioned for their roles in the play-action sequence. Unlike competitive sports, however, they're in a serious game of life bearing the highest stakes. Their goal is to transform the lives of children rescued from living situations so horrible that they almost certainly would have demolished any chance for the children to grow into healthy, well-functioning adults. Superstar pros like Mariene as psychologist, Isabel as private tutor, Fabiana as speech therapist-audiologist, and Kénia as social worker have contributed much toward developing the CHAIN of Love.

Newest on the team is Kénia, who was recruited onto the CHAIN's roster in October 2004. Her home church in

Porto Alegre, a city of 250,000 thirty-one miles south of the CHAIN'S site in Campo Bom, is the world's first to begin patterning a ministry to children after the Bayers' *Lar Colméia* prototype. The Christian and Missionary Alliance, as recorded back in chapter one, is several years off the ground constructing homes for boys and girls and in 2005 had two, each about six times the size of a single house on the *Lar Colméia* site. Since its launch, social worker Kénia has been serving as the Alliance's legal representative before the courts, Social Services, and government agencies on matters concerned with proposed guardianship of certain children or those already in the ministry's care. Now Kénia is doing the same for the CHAIN of Love, splitting her duties with the two ministries, shuttling back and forth between Porto Alegre and the Campo Bom-Novo Hamburgo area. Kénia, twenty-seven and single, was born and raised in Porto Alegre and is a 2003 graduate of that city's Pontifical University.

To both the CHAIN and Alliance teams, she might best be described as a "quarterback" of sorts. As the person responsible for the assessing and placement of children, she oversees and monitors the comings and goings of children into and out of legal guardianship. As Pastor Ken emphasized during our last interview in Kelowna, Canada, the major strengths Kénia brings to the CHAIN are her extensive network of contacts and her comprehensive knowledge of available resources and the intricate workings of the entire framework of government, public, and private agencies. That produces both time and money savings. "She has saved us a lot of money already," Pastor Ken says. "About $1,000 alone in medical expenses during her first month." Everything Kénia is doing now had been shouldered previously by Ken, Jerilyn, and the Bayers' administrative assistant, Clovis Scheffel. Lacking Kénia's education and experience, their efforts, naturally, were slower, more laborious, and less efficient. Now, the three are freed up to concentrate more intensively on other major responsibilities.

"Isabel, Fabiana, and I all go to lunch together, and even then we're always discussing our work with the children," says forty-three-year-old psychologist Mariene. Their offices are closely quartered in the technical-vocational center at *Lar Colméia,* making for a continuing exchange of views and information. The three are in pivotal roles, since they almost always are among the earliest spark plugs in the life-recharging process of the CHAIN's children. Out of the ruins of their past misery, they're being overhauled mentally, physically, emotionally, spiritually, and psychologically.

Psychologist Mariene Tammerik uses many toys and figures in helping kids overcome their difficulties.

One small incident is revealing of that gradual process in reconstructing young lives. It occurred when Altamir Matias, then seven, turned up at Mariene's office while teammate Sara and I were interviewing Mariene. She answered Altamir's insistent door pounding, kissed him tenderly, apologized for having forgotten their appointment, and rescheduled another with the promise this one would be kept. While sour-faced, Altamir accepted Mariene's explanation and left silently. A few years earlier, that would have provoked him into a screaming protest. "This shows the progress he has made," Mariene noted. "He accepts the fact I simply forgot, that I also can err, and that my forgetfulness has nothing to do with him." Remember, Altamir is the boy who cannot hear or speak, described in earlier chapters as having arrived into the CHAIN's care as a three-year-old in 2000. He had been neglected and abandoned several times by a seventeen-year-old mother who never wanted him. Her severe beatings finally compelled civic officials to shelter him until the CHAIN was granted legal guardianship. As Mariene explained, Altamir had come into care incapable of understanding or accepting the concept of authority over him, that someone should police and put a check on his behavior. "This is a boy who requires limits, and now when things are carefully explained, Altamir knows that for his own good he should obey adults in authority." *Lar Colméia* driver Tadeu, for example, has learned enough sign language to convey authority to Altamir, and houseparents Romilda and Sérgio have become skilled enough in sign language to communicate easily with him. "Altamir still has difficulties with other children," Mariene said. "When he gets frustrated, he sometimes regresses and lashes out at other children. He still wants to have his own way, and he can hurt others trying to get it. Still, Altamir has come a long way."

Speech therapist-audiologist Fabiana is also impressed with Altamir's progress.

"In his first days here, Altamir was extremely aggressive; he dribbled at the mouth and was terribly stubborn. He was wild, isolated himself, and wouldn't talk or play with anyone. After three years of working with Altamir, we see him now participating in organized games, always trying to express himself, and trying constantly to communicate with others in sign language."

Altamir's growth is a shining testimonial to the value of all those ongoing meetings and lunchtimes shared by Fabiana, Isabel, and Mariene as well as their involvement with all volunteers helping him and other children. In 2003, Isabel and Mariene completed a sign language course, and Fabiana has taken three such courses over three years. Theirs is a professionalism above and beyond the call of normal duty, all for the love of God's children.

When interviewed in May 2004, Mariene had been working with twenty-six children at the CHAIN, Isabel with thirty-five, and Fabiana, during her two years of service to that point, another thirty-five. By 2005, easily several hundred had been helped by this awesome threesome. Mariene has been serving the ministry more than eight and a-half years, Isabel eight, and Fabiana six.

How did their professional roads converge at Campo Bom? First consider Mariene. All her professional words and seemingly every niche of her office are purposely targeted at stripping away every shred of psychological damage weighing down the children brought aboard the CHAIN of Love. For example, all wall shelves are stocked with toys and games designed to promote therapy. A typical session has a child choosing his or her own toy or game for play. But it's all meaningful activity in the process, as Mariene explains.

"With the toys and games, they're responding like fish out of water. Instead of verbally expressing their problem, a boy or girl plays or acts it out. What they reveal are the feelings going on inside. By pretending to be Mommy or Daddy, they show how they perceive themselves as children. They also disclose what their biological mothers and fathers are like, and, beyond that, how a mother and daughter relate with each other, for example."

Growing up in São Paulo as the seventh in a family of nine children surely prepared her with some basics. "Even as a young child, I was interested in psychology. And, now not even the most difficult moments professionally will stop me from loving what I do."

Mariene attended United Metropolitan University in São Paulo and graduated in 1997 with a bachelor of arts degree and a teaching certificate in psychology from the University of Ijuí. That's also the alma mater of her husband, forty-nine-year-old Edson, currently the worship and music minister at Porto Alegre's First Baptist Church. As a student intern, Mariene worked as a psychologist for a human resources company and during that final university year hung up her own office shingle as well. Hired by the human resources firm upon graduation, Mariene also continued her private practice. After a year, she joined a computer-education firm in 1999. She left in 2001 to devote all of her time to her practice, church work, and family. She and Edson have two daughters, Evelyn and Karoline, now twenty-three and seventeen. Evelyn is a university psychology major in Porto Alegre, where the Tammeriks live.

One particular incident highlights her passionate professionalism. Mariene had been told by government officials that financial cutbacks would necessitate suspending her sessions with a young girl. Within two weeks, there would be no money in the government vault to pay her fees. "I just felt I could not cancel those sessions. So I continued counseling her for the next two months without charge." What a demonstration of her commitment to children and the concern and softness of her Christian heart!

Word of her Christian professionalism spread quickly. Mariene had been teaching two classes at the Baptist seminary in Porto Alegre in 1999 when a seminary student, who was in neither of her classes, sought help from the seminary president. At that time the student just happened to be a housefather at the CHAIN of Love and was having problems with a certain child in the household. Call on Mariene, the president immediately recommended. That produced counseling sessions with not just the one kid in the house family but two—a ten-year-old girl and a six-year-old boy. Mariene helped the children overcome their difficulties. That former housefather, Carlos Valentin, is now a pastor. Pastor Ken got word of Mariene's skilled professionalism that same year, 1999. A telephone call from him in July brought the invitation to counsel children at the CHAIN on a fee-for-service basis. Mariene accepted, and the opportunity launched her into a bit of self-analysis. "I wondered where this ability to hear people out and help them came from. Guess it comes from having grown up with a lot of people constantly in our house for company. And my teenage friends always enjoyed talking with me." It seemed natural as well that this innate ability found still another outlet in volunteer work during Mariene's final university year. She counseled mothers and children belonging to her church in Ijuí. Indeed, the Lord has gifted the CHAIN enormously by delivering her.

Mariene has been driving the sixty-two-mile round trip between Porto Alegre and *Lar Colméia* for more than seven years. "At first, it was a half-day once a week, then a full day, then two days weekly, and now two and a half days, and still that's not enough." She strives to be as supportive to the housemothers as possible within that available time frame, realizing that guidance is needed as children within the families grow older. Her counseling requires only a telephone call. "Or they could phone Ken in an emergency, for example when a child has run away, or when two children are arguing." In any case, Mariene will rush to the home immediately if she is at *Lar Colméia*. Often, she advises Ken by phone from Porto Alegre.

> "We have strong communication. Ken, Clovis, and I meet once every two months to discuss the children. Isabel or Jerilyn also have been called in occasionally. I also meet with the housemothers once every two months to discuss their roles with their children. I would like these meetings to be more frequent, too."

Broadly, and especially professionally, how does she view the CHAIN of Love? "I feel this ministry is part of the dream of God. It's a channel of blessing to these children. God has a goal for them. Just think, here are children who were taken out of chaotic, unstructured backgrounds and who are now gaining better perspectives on life. The pieces of their lives are being put back together."

Mariene concedes small losses have occurred, but they are negligible in relation to the net gain. There are fewer runaways, for example.

"The greatest riches come in seeing how successfully children have overcome their initial problems, particularly in those who are now teenagers. Our major challenge here now with the increased number of teenagers—and we are researching this—is to help prepare them for healthy living and further social roles in the larger community once they leave here."

What do the children need, more than anything? "Above all, that they internalize the new values and new patterns learned here." Signs are strong that the process is taking root. It's not really that surprising that some of those children aspire to become psychologists.

Mariene's teammate Isabel is a born teacher. Although the children she tutors one-on-one don't say it exactly that way, their remarkable progress does, and so does the expressive panorama of drawings adorning the walls in her office. Their creations speak powerfully of their affection for Isabel. The Master Teacher's Hand surely steered this thirty-eight-year old into a role with the CHAIN. The Bayers' invitation in 1999 to join them came courtesy of mutual friend, who had been impressed by her small son's advances during three years of Isabel's tutelage and highly recommended her.

Isabel, who is single, seemed custom-made for the CHAIN's purposes since her extra duties outside daytime teaching in the Novo Hamburgo public school system involved private tutoring of what municipal education officials termed "children at risk." When Isabel accepted Pastor Ken's offer, she had already been tutoring at-risk children for about a year. She still does, in addition to the three days weekly serving at *Lar Colméia*.

Much of what Isabel does in the city program harmonizes with the tutoring at the CHAIN of Love. Most of the children in that municipal program, though, are with one or both their biological parents. But their households are miserable compared to the safe, wholesome, encouraging places of refuge nurturing children at the CHAIN of Love. Remember Rusty, the filthy, hungry, homeless fourteen-year-old waif whose murder on Novo Hamburgo's mean streets in late 1993 sparked the birth of the CHAIN of Love? Well, the dirt-poor children being tutored by Isabel in that municipal program are included in the disgraceful statistical disparity between rich and poor cited earlier by Pastor Ken—8 percent of Brazilians fighting to survive on just 10 percent of the nation's wealth. As stated previously, Brazil accounted for fully 20 percent of an estimated forty million homeless children roaming the world's urban streets, according to an admittedly outdated study from 1997. God only knows how many more millions of hungry, homeless children are hopelessly wandering streets today, especially since the tsunamis of December 2004 and the Indonesian earthquake of May 2006.

That's why many more Isabels and many more CHAIN-like outreach ministries are needed across the world. Isabel and the Bayers' ministry are proving what can be accomplished by any church or worship assembly willing to step out. Of her children in the municipal program, Isabel says,

"Many have no one at home much of the time, and a lot of them must go out begging for money and food for their parents, themselves, and their brothers and sisters. Some of them also are beaten by their parents. This government-funded program at least gives them safe shelter and provides some food for the family. We teach them basic hygiene and life skills, as well." Isabel's imaginative teaching has proven itself. "I brought in a lot of fun activities into the lessons, and the children loved it." Municipal officials balked at the innovative teaching at first, but the swift learning progress of her students quickly won them over.

At *Lar Colméia,* Isabel employs the same techniques. She emphasizes that she always matches her private tutoring to the grade the boy or girl is currently in at school. When interviewed in May 2004, Isabel was tutoring thirty-five students, either one-on-one or in groups of two or three, ranging in age from six to eighteen. She confers constantly with Mariene regarding the specific needs of each student and the difficulties or handicaps each is coping with. Meeting those needs and dealing with those difficulties as a team are included in her prayers. "I bring God and Jesus into my sessions, and I find the children are most willing to open up. Our fellowship and closeness always grows. And with each student, I try to emulate how I imagine Jesus would tutor that particular boy or girl."

Isabel was the youngest of four children in a traditional, middle-class family. Her dad was a leather-treatment worker, and her mom cleaned houses.

"My mother was the first to accept Jesus, and that was after she retired. That's when she started taking me to church. Thinking back, I consider tutoring more than a job. I feel it was God's calling. I was just fourteen when I began teaching Sunday school at the church. I was led by the Holy Spirit then, and I know God was giving me the wisdom to say the right words at the right time then, just as He does today. Always relying upon Him has become part of me."

Tutoring at any time and anywhere obviously comes as naturally to her as breathing. Her flexibility and versatility are proven by her shifting appointment hours and weekly schedules to accommodate time frames convenient to both the children and houseparents. At first, Isabel taught in *Lar Colméia*'s gymnasium. Then she taught in a tiny, cramped building near the gym until the technical-vocational center was completed in 2003.

"I strive to convey God's love for these children through my teaching." To illustrate, Isabel cited the example of an embittered teenage girl who confronted her with some pointed questions. The girl couldn't fathom why her mother had rejected her and four other siblings, why God would allow that, and why God would allow her dad to murder her mom. "I patiently explained that none of this was God's doing, but that they were the awful acts of people having free wills." As tutoring progressed, Isabel told that same girl about life changes, even in older people, once they invited Jesus into their lives—housefather Sérgio and others at *Lar Colméia,* for example. "It's so gratifying to see how God has taken charge of this sixteen-year-old girl's living. She's now doing so much better in school, and she is with a house family that gives her all the love and attention she needs."

As Isabel declares, the children really do blossom when God's love for them is demonstrated in such small tutoring details as placing a cute sticker on a child's notebook. For example, an eight-year-old boy's eyes lit up when Isabel complimented him on the work in his notebook and rewarded his accomplishment with a sticker. This child, once so aloof from everyone, including all the other children, is now thriving educationally and socially. "Stars and other neat stickers are how I pay tribute, and they also serve as constant reminders for motivating the children."

In turn, the artwork covering Isabel's office walls speak of the children's gratitude and love for her. There are scenes of adults, children, animals, and biblical scenes, such as a cartoonish Samson and lion. Most expressive, though, is a girl's written message: "I love you. I love you a lot. God loves you very much."

Like Isabel, Fabiana is surely born for her calling. As a speech therapist and audiologist, she is dedicated to building communication abilities and self-images of children who are hearing- and speech-impaired. The thirty-year-old single mother of a five-year-old son, Gabriel, has been serving the CHAIN of Love since April 2002. By the time of our interview in May 2004, Fabiana had helped thirty-five children— all now far more socially at ease, expressing themselves much better, and advancing in school and learning.

Again, surely the Divine Strategist made the connections that brought Fabiana to the Bayers' team. Two other speech therapists from Mariene's church in Porto Alegre had rejected the chance to work at *Lar Colméia,* but somehow an American missionary couple who had worked at *Lar Colméia* years earlier got word of the job opportunity. Ten years earlier that couple, Dick and Beth Rabenhorst, had initiated youth-group Bible studies at Fabiana's church in Porto Alegre and, as Providence would have it, were neighbors then to Fabiana and her family.

The Rabenhorsts' daughter knew that her friend Fabiana had become a speech therapist and informed her parents of that when they mentioned the opening at *Lar Colméia*. Fabiana had graduated from university in December 2001 and had been working as a speech therapist-audiologist in a small medical clinic in a nearby city. Her major duty there was conducting hearing tests. She had already been told of the job opening at *Lar Colméia* by one of the two speech therapists who had rejected the opportunity. "I wasn't very interested then, because I had been focused more on a career in audiology than speech improvement, and, for that, Porto Alegre is better for advancement." (An audiologist is a licensed health-care professional who diagnoses, treats, and manages individuals with hearing-loss or balance problems.) Fabiana dismissed the *Lar Colméia* opportunity when Dick Rabenhorst talked with her. Nonetheless, some time later he handed her a slip of paper with Pastor Ken's number.

> "At the time, I struggled with the thought of having to make a lot of changes. But then the sequence of events and circumstances made me feel God wanted me with the CHAIN of Love. The speech therapist had said I would have to deal with a broad range of speech difficulties. That sounded appealing and challenging. And I recalled Dick Rabenhorst's encouraging words. But I was still unsure of myself, so I prayed for an answer. Then I again reviewed how everything had happened, and I guess the answer was that I should be with the children at the CHAIN of Love."

Her decision made, Fabiana had to wait a month before

telephoning Pastor Ken, as the Bayers still had a month remaining in their home assignment to Canada. "We met on a Saturday finally, and after interviewing me, Pastor Ken handed over a list of ten children and detailed what he had observed to be the problem with which each was coping. He said, 'This is what you're going to do.' And I said, 'Yes, I'm going to do that.'

> "Looking back, it has been, and remains, every bit as challenging as I had anticipated. I studied their background files and knew how and why they had come into guardianship. Some of the children have stuttering problems initially, and I have made some progress teaching them how to deal with the pressures that accompany stuttering. I managed, despite the fact we didn't get very deeply into stuttering at university or during our internship."

Many theorize about but don't really know what causes stuttering, Fabiana said. "Some say its roots are psychological, others say physiological, but no one really knows, and it's more common in males than in females." Mentioning an eighteen-year-old girl, Fabiana said flatly that the girl would never completely overcome the affliction, but her stuttering had markedly diminished and she was now more at ease socially.

On the other hand, there was the seven-year-old girl who had been coldly aloof and wordless with everyone. Mariene and Isabel had drawn blank stares from her when they questioned whether she liked being with her new family at the CHAIN. This child had been a victim of sexual abuse by her stepfather. Fabiana tried a different approach—no questions, simply the request to draw things with crayons and coloring pencils. The girl drew two dwellings, the larger *Lar Colméia* house in which she lived and a much smaller one with an open door, actually representing Fabiana's office. Walking into the office through the doorway was a smiling little girl representing herself. The girl broke into a beaming smile of pride as she completed her creation. A breakthrough at last! Fabiana had opened the door, and that girl, her fears swept away, is now talking with everyone.

The only child Fabiana couldn't reach at first was Linda Débora de Lima, eight when Fabiana began seeing her in 2002. As related in chapter nine, she was rescued out of the "bush" when brought into the CHAIN's loving care two-and-a-half years earlier, an extreme example of social retardation. Afflicted with a neurological disorder, Linda had never been taught to speak by her neglectful, alcoholic parents. And for months after her mom's death, she roamed the streets, much like a stray animal, and taught herself to walk by hanging on to the tail of a neighborhood dog. Fabiana began by employing the few words Linda could speak for one-on-one games. During that early period, Linda underwent cranial surgery to control convulsions, so their weekly sessions were interrupted for several months. Still, Fabiana and Linda built a bond of mutual affection. Linda continues taking medication for behavioral control, but the winsome, toothless girl with the ever-present smile bears the stamp of the loving professionalism practiced by Fabiana. Fortified by a caring *Lar Colméia* family, daily lessons in a Novo Hamburgo school for children with special needs, and Fabiana's devoted attention, Linda's social skills are blossoming.

Looking back on results with children helped to date, Fabiana said the "greatest need" now is to teach them not only to expand their speaking abilities but to carry those abilities over into learning how to write.

Fabiana hails from a Porto Alegre family of four sisters and inherited an early impetus toward a profession now benefiting God's children at *Lar Colméia*. Her mom, following high school graduation, had been interested in studying speech therapy. While she neither went to university nor learned sign language, she did learn how to lip-read and taught that to deaf children in São Paulo. "So I have always been interested in dealing with deaf children."

Fabiana's decision to study speech therapy and audiology in university crystallized thanks to a high-school science teacher who advised that she advance beyond lip-reading and learn sign language. "He knew some sign language himself and explained it. As he said, I could be teaching and talking with my hands. And that piqued my curiosity." Thus Fabiana went on to be custom-crafted for the love of God's children.

16

GOING THE DISTANCE FOR GOD'S KIDS

Reverend Ken and Jerilyn Bayer are trailblazers. Because they ventured out bravely and faithfully for God and the love of His children, these Canadian missionaries have forged a CHAIN of Love in Brazil that gleams as a global prototype for loving ministry to homeless, abused, and abandoned children. And, as teammate Sara and I have contended and emphasized throughout this book, that Christian enterprise could be emulated by any worship congregation anywhere. The pattern has been sewn by the Bayers. Worship assemblies of any faith need only to modify, alter—or expand—that pattern as they decide their own outreach objectives and, of course, do that in a way consistent with potential and available resources. The bigger challenge, though, is becoming gutsy enough to step out as boldly as the Bayers did in 1994. We all know from the 2004 tsunamis, the Indonesian earthquake of May 2006, and sundry other disasters—natural and man-made—that there are millions of victimized children on the world's streets starving for loving, sheltering, long-term care.

Sure, it was scary for Pastor Ken and Jerilyn, taking that courageous first step, one taken only because of a tragic turn of events—the shooting murder by a shopkeeper of an obscure and homeless fourteen-year-old street kid known then only by the nickname of Rusty. Rusty had been turning up almost daily for a morsel or two of sustenance from the caretaker of the Bayers' Good News Baptist Church in Novo Hamburgo. But their Christian consciences hammered them and their church board into compassionate action. They were taking that risky step in the nation most notorious of all for its enormous gap between rich and poor, its millions of homeless children making up fully one-fifth of the global total at that point. As servants of Jesus, the Bayers and their supporters knew these Brazilian wanderers were so detested that they were targets of "death squads" hired by merchants to "clean up" the streets. Figuratively, they were entering a lion's mouth. Their rescue ministry was being launched in a nation whose class and income disparities fostered the term "Brazilianization"—a label derisively used by economists and sociologists as a warning signal to other nations. As Uruguayan writer Eduardo Galeano asserted in 2000, "There is no country in the world as unequal as Brazil."[38]

For a moment or two, assume a global overview, and, from that perspective, ponder that figurative lion's mouth called Brazil into which the Bayers jumped. About one million children younger than five die each year in that nation, with its northeastern section accounting for about 25 percent of those deaths, a section having one of the world's highest infant mortality rates at 116 of every 1,000 live births. And it's estimated that two-thirds of those infants go to the grave without a medical diagnosis. All of this from hovels like those that so many of the CHAIN'S children lived in before being rescued by the Bayers' ministry. You have already read their stories. Hunger in the midst of plenty. Hunger so desperate it drives children like Paulo to sift through garbage dumps for their younger kin. The statistics cited here are from *Global Problems and the Culture of Capitalism* by Richard Robbins and *Death Without Weeping: The Violence of Everyday Life in Brazil* by Nancy Scheper-Hughes. These books confirm and reinforce what both Ken and Jerilyn said in earlier chapters about Brazil's glaring disparities. It is hardly a poor country, since it ranks among the world's top ten to fifteen economies. Some Brazilians have become very wealthy, while poverty ensnares 80 percent of the nation's population—43.5 percent of whom live on less than $2 U.S. per day. Despite all those daunting numbers, the Bayers dared the unknown, knowing that God is the God of breakthroughs and that they could do all things through the Christ who strengthens them (Philippians 4:13).

And from the perspective of a dozen years, those breakthroughs came repeatedly because the Bayers and their team faithfully heeded their Master's Voice. Those breakthroughs were delineated by the Bayers during a CHAIN of Love progress review on January 19, 2005, at a seniors' brunch in this author's church, Trinity Baptist in Kelowna, Canada. Breakthrough after breakthrough punctuated the Power Point presentation of construction scenes over the years at the *Lar Colméia* campus and Ken's accompanying commentary, as well as accounts by both Ken and Jerilyn of certain children whose lives had been transformed. Jerilyn led with a breakthrough heartwarming to her personally and received touchingly by the seniors—grandmothers and grandfathers themselves who identified with Jerilyn's debut as "a grandma," not biologically but by appointment of the baby's mother. She is "grandma" to Ana Raquel Moreira, born on October 6, 2004, to Adriane Ferreira Capeletti Moreira and her husband, Nei. Only God's miraculous Hand could have engineered this breakthrough for twenty-three-year-old Adriane, who was thirteen years old when rescued by the CHAIN in 1994, her sexual organs so atrophied by sexual abuse that a gynecologist determined she might never develop normally. Dear reader, you know Adriane as the radiant bride from the wedding account that opened chapter eight. Remember that scene of her and the Bayers hugging tearfully after the ceremony performed by Ken on November 23, 2002? "How blessed we have been over the years," Jerilyn told the seniors at Trinity Baptist. And, in listing those blessings, she led off with her joy of nestling infant "granddaughter" Ana in her arms for the first time. Then the others: her loving pride in Adriane and her husband, Nei, a school teacher now in seminary; the two churches she and Pastor Ken launched over twenty-one years; more than ten years then as cofounders of the CHAIN of Love. "God is expanding His kingdom."

Then Ken stepped up for the Power Point presentation. There he stood, passionately delivering for God and His children at the CHAIN of Love while submerging an aching heart and a mind beset with worry over the medical condition of his mother, Irma, deathly ill with liver cancer back in Edmonton. Ken's family had called him home to Canada, and he had been within the comfort of the Bayer family circle from November 23, 2004, until he and Jerilyn set out from Edmonton in the new year to call upon ministry "support" and "interest churches" in five Canadian provinces and the U.S. states of Michigan and Illinois. The emergency call caused Ken to miss by three days the CHAIN's lively tenth-anniversary celebration on November 26. However, Jerilyn stayed behind to lead the program in Ken's absence.

In subsequent paragraphs you will read her description of those events. A week later, Jerilyn and their three daughters were with Ken and his family. Because of the family emergency, North American Baptist Conference headquarters had agreed to Ken's suggestion of advancing by a year his and Jerilyn's scheduled furlough. These furloughs every few years are to gather support for both the CHAIN ministry and themselves as missionaries. So here were these two stalwart trailblazers in Canada, going together to some churches for presentations but otherwise splitting most of the total by making separate visitations. This time around they called upon fifty-five churches, three or four weekly, and made sixty-eight presentations. In past years the number visited had reached about one hundred, or six or seven weekly. "The purpose of home assignments is to renew a missionary's vision, and they're usually for a full year every four years," Ken pointed out.

"But, unlike other missionaries, our home furloughs are more frequent and much shorter. They must be carried out quickly and intensively because our legal obligations to the Brazilian government demand that we're back promptly. We're bound as legal guardians of the Brazilian children at the CHAIN of Love."

Jerilyn returned to Campo Bom on February 15, 2005. Irma Bayer died on March 9 in an Edmonton hospital, her family at her side. Ken returned to Campo Bom just a few days after his mom's funeral.

For his presentation to the seniors' brunch in my church, Ken dressed in the typical garb of a Brazilian male villager. He reeled off these "power points" matching the scenes on the screen:

* Gym construction, 1997
* New playground started, 1999
* Fourth home under construction, 1999
* Sixth home under construction, 2001
* Greenhouse, 2002
* Beginning of seventh house, 2004
* Ninth house off campus
* Tenth family off campus

Then Ken zeroed in on what drives the ministry's labor of bringing children into Christian guardianship. "These are children who had been in the wrong reality, prone to the lower calling of the enemy and being subjected to Satanic success." He quoted, in part, from Romans 8:29 to emphasize where and with whom such children are ultimately meant to be: "For those God foreknew He also predestined to be conformed to the likeness of his Son." Next came Colossians 1:15-16: "He is the image of the invisible God, the firstborn over all creation. For by Him all things were created: things in heaven and on earth, visible and invisible, whether thrones or powers or rulers or authorities, all things were created by Him and for Him." Then Ken gratefully addressed the Lord. "Lord, You created these for us, and now we are recreating them for You so that You will have control and sway over their lives."

As Ken recalled, it was a tough grind mentally for everyone once the decision had been made to launch the CHAIN of Love.

"We really struggled with the questions 'Where do we begin?' and 'How do we begin?' But we have learned two major lessons after ten years. One: the focus is consistency, not necessarily the right answers. Two: the focus is love, not necessarily being right. It's not, for example, using a spoon on a naive, disheveled child, because the only thing these children have not known is love. And, in the end, we see Christ win over."

Surely no single event in the CHAIN's history packaged the aggregate victory of Christ's love as largely and powerfully as that rollicking tenth-anniversary celebration of everyone's gratitude to Him. Judging by e-mailed reports from Jerilyn Bayer and staff members Cal and Katie Taylor, it seems as though Heaven in all its magnificence had flown into a packed Good News Baptist Church in Novo Hamburgo for a few hours that Friday night of November 26, 2004. Angels were there, at least earthly angels. So was Jesus—in the hearts of the celebrants, especially the children. Their luminous smiles spotlighted His Presence. Organized by God's children—young, older, and old—this was, above all, a gala marking transformed lives.

For the children, the day leading up to the celebration was electric with pent-up anticipation. All were dressed in their finest, smiling, laughing, and chattering non-stop while awaiting housefather José and the bus for the ride to church. On arrival in the hot early dusk, they were momentarily wonder-struck, viewing the multicolored Christmas lights beautifying the church's exterior. After a mad rush inside, they cruised among the tables in the foyer, proudly pointing to items they had created in classes at *Lar Colméia*'s technical-vocational center and informing others of what that involved. Their creations included quilting, cross-stitching, sewing, drawings, paintings, clay and wood sculptures, belts, shoes, and baked and cooked foods.

Heads held high and walking briskly, everyone appeared to be riding a wave of celebratory expectation as they filed into the sanctuary. Special guests included volunteers, former houseparents, prayer supporters, and children formerly with the CHAIN of Love. On stage, program leader Jerilyn began by thanking God for ten years of joy and growth, for the challenges and victories, and for the wonderful children with whom they had been blessed. Then she read a story that brought a tear or two to some older folk. It was about a man on a Mexican beach watching another fellow hurl starfish after starfish back into the ocean. The beach was littered with thousands of starfish. The onlooker asked, "Why bother throwing them back? With so many starfish, what difference will it make?"

The starfish pitcher then picked up another, held it out to his questioner's face, and said, "Makes a difference for this one." Then he pitched it into the ocean.

As Jerilyn observed, "Yes, we cannot change the world, but we can change the world one person at a time."

Following Jerilyn's story was a talent show perhaps unequaled anywhere in Brazil for the zest that went into the performances. Children and houseparents from each of the CHAIN's ten families did something special in song, dance, or instrument playing. A teenage choir sang, and a teenage band played. A gang of little ones were greatly amusing with their cute choreography. Other children acted out short plays. Recorder and classical guitar numbers were lovely. As well, there was an inspiring round of songs by a quartet, psychologist Mariene, social worker Kénia, private tutor Isabel, and speech therapist Fabiana. A short video traced the years, igniting waves of laughter through the audience as older children saw themselves and their "brothers and sisters" as little ones. It was a night filled with resounding applause for each feature and each performance. And, naturally, there was a windup of thanksgiving to God for the vision He had given the Bayers, for bringing people along to fulfill that vision, and for the children's lives that were salvaged as a result. The social that followed provided a sweet sequel to the celebration—ice cream, and lots of it. Two or three bowls for some!

Less than a month later, trailblazer Ken was describing the amazing life changes in several of the very same children who had demolished that ice cream. And those Canadian seniors in Kelowna's Trinity Baptist Church sat fascinated as Ken told of the transformed lives of Graziele Victor dos Santos, André da Silva, Quéli Regina dos Santos, and Karine Luciana Lesing. As Ken observed, the children come into the CHAIN of Love from such broken situations that you just keep working and praying that the pieces of their lives can reassembled. Listeners could feel the thrill in Ken's voice as he declared, "Then, all of a sudden, there's a breakthrough! And you see Christ win over!" Spectacular transformations include that of sixteen-year-old Graziele, who came into the ministry's guardianship as a six-year-old in 1995. "She told us she wanted only to finish grade two and go to work. That was all she felt capable of. Today, this girl is baptized and a leader in the church youth group. Now, she wants to be a judge." As Ken explained later, what Graziele had meant by "going to work" was to "entertain" men, just as her mother had (prostitution). I wonder what Graziele's life would have been like today had she and two sisters not been rescued by the CHAIN ten years earlier.

Flash back a decade earlier to April 30, 1995, when the CHAIN's life-salvage operation began for Graziele and older sister Darciana and younger sister Marciele. With the entire family starving, the mother was driven to a decision. She surrendered the girls to government social workers to ensure the survival of their baby brother, then only two months old. Graziele and her sisters are the girls unidentified in chapter seven. Theirs was a pitiful plight. They arrived with lice infesting their heads and worms invading their bodies. These were the ravages of living in a dilapidated hovel shared with other families and sleeping with their mother and baby brother, five in a single bed. Their only other possessions were a small stove and a table. How on earth could Graziele's mother cope? Graziele's alcoholic father had abandoned the family during her mom's last pregnancy, and her mom could earn just twenty dollars a week, at best, scrounging for salable items in a garbage dump.

Ken pointed out that André, then twenty-one, has forgiven his past and is long past being hell-bent on somehow avenging his mother's murder, a crime he had witnessed as a toddler, one so horrific that he refuses to share its details with anyone. Whoever killed her, it wasn't André's father, since he had been long gone during those early years when André was being raised by his mom. André was certainly ripe for an identity crisis. His father is unknown, rumored only to be a nameless vagabond. Following his mom's death, his grandpa sheltered him, but he was simply too old to look after him properly. André wasn't attending school and was pretty much a homeless street kid when government social workers arranged for the CHAIN's legal rescue in 1995. What a world of difference there is in him after ten years with a loving Christian family of houseparents and "brothers" and "sisters" at *Lar Colméia!* What a breakthrough! André's future looks promising, as Ken observed. Since December 2004, André has been sharing the rental of an apartment in Novo Hamburgo, with another boy formerly with the CHAIN and the two sons of André's former houseparents. He's working in a sheet-metal finishing company owned by his ex-housedad of almost ten years, Raimundo de Jesus. His job involves applying resin to metal parts used in the shoe and leather-purse industry. It's a great follow-up to the leather-making trade he learned at *Lar Colméia's* technical-vocational center.

Another breakthrough is the "extreme makeover" of Quéli Regina dos Santos from the angry and pugnacious girl brought into guardianship with three younger brothers on January 18, 1997. This child of almost eight had been so boiling with internal rage that she viciously pushed away the arm of the barber trying to trim her hair as a first step toward ridding her of lice. And she and her brothers had scrapped so furiously that blood was drawn. Now envision the then-sixteen-year-old Quéli described by Ken to the seniors in Kelowna, a high school student so nurturing in temperament that her sights are fixed on a nursing career. She is studying practical nursing and is determined to go on to university for a bachelor's degree in nursing. She is so in love with Jesus that she teaches Sunday school and is taking extension studies in theological education. The CHAIN certainly had to be Divinely empowered to flush all that seething rage from Quéli. It is understandable why it invaded her, along with an army of lice.

The family of seven children had been immersed in unbelievable squalor until the CHAIN took in Quéli and her three brothers and a grandmother took in the two oldest children and the baby. Social workers had forcefully taken the children away from their fifty-six-year-old father, a widower and alcoholic who later died of alcoholism. Never had their dad worked, since he was an around-the-clock drunk. Their mother had died at age thirty-eight when she keeled over while washing clothes at her outdoor scrub board. The cause of death was internal bleeding, a condition that had lingered since the recent birth of her youngest child. Thereafter, their father left the children to their own wits as he submerged himself in booze. Since their shack had no beds and a dirt floor, Quéli and her siblings often chose to sleep in a cow pasture next to a neighbor's cattle. They quenched their thirst drinking polluted river water.

What a dreadful sight she and brothers Magnus, Robson, and Roni were that first day in guardianship. They were loaded with lice, undernourished, their bellies swollen from worms, their bodies bearing many open wounds, principally on the feet. Quéli's push of the barber's arm had clipped out a whole swath of her hair. She wore a hat for weeks until the hair grew in again. Over the years, though, there has been a much more luxuriant growth in Quéli. It sprouted in her heart and soul from day after day of love from houseparents Nair and Enaldir and her family of "brothers" and "sisters." Thanks to Jesus and the CHAIN, Quéli has been completely healed, and her patients will benefit from a nurse who knows much about the powerful medicine of love, nurturing, care, and restoration.

Our God of breakthroughs was also directing the action as His CHAIN of Love erased the wounds and lifted Karine Luciana Lesing out of her tormented past. Pastor Ken's pride was aglow as he told Karine's story to those Canadian seniors in Kelowna's Trinity Baptist Church. Karine, now eighteen, has been baptized, teaches Sunday school, has won debates in high school, is working as a librarian, and has her heart set on a career in social work. "I told her, 'You will be good because you will be doing it with your heart.'" This young lady indeed is blessed with an sensitive heart. It was Karine who delivered her beautifully composed poem to all mothers, and particularly housemother Eva Rosa do Santos, during the Mother's Day service in Good News Baptist Church on May 9, 2004, as described in chapter ten. Love from an army of devoted servants of Jesus over eight years have brought a glorious vision of the future into Karine's eyes.

Mariene Tammerik, the psychologist, was among the first to set Karine's restoration into motion. Ten-year-old Karine didn't even know her real name when she came into the CHAIN's care in May 1998. The name she gave was quite different than the one registered on her birth certificate. Karine's birth mother had abandoned her almost simultaneously with the exit of her mentally deranged dad. Then she was repeatedly raped, since the age of five, by a stepfather and his "buddies." Social workers yanked her out of this depravity, only to be frustrated once more by her placement into the family of Karine's remarried mother. There she was raped by her mom's new husband. Again, social workers took her out and placed her in a municipal shelter for girls (most older). Actually, that shelter was pretty much an ideal school of learning for street prostitution. Thankfully Karine's caseworker recognized the danger and called upon the Bayers' ministry. And today we have a Karine Luciana Lesing planning to go into the world as a social worker bent on salvaging lives of children, just as her own had been salvaged and transformed.

Ken's concluding remarks to the Canadian seniors in Kelowna captured the spirit of the Great Transformer's mission. "We look at these children in awe. God started it, and they are works in progress. Boys and girls have been restored, have forgiven their past, and are to free to develop into what God intended them to be." He pointed out that of the forty-three baptisms in a recent ceremony at his church, fifteen were of children from CHAIN of Love homes. "We are reaping the fruit of our prayers."

Reflecting back to 1993, Ken made a confession. "I sometimes wonder," he told the seniors, "if we might have said 'no' had we been able to foresee what we were getting into and where we were going." In our interview three days later, Jerilyn reminded Ken, "But God doesn't show us or anybody the whole picture, and for good reason." That reminded me of Jerilyn's words during our interview eight months earlier in Brazil. She admitted that she, not Ken, had been hesitant about venturing into the unknown of a CHAIN of Love—potentially an around-the-clock undertaking that could prove much too exhaustive and all-consuming, especially for her. But, then, she emphasized, "You just go through open doors, work hard, obey, and trust, because all the resources are in God's Hands. All our changes have been from good to better."

The Bayers surely wouldn't have gotten past the start line had they fearfully imagined potential disaster and disappointment. Far too many of us never scale the mountain peaks nor navigate the oceans of our dreams because we permit imagined fears to sideline us permanently. The Bayers didn't. Nor did Dr. Martin Luther King Jr., whose 1960s civil rights movement was equally a Christian crusade and whose entire life of fearless service was, as one biographer described, his "greatest sermon." Nor did President Franklin D. Roosevelt, who rallied Depression-demoralized Americans, declaring that "We have nothing to fear but fear itself," and forged ahead with New Deal policies that restored hope and helped bring recovery to the United States in the 1930s. Nor did Nelson Mandela, who spent twenty-seven years behind bars in South Africa but whose cause ultimately triumphed in dismantling apartheid. As Mandela said,

> "We were born to make manifest the glory of God that is within us. It's not just in some of us; it's in everyone. And as we let our light shine, we unconsciously give other people permission to do the same. As we are liberated from our own fear, our presence automatically liberates others."[39]

Those beloved children at the CHAIN are being liberated from the negativism of their backgrounds and self-images to develop their God-given potential, thanks to the light projected upon them by all those servants of Jesus in the Bayers' ministry. Ken, Jerilyn, and all their supporters are fortified by God's biblical assurance to everyone that they are capable of enduring any assignment made—that He would not assign more than they could handle. They are also heartened by Paul's declaration to the Philippians while imprisoned: "I can do everything through Him who gives me strength" (Philippians 4:13).

As previously mentioned, there is an endless number of potential assignments worship assemblies can undertake for the love of God's children around the globe, using the Bayers' CHAIN of Love as the prototype upon which to build their service. Ponder the need in light of UNICEF's estimate of 50,000 children orphaned by the earthquake and resulting tsunamis of December 26, 2004. An estimated 50,000 other children were among the death toll of upwards of 175,000 people. Ponder the despairing hopelessness of those 50,000 orphans against the larger reality of 500,000 left homeless. Those children have been tagged the "tsunami generation," surely to be haunted throughout their lives by traumatic memories. That terrible prospect exacerbates the initial suffering from physical injuries, psychological trauma, diseases brought on by lack of clean water and sanitation, plus being exploited by those who, sniffing quick cash, crawled out of hell to sell the children to sex-industry bidders.

Nations can be proud of their neighborly aid to those stricken Southeast Asian countries in both cash and relief volunteers. It was an outstanding response, ranging from teddy bears sent overseas by school children to celebrity fund-raising concerts to millions sent by governments. Still, as Ken and Jerilyn Bayer observed during our Kelowna interview, the ongoing tsunamis tragedy is a natural disaster that, deservedly, will continue receiving monumental news coverage worldwide. But, as they emphasized, let's not be blind to the fact that even the magnitude of the tsunamis (and, most recently, the 2006 Indonesian quake) is minimal alongside the continuing everyday devastation from countless man-made disasters that go uncovered, unseen, and unheard of. The Bayers pleaded that churches and worship assemblies, especially, should not blind themselves to that reality, either in their own communities and nations or anywhere in the world.

Their comments were offered in response to the question "What does the fallout from the tsunamis say to the world's Christian churches and, in fact, to worship assemblies of all faiths?" Granted, as Ken said, religious faiths went all out in response to the 2004 emergency. "Many of our Baptist churches were in Sri Lanka immediately to help sister churches that had been washed away." But he felt regretful that churches generally haven't responded all that well to man-made disasters such as AIDS, hunger, starvation, and the homelessness bred by war, poverty, and family abuse.

> "Most of our churches ignore these man-made catastrophes. For example, evangelical churches in Brazil aren't helping us. Very rarely, anyway. They think we're competing with them. Actually, we're getting much more help from non-Christians."

Jerilyn agreed, adding: "Churches must open their eyes and come together for these man-made disasters. The hearts of our churches have to change."

These man-made disasters, Ken emphasized, are neither subject to political solutions nor primarily the responsibility of governments.

> "Politicians all over the world rushed out in response to the tsunamis, but I suspect their reasons. They did so for the right reasons, yes, but let's not overlook their wrong reasons. Let's acknowledge that a lot of self-promotion was involved as well. Elections, for example."

Ken doubted that he would get an audience with any national leader anywhere to discuss, for example, the man-made disaster of eight million homeless street children in Brazil.

> "Anyway, we shouldn't be looking to governments and political leaders seeking reelection to deal with these man-made disasters. People are losing out on the blessing that goes with being directly involved. Almost everybody acts as if they're incapable. They want to centralize the responsibility for dealing with these man-made disasters to governments. Actually, that responsibility should be decentralized. It's our responsibility as God's people, not the government's."

Ken and Jerilyn's challenge to God's people cannot be shrugged off, considering the breadth of those man-made disasters. Two accounts published a few weeks before their remarks provide a revealing glimpse of why the Bayers' rallying cry is for everyone's ears. One is by columnist Marcus Gee in the *Globe and Mail* (one of Canada's national newspapers) on December 29, 2004. The other is a letter to the editor in the *Kelowna Daily Courier* on January 8, 2005, from Dr. Bob Dickson, of Calgary. The subheading over Gee's commentary is: "The Asian tsunamis have swept away the rich countries' excuses for ignoring the world's neediest." As Gee points out,

> "Despite the enormous progress recorded over the past few decades—a doubling of average income in developing nations since 1975; a rise in global adult literacy from 47 percent to 73 percent today—ten million children still die each year from completely preventable causes. A billion lack clean and accessible drinking water, and two billion cook their

food on open indoor fires. The existence of such want in the midst of plenty is the scandal of the twenty-first century. The Asian disaster is a perfect chance to make things right by launching a global war on poverty."[40]

Dr. Dickson, while commending the generosity of Canadians in the tsunami crisis, also reminds them,

"Give or take a couple of pennies, we average twenty-seven cents per Canadian per day in official development assistance to combat, to name just a few: 29,000 children dying every day from preventable diseases and starvation, 2.7 million people dying of malaria yearly, 2.2 million dying of tuberculosis, three million dying of HIV/AIDS, 940 million illiterate, 800 million going to bed hungry every night, the billion without fresh water, the 2.3 billion without sanitary services, millions of refugees, millions of orphans, removal of land mines and, on the positive side, to provide micro-credit loans to the poorest women with children whose families live on less than one dollar per day and to forgive onerous loans to the world's poorest countries. Through charities and philanthropic ventures, we contribute another thirty six cents daily, and corporations and foundations add another seven cents to the total. So, now we're all the way up to, well, let's see, about half a can of soda pop a day or a quarter of a fancy coffee... I only ask that we in the wealthy world commit a small percentage more of our personal and national wealth to overcoming the perverse and monumental disparities that persist today. And, please, not another word about tax cuts until all the above are rectified."[41]

In contrast, therefore, it was "perverse," using Dr. Dickson's word, reading of the record highs posted on Latin America's two biggest stock exchanges just two days after the tsunamis.[42] No doubt a healthy number of those investors posting gains in São Paulo were from that 3 percent of Brazilians Pastor Ken cites as controlling 70 percent of the nation's wealth.

Never mind just the tsunamis, the earthquakes, and all of those man-made disasters that become virtually invisible to us as their newsworthiness fades, it seems that each new day stretching back to time immemorial brings a new crop of disasters—and opportunities for humanitarian intervention and rescue by God's faithful people. Consider the news of just one day, February 28, 2005: a suicide bomber in Iraq killed 125 and wounded 130 by detonating a car in a crowded market; a setback occurred to the United Nations peace process in western Ivory Coast when pro-government militia attacked rebel fighters, the first outbreak of hostilities in four months in the on-off civil war; the pro-Syrian government in Lebanon collapsed just two weeks after the assassination of a former Lebanese prime minister.

What's all of this have to do with children, or homeless children? Short answer: everything! Because children are always—*always*—caught in the crossfire of these adult-caused tragedies. They're the innocent and often the most suffering victims of these man-made disasters. You have the Bayers' word for that in Brazil, and you would have to conclude the same from another news story of that same day of February 28, 2005. Haiti, the poorest country in the

Americas, was reported as being torn with political instability and violence a year after former President Jean-Bertrand Aristide was ousted from power. Armed and hooded vigilante gangs roamed the slums, former soldiers controlled small towns, and bystanders died in street fights. Police fired on thousands of demonstrators in a Port-au-Prince slum, killing three and bringing to twenty-eight the number killed in the slums over the five days leading to February 28. The death toll over six months was 278. Some slum dwellers claimed their poverty has worsened. Impact on children? One father said, "Last year, I sent all three of my children to school. This year I could only afford to send one. I can't even feed them."[43]

Remember that man-made disaster at the Auschwitz death camp in Poland of more than sixty years ago, those gas chambers where millions were incinerated during the Second World War? Well, a newspaper editorial page cartoon in the *Vancouver Province* a month earlier than those February 28 news stories is instructive on the human condition. Its overline notes, "What we've learned since Auschwitz." Vertically listed on a classroom blackboard are "Darfur, Congo, Ivory Coast, Yugoslavia, Rwanda, Uganda, Cambodia, Tibet, East Timor, Guatemala, Bosnia." Likely, many more places could have been chalked onto that blackboard: Vietnam, Iraq, Nigeria, and Haiti, to cite just a few.

Notice the names of those countries, and one dreadful reality jumps out—all are nations whose average citizens are so impoverished that they cannot buy a shred of what we North Americans so conspicuously consume. Reader, work out the percentages yourselves based on what economists call "purchasing power parity." The purchasing power parity (PPP) of a nation per capita reveals the average amount of money each citizen has available to buy a certain basket of goods and services. The nation's gross domestic product—the value of all goods and services produced by that nation—is the aggregate total from which the PPP (expressed in U.S. dollars) is calculated. The basket of goods and services priced for the PPP is a sample of all goods and services covered by the GDP, the most basic of which are food, shelter, clothing, and health care. The following figures are those of the Organization for Economic Cooperation and Development for 2002. With an average purchasing power of $35,056 for that consumer basket, the United States ranked third in OECD's measure of 181 nations. Canada ranked seventh with $29,328. The U.S.— no surprise—is the world's highest-producing economy at $10.4 trillion. Contrast that with hapless Haiti in 147th place with the average citizen having $1,631 yearly of buying power to keep life and limb together. Moreover, consider the average Joe Blow in these countries: Sudan (155th), where Darfur is located, hanging on to life precariously at $1,442 yearly; the Congo (175th) at $883 yearly; Rwanda (170th) at $1,080 yearly; in Uganda (161st) at $1,280 yearly; Cambodia (149th) at $1,586 yearly; in Bosnia (141st) at $1,805 yearly; Vietnam (133rd) at $2,237 yearly; Iraq (130th) at $2,323 yearly; Nigeria (178th) at $854 yearly. There's worse—the average fellow living on the eastern half of the Southeastern Asian island of Timor-Leste, a democratic republic, has all of $500 yearly to splurge away. This fact, gleaned from the *New York Times Guide to Essential Knowledge,* hurls the average Joe Blow there into 181st, and last, place.[44]

Remember that all these statistics of deprivation are from 2002. God only knows how much more unbalanced our planet is today, more than four years later, as we have since had the tsunamis and the 2006 Indonesian quake added to our plate. Likewise, remember the Sudanese crisis in which more than 1.2 million refugees fled to more than 100 makeshift refugee camps in Darfur province and across the border into Chad. Up to 300,000 were on the brink of starvation and 50,000 had been killed by August 2004. They were citizens caught in the crossfire of a then eighteen-month-old civil war between Black Sudanese rebels and government-armed Arab militias who raped and tortured as they plundered and terrorized villages. The United Nations termed it the "world's worst humanitarian crisis with catastrophic levels of suffering." Those grim words were from Mukesh Kapila, the UN's humanitarian coordinator in Sudan. As one refugee desperately cried to a relief agency worker, all she received was a five-pound bag of grain with which to feed her four children for a month. World leaders were denouncing the violence as the worst case of African ethnic cleansing since the Rwandan genocide of 1994 extinguished hundreds of thousands of lives in just a few months.

Don't forget Uganda either. In that nation's chaotic north, about 1.6 million Ugandans have abandoned their homes to escape rebels with the Lord's Resistance Army. Half of those 1.6 million are children, and they're the ones the rebels are indoctrinating and using to carry out killings. Up to 90 percent of the rebel army's soldiers are children and teens, the UN estimates. And UNICEF claims about 12,000 children have been abducted in the past two years. These alarming numbers are described by Canadian, David Suzuki, in a syndicated column in the *Kelowna Capital News* on September 10, 2004. The Democratic Republic of the Congo shouldn't be dismissed as no longer of concern. Despite the end of five years of civil war and a loss of millions of lives, the Congo is still flirting with anarchy as various factions wrestle for governmental power. We should be mindful, too, that 95 percent of the forty-three million people infected with HIV/AIDS across the globe live in the developing world, and that there is still no effective vaccine available to them.[45] That statistic on AIDS was cited in a special Focus section feature on June 21, 2004, by Africa correspondent Stephanie Nolen in the *Globe and Mail*. The compassionate thrust of Nolen's account echoes those delivered in a CHAIN of Love child-sponsorship leaflet and Suzuki's aforementioned column. The CHAIN's leaflet quotes Psalm 82:3-4: "Defend the cause of the weak and the fatherless; maintain the rights of the poor and oppressed. Rescue the weak and the needy; deliver them from the hand of the wicked."

Suzuki's prodding and challenging observations reinforce a conviction that we North Americans live all too insulated and sealed off from the developing world, ensconced in our continental cocoon of self-centered me-ism and unceasing, grasping materialism. He chides Canadians for turning a blind eye to suffering in large parts of the developing world.

> "Most of the human population increase over the next fifty years will be in the developing world. It's also where the greatest resource stress will be found. But in today's interconnected world, that kind of instability cannot be contained or walled off. Their world is our world."

Sara and I concur that their world is our world, as Suzuki emphasizes. It seems to us that you must meet the basic needs of people's bodies before awakening any anaesthetized souls into being receptive to hearing of potential glory with the Almighty Loving Lord in the hereafter. Remember that Jesus urged everyone within earshot to feed the hungry, shelter the homeless, and comfort the sick (Matthew 25:31-46). And that the CHAIN of Love has been doing and continues doing, forcefully demonstrating it can also be done by other faithful congregations—given the will, the forethought, and the determination to persevere.

That implies that worshippers will have to get their hands dirty while sharing our world without walls with all those unfortunate brothers and sisters cited by Suzuki. That involves stepping out of their religious buildings and venturing out of their cultural, social, and religious milieu to consort with those deemed "different." Herb Vander Lugt reinforces our conclusion in his insightful devotion for March 10, 2005, in the *Our Daily Bread* booklet published by RBC Ministries. Vander Lugt urges Jesus followers not to be what he labels "rabbit-hole Christians" especially unsociable and condescending toward unbelievers. As he notes, "No wonder unbelievers equate being a Christian with a kind of aloof self-righteousness." Didn't Jesus befriend "sinners" and those despised tax collectors of His day? After all, the whole ball game for anyone claiming devotion to God centers on enabling health of body and soul—both his or her own and that of all brothers and sisters sharing this planet.

And that's what Ken and Jerilyn Bayer and the CHAIN families and supporters have been concentrating on since 1994. The Bayers label their program as one of "prevention." Prevention for the health of body and soul...for children like Paulo, Taís, Graziele, Linda, Altamir, Alexandre, André, Ana Paula, Deneclei...and on and on. One after another, these children were rescued from straits so desperate that, if prolonged, undoubtedly would have broken down—if not destroyed—body and soul.

As the Bayers were making their rounds of Canadian and U.S. churches in February 2005, word came via e-mail from Brazil of how Paulo and other children were looking forward to heading off to summer camp. The nation was revving up for one of its rip-roaring, yearly celebrations, carnival—a grand spectacle during which murder, adultery, and much drunkenness are common. Here was this hearty child, twelve-year-old Paulo, beaming happily out of the digital color photo on that e-mail, a lifetime removed from that starving five-year-old sifting through garbage heaps to sustain himself and two younger siblings before God's servants entered their lives. The letter reported that Paulo had rushed up to staff member Cal Taylor asking for a suitcase. For when? Cal asked. "I need it now—camp is just three weeks away!"

Paulo's life change is just one illustration of what Sara and I feel to be two biblical passages driving Ken and Jerilyn's Bayer's ministry and earthly journey with Jesus. One is from Hebrews 12:1: "Let us run with perseverance the race marked out for us." The other is from Colossians 3:23: "Whatever you do, work at it with all your heart, as working for the Lord, not for men."

During our interview in Canada in January 2005, Ken said more of the older children, once they have been equipped with vocational skills and education, will be transferred into pre-arranged boarding and apartment quarters where they will share rental payments. He pointed out that forty-eight of those then in guardianship were over fourteen and in various "professionalization" classes at *Lar Colméia's* technical-vocational center. Reviewing the CHAIN's envisioned program to 2005, Ken said the first ten-year phase had been pretty much on schedule. Many children were now nearing completion of elementary school and soon would be into the third phase of their "formative years and graduation." As Ken was offering the CHAIN's overview in Kelowna, word came by e-mail from staff members Cal and Katie Taylor "happily" reporting that exterior construction of House 7 at *Lar Colméia* was almost complete. "Now come all the finishing details—electricity, water, doors, etc." It was fascinating watching each day's progress, the Taylors wrote. They urged the continuation of prayers for job-site safety and funds needed for completion.

Meanwhile, Ken added that houseparents Enaldir and Nair and ten children would move into that house from their off-campus home in August 2005. "We are delaying the move purposely because moving in the middle of a school semester would disrupt the children's education." In that same month, Ken said, construction would begin at *Lar Colméia* on another house for the tenth family, the only remaining one in a rented home off campus. That would be for houseparents Cezar and Marli and ten children.

> "When the infrastructures are done, we will be pushing for more involvement by North American volunteers—people with skills who can teach children in our technical-vocational center for whatever periods of time they can devote during any given year. Electronics, new hobbies, name it—we hope to develop as wide a spectrum of instruction as possible."

As for the Bayers' personal plans, their hope is to eventually train a Brazilian missionary couple to administer the CHAIN's day-to-day affairs. "The transition would take some time," Ken said.

> "But we would be looking at candidates for administrative director, and, hopefully, I could then become administrator emeritus. Naturally, I would continue as pastor to the children in guardianship through Good News Baptist Church. Jerilyn and I are determined to start new churches. We would be concentrating on Good News Baptist becoming a multiplying church."

In the meantime, Ken stresses that the ministry is open to using any resource and skill capable of enhancing and expanding the CHAIN's outreach. Doctors, dentists, factory managers, and a veterinarian have been volunteering their services for years. Ken further emphasizes that the CHAIN is almost wholly a Brazilian operation. "Katie Taylor, Jerilyn, and I are the only foreigners involved. The rest of the staff and all houseparents and long-term volunteers are Brazilian. In contrast, volunteers from North America come for short-term projects." (The Taylors have since left the CHAIN for another assignment.)

Word of the ministry's contributions to the community has attracted ever-increasing help from locals and churches. One church provided a large inventory of groceries for the CHAIN's homes; another contributed all the school supplies needed for an entire semester. Children in the homes also got bundles of used clothing—proceeds of a Christian school art fair whose admission was one good article of used clothing. And the local district attorney's novel idea paid off as well. In lieu of money fines, the levies for some traffic and other violations were groceries and other useful items for the CHAIN.

As the examples above indicate, it all starts with one,

one person's idea in one place, another person's idea in one other place. One by one by one by one, it can be done. You have Mother Teresa's word on that. As she is quoted by Tricia McCary Rhodes in *Taking Up Your Cross,*

> "I never look at the masses as my responsibility. I look only at the individual. I can love only one person at a time. I can feed only one person at a time. Just one, one, one. So you begin...I begin. I picked up one person—maybe if I didn't pick up that one person, I wouldn't have picked up the others. The whole work is only a drop in the ocean. But if we don't put the drop in, the ocean would be one drop less. Same thing for you. Same thing in your family. Same thing in the church where you go. Just begin...one, one, one..."[46]

Face it, this power of one is unstoppable if we all do it, one by one as people, and one by one as religious faiths and worship assemblies...for the love, one by one, of God's children. There is nothing new in that power formula, for various expressions of it have been expressed for millennia. Lucius Annaeus Seneca (4 B.C.—A.D. 65), the Roman philosopher, statesman and dramatist who despairingly said, "What fools these mortals be," also urges us, "Wherever a human being exists, there is an opportunity to do a kindness."[47] Likewise, as God's Word emphasizes and so many notables have echoed throughout history, all of humanity suffers if even one suffers. So, whether you read these lines this year, next year, ten years hence, a century or even ten centuries from now, so long as there is one homeless, abused, or abandoned child somewhere on earth, you will have a one-on-one ministerial opportunity of loving rescue.

Yet, today, we don't have just one child hanging on to life by the fingernails. Countless millions are scattered across the globe crying out for one-to-one loving kindness. There are countless millions of one-to-one ministerial opportunities. From the looks of unfolding events in 2005 and 2006, individuals and worship assemblies may even need to reach out compassionately in the face of obstructionist politicians. How depressing, for example, to read that Zimbabwe's children are paying the price for attempts to punish their government for its human rights violations. Again, children caught in the crossfire of a political war between adults, if indeed the accusation by UNICEF executive director Carol Bellamy is valid. "Look for other ways to make your point—don't take it out on the world's children," Bellamy said, denouncing the fact donor organizations are giving Zimbabwe just a fraction of the funding lavished on its neighbors. That aid is being diverted, Bellamy contended, because of concerns an autocratic Zimbabwean government under President Robert Mugabe would use such aid only to strengthen its political hold. On March 17, 2005, Bellamy decried these deplorable realities: no support from the U.S. initiative on AIDS or the World Bank's AIDS program for 2004-2005 and only limited funds from the Global Fund to Fight AIDS, tuberculosis, and malaria. This was in a nation that Bellamy notes has one in every eight children dying before the age of five—a 50 percent increase since 1990. A child dies every fifteen minutes from AIDS complications, the tragic fate of being amid a population in which an estimated 26 percent of 12.5 million are infected with HIV and one million children have lost one or both parents to AIDS. That's heartbreak for one in every five Zimbabwean children.[48]

Just two days later—on March 19, 2005—came the one-year anniversary of a remark naming Darfur, Sudan, as the site of "the world's greatest humanitarian crisis." That's how Mukesh Kapila, the UN's humanitarian coordinator in Sudan, described the violence and forced displacement of people in the African nation's western province. In just one year, two million people had been uprooted from their homes, twice as many as when Kapila pleaded for international help. Malnutrition and disease were claiming 10,000 lives monthly in March 2005. God only knows how many children have been and are being victimized in what Kapila had labeled a year earlier as a process of "ethnic cleansing." There was no international presence in the region when Kapila made that statement, but by March 2005 almost every major relief organization and many smaller ones were there working furiously. Still, hundreds of thousands of people weren't being reached, because lack of funds, logistical challenges, and insecurity had stymied aid efforts by these organizations.[49]

But remember that the Zimbabwean and Darfur catastrophes are just two of numerous man-made disasters—man-triggered calamities that, as the Bayers emphasized earlier in this chapter, worship assemblies generally have either overlooked or been all too lukewarm in responding to. As Pastor Ken further emphasized, God's people, not governments, should step out and seize primary responsibility for dealing with these man-made tragedies, rather than observing them idly from the sidelines and allowing some world politicians to politicize those misfortunes.

For more than twelve years in Brazil, the Bayers have been ministering through their CHAIN of Love with our God of breakthroughs. They would love to pass the baton to you in a worldwide relay for all those millions of children. Be a servant to them. You may even have to wash the grime off the feet of these unwashed children, much like Jerilyn did after rooting the chiggers and worms out of those little feet belonging to sisters Ana Paula and Taís, just as Jesus so humbly washed the feet of His disciples in one of His last great lessons of servanthood before going to Calvary's cross.

Faithful people, you need only look to Paulo and Paul the Apostle as inspirational beacons for servanthood to God's children. Like his namesake, even Paulo, not yet five years old, had finished his own race of sorts for the love of God's kids before being rescued by the CHAIN of Love in 1997. He had kept younger sister Vanessa and baby brother Sidinei alive by scouring garbage dumps for the morsels and liquid sources with which they sustained themselves. Here was a tyke fulfilling a three-way role of dad, mom, and older brother. As readers may recall from chapter three, that went on for about a year, thanks to a mom who frequently left them alone for days in one abandoned hovel after another near a garbage dump. Thanks to Paulo, baby brother Sidinei survived long enough to be rescued with his siblings—a day later, a hospital report noted, and Sidinei would have died of dehydration. And the apostle Paul, once among the most ruthless of Christian persecutors, declared in 2 Timothy 4:7: "I have fought the good fight, I have finished the race, I have kept the faith." Paulo and Paul: guts, grit, faith, and love.

It seems almost incomprehensible that, in this age of super-worldly abundance, there should be millions of Paulos aimlessly wandering the streets, poking through garbage dumps around the globe and dying—literally dying—without hope that the faithful people of churches and worship assemblies would run with perseverance and finish the race rescuing them. In the face of that enormous global challenge, why shouldn't churches and worship assemblies everywhere be unflinchingly bold and adventurous, like the Bayers? Step up and generously unleash your creative imaginations in a tsunami-like torrent for the love of God's children. Remember that God and his workers exult in making His breakthroughs. Be His human hands on Earth. Be His teachers, renovators, architects, masons, carpenters, and whoever else is needed, rebuilding His children for a blessed future on earth and, ultimately, His kingdom. Should you wish, as faithful servants of God, to erect your own specially designed earthly kingdom for the love of His children, you now have Ken and Jerilyn's prototype and road map for guidance.

As you mull over the possibilities, consider this motto from the Elks fraternal organization: "No person stands so tall as when he stoops to help a child." To which Sara, myself, and our friends at the CHAIN of Love add: "No worship congregation towers so godly as when it bends to uplift and help a child of God."

Also ponder the significance of this expression from Athenian poet Sophocles (495-400 B.C.): "One word frees us of all the weight and pain of life: that word is love."[50] Still, great as it is, *love* remains frozen as just another word in the dictionary until it's activated—activated, as the Bayers have, for the love of God's children.

One final word to all of you faithful people and worship assemblies, and what a gem of wisdom to God's glory! It comes from Dr. Oliver Wendell Holmes (1809-1894), American physician, poet, essayist, and father of the famous U.S. Supreme Court Justice Oliver Wendell Holmes Jr.

(1841-1935). "The mode by which the inevitable comes to pass is effort."[51] Now, go to the start line and build the inevitable as you run your race of perseverance for the love of God's kids. A world of children is waiting.

ENDNOTES

Chapter 1

[1] Tim Schroeder, "How many churches do we need?" *Focus on Faith, Kelowna Daily Courier,* 10 Sept. 2004.

Chapter 2

[2] Jesse Banfield and Nevine Mabro, comps., "Children as victims," 1997, on-line posting, http:boes.org/coop/censor1.html (accessed April 4, 1997).

[3] "Brazilian Street Children," May 31, 2002, on-line posting, http://www.jubileeaction.co.uk/reports/Brazilian_Street_Children. pdf (accessed April 18, 2004).

[4] "Street children being murdered in Brazil," *The Ottawa Citizen,* 29 September 1989.

[5] Ibid.

[6] "Brazilian Street Children."

Chapter 4

7 "Find more men to teach love," editorial, on-line posting, www.animalpeoplenews.org/93/7editoria11.html, (accessed April 18, 2004).

8 Ibid.

Chapter 5

9 Calvin Miller, ed., *The Book of Jesus: A Treasury of the Greatest Stories and Writings About Christ,* "One Solitary Life" [Dr. James Allan Francis] (New York: Simon & Schuster Inc., 1998) p. 450.

10 Ibid.

Chapter 6

11 Ardath Effa, e-mail to author Dennison, July 14, 2005. Ken Bayer, e-mails to author Dennison, June 13 and 26, 2006.

12 www.chainoflove.org/index.php?option=com_content &task=view&id=176&Itemid=44 (accessed June 27, 2006).

13 Paulo Romeiro, "Set Free from the Spirits: Paulo's Testimony," *Christian Research Newsletter,* Vol. 4, November 4, 1991, on-line posting, http://museltof.bravepages.com/setfree. html (accessed July 6 2004). Reginaldo Prandi, "African Gods in Contemporary Brazil: A Sociological Introduction to Candomblé Today," University of São Paulo, Brazil, on-line posting, www.prolades.com/prolades1/cra/brazil/candomble.htm (accessed July 6, 2004).

14 David St. Clair, *Drum and Candle* (Garden City, New York: Doubleday & Company, Inc., 1971) book jacket.

15 Ibid.

16 St. Clair, p. 203.

17 Voltaire, quotations, on-line posting, www.brainyquote. com (accessed July 1, 2006).

Chapter 9

[18] Ardath Effa, comp. and ed., *CHAIN of Love, Brazil, newsletter.* July 2006.

[19] Ibid.

[20] Ardath Effa, comp. and ed., *CHAIN of Love, Brazil, newsletter.* June 2006.

Chapter 10

[21] "Mother Educates, Cares for, Loves and Is Still Touched When Child Says 'I love you,'" *Campo Bom Gazette,* May 7, 2004, translated by Sara Esther Luna Cezar.

[22] Ibid.

[23] Ibid.

[24] Ardath Effa, comp. and ed., *CHAIN of Love, Brazil, Newsletter,* February 2006.

[25] Ardath Effa, comp. and ed., *CHAIN of Love, Brazil, Newsletter,* separate issues of November, 2005 and December 2005, mailed to author Dennison.

Chapter 12

[26] "John Newton, Servant of Slaves, Discovers Amazing Grace!" *Glimpses,* Issue No. 28, on-line posting, http://www.gospelcom.net/chi/GLIMPSEF/Glimpses/glmps028.shtml (accessed December 17, 2004).

[27] Calvin Miller, pp. 444-49, 458-61, 474-77.

[28] Wally Dennison, "The Return of the Prodigal Son, as recounted by a once-prodigal father, Rembrandt Harmenszoon van Rijn, March 1669," research paper, Fine Arts 241, Okanagan University College, March 6, 2000.

Chapter 13

[29] Ardath Effa, comp. and ed., *CHAIN of Love, Brazil, Newsletter,* July 2006.

[30] Bob Brown, "Brazil Changed Me," *NAB today,* Vol. 2. No. 5, 1998.

[31] Stacy Siedlecki, "Taught by Children" *NAB today,* September-October 2001.

[32] Ibid.

[33] Lisa Blackburn, "Building hope for children of Brazil," *The Peace Arch News,* March 4, 1995, p. 11.

[34] Shauna Jackson, "Chain of Love links Swan River to Brazil," *Swan River Star and Times,* April 11, 2000, p. B1.

[35] Ardath Effa, comp. and ed., *CHAIN of Love, Brazil, Newsletter,* September 2005.

[36] Carl Beck, of Leduc, Alberta, letter to supporters, autumn 2004.

Chapter 14

[37] "Striking a Different Kind of Goal," *NAB today,* January February 2004, p.8.

Chapter 16

[38] Eduardo Galiano, *Upside Down, a primer for the looking glass world,* "Third World Traveler," on-line posting, www.thirdworldtraveler.com/Eduardo_Galeano/Upside_Down.html (accessed July 3, 2006).

[39] Nelson Mandela, quoted in a Kelowna Singles Club newsletter, 2003.

[40] Marcus Gee, "Thirsting for more aid, The Asian tsunamis have swept away the rich countries' excuses for ignoring the world's neediest," *The Globe and Mail,* December 2004.

[41] Dr. Bob Dickson, "Disaster Relief, We should do much better," Okanagan Saturday edition of the *Kelowna Daily Courier*, Letter to the editor, January 8, 2005.

[42] "Latin America's two biggest stock exchanges climb to record highs," *The Globe and Mail* (Toronto), financial page, December 29, 2004.

[43] Joseph Guyler Delva, "Civil Unrest: A year after Aristide, Haiti Still Torn," *Kelowna Capital News/DAILY*. March 1, 2005, p. 10.

[44] "Purchasing Power Parities(PPP) Frequently Asked Questions," Organisation for Economic Development, on-line posting, http://www.oeced.org/faq/0,2583,en_2649_34357_ 1799281_1_1_1_1,00.html (accessed March 12, 2005); "GDP Rankings—Purchasing Power Parity Method (Numerically by Ranking)," on-line posting, http://aol./globrank.asp?TBLS= PPP+Method=Tables&vCOUNTRY=17&TYPE=GRAN (accessed March 12, 2005).

The New York Times Guide to Essential Knowledge (New York: St. Martin's Press, 2004) p. 824.

[45] Stephanie Nolen, *The Globe and Mail* (Toronto), June 21, 2004, p. F1.

[46] Tricia McCrary Rhodes, *Taking Up Your Cross* (Minneapolis: Bethany House Publishers, 2000).

[47] Lucius Annaeus Seneca, quotations, on-line posting, www.brainyquote.com (accessed July 3, 2006).

[48] The Associated Press, "Diversion of aid hurting children, says UNICEF, UNICEF urges world to help Zimbabwe's forgotten children," *Kelowna Daily Courier*, March 18, 2005, p. A12.

[49] Stephanie Nolen, "A year of dying in Darfur," *The Globe and Mail* (Toronto), March 19, 2005, on-line posting, www. care.ca/press/newsstories/dying_e.shtm (accessed July 3, 2006).

[50] Sophocles, on-line posting, www.quotationspage. com/quotes/Sophocles/31 (accessed July 4, 2006).

[51] Dr. Oliver Wendell Holmes, on-line posting, www. quotedb.com/quotes/3781 (accessed July 4, 2006).

BIBLIOGRAPHY

McCrary Rhodes, Tricia. *Taking Up Your Cross.* Minneapolis: Bethany House Publishers, 2000.

Miller, Calvin, editor. *The Book of Jesus, A Treasury of The Greatest Stories and Writings About Christ.* New York: Touchstone, 1998.

Robbins, Richard. *Global Problems and the Culture of Capitalism.* Toronto: Pearson Press, 2002.

St. Clair, David. *Drum & Candle.* Garden City, New York: Doubleday and Company, Inc., 1971.

Scheper-Hughes, Nancy. *Death Without Weeping: The Violence of Everyday Life In Brazil.* Berkeley, California: University of California Press, 1992.

Stockdale, Mary Jo, with Ken and Jerilyn Bayer. *Links in the Chain of Love.* University Place, Washington: Open Eyes Publishing, 2002.

The New York Times Guide to Essential Knowledge. New York: St. Martin's Press, 2004.

Questions on sponsorship and possible participation in the
CHAIN of Love may be addressed to
Rev. Ken and Jerilyn Bayer at:
CHAIN of Love Homes
C.P. 2040
93.511-970 Novo Hamburgo, R.S.
Brasil

Or e-mail the Bayers at bayer@sinos.net or col@sinos.net

Or visit the CHAIN of Love's Web site at
www.chainoflove.org.